A PLACE TO BE NAVAJO

*Rough Rock and the Struggle
for Self-Determination
in Indigenous Schooling*

Sociocultural, Political, and Historical Studies in Education
Joel Spring, Editor

A PLACE TO BE NAVAJO

Rough Rock and the Struggle for Self-Determination in Indigenous Schooling

Teresa L. McCarty
University of Arizona
Department of Language, Reading and Culture

With Photographs by
Fred Bia
Rough Rock Community School

2002

LAWRENCE ERLBAUM ASSOCIATES, PUBLISHERS
Mahwah, New Jersey   London

Lawrence Erlbaum Associates, Inc., Publishers
10 Industrial Avenue
Mahwah, NJ 07430

Cover design by Kathryn Houghtaling Lacey

Cover photograph: "School children at Rough Rock in 1983."
(Photograph by Fred Bia, courtesy of Rough Rock
Community School).

Library of Congress Cataloging-in-Publication Data

McCarty, T. L.
  A place to be Navajo: Rough Rock and the struggle for self-
  determination in Indigenous schooling / Teresa L. McCarty;
  with photographs by Fred Bia.
  p. cm. — (Sociocultural, political, and historical studies in
            education)
  Includes bibliographical references and index.
  ISBN 0-8058-3760-4 (cloth : alk. paper)
  ISBN 0-8058-3761-2 (pbk. : alk. paper)
  1. Rough Rock Demonstration School.   2. Navajo Indians—
  Education. 3. Navajo Indians—Ethnic identity.   I. McCarty,
  Teresa L.   II. Bia, Fred.   III. Series.
  E99.N3 .M2978   2002
  371.829'97'2 —dc21   2001033346
                                                            CIP

Books published by Lawrence Erlbaum Associates are printed on acid-
free paper, and their bindings are chosen for strength and durability.

Printed in the United States of America
10   9   8   7   6   5   4

To the people of Rough Rock,
whose belief that school could be a place to be Navajo
sparked the movement for Indigenous education control.
—Teresa L. McCarty

* * * * * * * * * *

"[A]s people fashion places, so too, do they fashion themselves."
—Steven Feld and Keith Basso,
Senses of Place, 1996, p. 11

Contents

Series Editor Foreword

This beautifully written account of the community-controlled Rough Rock School highlights the current struggle of Native Americans to gain control of their destinies. Since the European invasion, the evolution of Native American cultures has frequently been influenced by cultural intervention from outside forces. Often, violence and force accompanied these interventions which included forced conversions to Christianity, forced changes in economic relationships from community to private property, military incarceration on reservations, and, most importantly for this study, the imposition by the United States government of schools whose purpose was to replace tribal languages, customs, and religions with English and Anglo-Saxon values.

I often wonder what Indigenous cultures would be like today if there had been no forced cultural interventions. In the same vein, I wonder what Native American tribes will be like in the future as more power is given to tribes to operate their own schools, such as in the Rough Rock community. The calendar can never be turned back to pre-invasion days and the effect of European cultural violence can never be erased from existing tribal cultures. Whatever happens in the future will be a product of remembered tribal cultures, the forced adoption of European customs, existing tribal cultures, and the new hope that tribes can maximize control over their destinies. Teresa McCarty's wonderful book sets the stage for understanding the present and future of tribal cultures.

—*Joel Spring*
New School University

Foreword

American Indians have been through so much: so many ups and downs, so much promise and so many disappointments, so much hope and so much hopelessness, so much unforgivable agony and so much forgiving, so much mature independence and so much infantilizing patronization, that a sympathetic observer and advisor—especially one who is an outsider—must take particularly great care not to repeat and prolong the process of interminably shuttling between extremes. Accordingly, I cannot begin these few words of introduction without honestly asking two questions: Shouldn't a Native person have written this book, and shouldn't a Native person be writing its foreword? In my heart, I know that the answer to both of these questions is "Yes, but ... " A Native person *should* have written this book, but if a non-Indian had to write it, and apparently the Navajo school board at Rough Rock thought that such was the case, I can think of no one better qualified to do so than Terri McCarty. Emotionally, attitudinally, philosophically, cognitively, experientially, and professionally, there is no one who can match her, all-in-all, for this task. And no Indian or non-Indian today can come close to doing so, insofar as involvement in and dedication to the Rough Rock Navajo School are concerned. Her 20 years of service to the school constitute an unrivaled record, as does her simultaneous excellent record as a university-based educator and anthropologist of Indian life and education throughout the American Southwest. Rough Rock is very fortunate to have attracted a psychological, anthropological, and sociological biographer of her refined talents and advanced professional distinction.

My only claim to some justification for being asked to write this foreword is having visited Rough Rock both early (in the late 1960s) and recently (in the late 1990s), thus being able to personally compare it at two crucial points in time. In addition, I have had the further good fortune of being a colleague and/or instructor of some of the school's leading teachers, researchers, and administrators, thus putting me in a favorable position to ask questions about the school's progress during a 30-year period. I have tried to view the school from a perspective of the general sociology of bilingual education throughout the world and, as a result, have ventured in past years to express some favorable opinions about its sociocultural-communal anchoredness and its readiness for principled pedagogical experimentation.

A Place To Be Navajo is a sensitive intertwining of ethnography, history, and pedagogy, as well as an extremely thoughtful evaluation of an ongoing 30+ year educational experiment that has worldwide implications. Typical of its unsurpassable refinement is its recognition that a minority language desperately needs "a place" it can call its own—indeed, "its own" without reservations, qualifications, or uncertainties. McCarty is to be applauded not only for this all too rare recognition, but also for suggesting that the Rough Rock School could both be such a place and yet *not* be such a place in any ultimate, all-encompassing and totally acceptable way. Languages are not just abstract and abstruse subjects, like arithmetic, spelling, and history, that can be perfectly tamed by their segregating school institutions and taken out for display purposes (e.g., for an examination or a report card) whenever there is a formal occasion to do so. Languages do not really attain their proper shape or function in schools. *Their proper "place" is really out of school* (both in days and in years before school and after school). While the facility achieved in them can also be displayed at examinations and on report cards, their true rationale is personal and interpersonal expression and participation within a complex sociocultural-communal communication network. Thus, to foster a language and to develop true facility in it is to both expand its "place" and to implement its appropriateness for all of the functions, statuses, and roles with which this "place" is and can be regularly associated. *Thus a language cannot and should not just be invoked at school,* for to do so would be to compartmentalize it beyond any recognizable naturalness, authenticity, or vitality. McCarty brilliantly demonstrates this by presenting the active actors on behalf of and in opposition to Navajo at Rough Rock, Indian as well as non-Indian, in all of their communal poignancy and interrelatedness. She does so because she implicitly knows that the "place for Navajo," just as the "place to be Navajo," is not just the school but *the Rough Rock community as a whole.*

However, if that is the case (and it is), then it must also be granted that Rough Rock will always be a bilingual community. Many of the functions of Navajo will have to be shared (even between Navajos) with English. This puts Navajo face-to-face with the greatest power-linked language of the modern world. In order to survive this competition, Navajo must also have some functions and statuses that are entirely and exclusively its own, and to which powerful English will simply not be admitted. The school may need to be bilingual, but perhaps the intimate and identity-forming family setting should not be. The shopping expedition to a larger town (on- or off-reservation) may well be bilingual, but perhaps the religious rite should not be. The open sessions of the Navajo Tribal Council may be bilingual, but perhaps its governing working committees should not be. Many of these functional differentiations are sociocultural-communal arrangements that still need to be normatively "worked out" and authoritatively established and implemented.

Let us hope that the aforementioned additional interactive settings, especially those that are somewhat more removed from the school, will also have their sympathetic, able, and intelligent observers and reporters during the years ahead. With the admission and cultivation of the bilingual/bicultural school at Rough Rock, the full story of the "place[s] to be Navajo" will doubtlessly have to be updated and told again and again during the lifetimes of Rough Rock's present and future Indigenous generations. McCarty's chapters set a very high standard indeed for the subsequent expansions and detailizations that the "place[s] to be Navajo" will need to undergo during the decades ahead.

—*Joshua A. Fishman*
Distinguished Professor, Social Sciences, Ferkauf Graduate School,
Yeshiva University and Visiting Professor, *Stanford University,*
New York University, CUNY Graduate Center,
and *Long Island University* (Brooklyn Campus)

FIG. P.1. "[P]laces consist in what gets made of them—in anything and every-thing they are taken to be."—Keith Basso, "Wisdom Sits in Places" (1996, p. 56). Black Mesa and Rough Rock area, the place of the first American Indian commu-nity-controlled school. (Photograph by Fred Bia, courtesy of Rough Rock Com-munity School.)

Preface

On July 7, 1966, five leaders from the Diné community of Rough Rock, Arizona, met to chart the direction of the new local school they had been elected to govern. Yazzie Begay, John Caboni, John Dick, Teddy McCurtain, and Ada Agnes Singer had been chosen to inaugurate a different kind of school—one to be controlled by Navajo people (Diné), which would position parents and community members at the center of children's formal education.

That first school board meeting began a course of action that forever changed Rough Rock and Indigenous schooling in the United States. This book is one story of those transformations. Although it is ethnographic, it is not an ethnography (see Wolcott, 1999). I choose instead to call it a critical life history. The unit of analysis is a single and singular community-based school. The text is unfinished, as all histories are when the life of the individual or institution continues to unfold. And it is partial, situated, and perspectival, reflecting my location as an invested outsider and "knower in the work" (Lather, 1999, p. 3).

As Levinson and Holland (1996) note, the critical perspective "has always been informed by a strong commitment to ideals of equality in education" (p. 4). More than a story of a single community and school, this is an inquiry into Indigenous schooling and the larger struggle for self-determination by Indigenous and minoritized communities.[1] My goal is to listen and to tell, through the multiple lenses of Indigenous oral testimony and critical ethnography, how that struggle has been lived in one time and place, and what its broader implications might be. Listening and telling *can* be forms of emancipatory practice: When we truly listen with "ears to hear" (Nietzsche, cited in Babich, 1994), we open ourselves to new understandings. When we truly understand, we are freed to

---

[1]Throughout the text, I use the term "minoritized" rather than "minority." As a characterization of a people, "minority" is stigmatizing and often numerically inaccurate. Navajos living within the Navajo Nation are, in fact, the numerical majority. "Minoritized" more accurately conveys the power relations and processes by which certain groups are socially, economically, and politically marginalized within the larger society. This term also implies human agency.

enact a vision of education that is democratic, just, and uplifting (see, for example, Espín, 1995; hooks, 1994).

A Place To Be Navajo grows out of 20 years of ethnographic and collaborative work at and with the community of Rough Rock. The title derives from a comment by colleague and friend Galena Sells Dick, a native of Rough Rock and a bilingual teacher who currently directs the school's pre-K–12 bilingual/bicultural program. In the course of our long-term work together, Galena and I became involved in reconstructing her personal literacy history. The eldest child in a large extended family, Galena was urged by her father to complete an education in Anglo-American schools. *Ólta'*, school, she explained, means "a learning place associated with the Whiteman's world." In Federal boarding schools miles from home, Galena Dick learned a new way of life. The most difficult change, she told me, was the language: "We were forced and pressured to learn English. We had to struggle" (Dick & McCarty, 1996, p. 72).

Children caught speaking Navajo were slapped with rulers or made to scrub floors with a toothbrush; some had their mouths "washed" with yellow bar soap. These practices were meted out by White teachers and Navajo dormitory personnel alike. "This shows that even for Navajo educators and school employees," Galena pointed out, "school was not a place for Navajos to be Navajos" (Dick, 1998, p. 24).

Founded and nurtured during the Civil Rights movement and a period of intense Indigenous activism, Rough Rock is called *Diné Bi'ólta'*, The People's School.[2] It represents a turning point in Indigenous education. In the words of one prominent bilingual educator, never again could educators justify why they "were not attempting to have community-based curriculum" in Indigenous schools (Wayne Holm, interview, January 31, 1996).

Although Rough Rock's development has been far from untroubled, the school was and is about Indigenous language, culture, and education rights. Given this, the book's title, I hope, speaks for itself. In July 1966, for the first time and at Rough Rock, one community began a journey to make school a "place for Navajos to be Navajo."[3]

---

[2]The literal translation of *Diné Bi'ólta'* is The People (Navajos) Their School. As used here, Diné Bi'ólta' also can refer to The Rough Rock Community's School.

[3]To preserve the integrity of the quotation from which the book's title derives, I have retained the European-influenced tribal designation of *Navajo*, just as Galena Dick spoke it. *Diné*, The People (i.e., Navajos), is the Indigenous collective term used self-referentially. Both Navajo and Diné are commonly used in the community, across the reservation, and in the literature. I use both terms throughout the book. Readers also will note the spelling, *Navaho*, by some authors cited here.

ABOUT THIS BOOK

As is evident from the title, this is a story strongly rooted in the relationship of people to place. In this sense the text is "relentlessly local," rejecting "totalizing theories that are blind to local conditions and understandings, and which proceed as though the meanings people make of their lives are without significance" (Levinson & Holland, 1996, p. 22). This is a book in search of local meanings.

At the same time, local meanings cannot be divorced from the larger network of power relations in which they reside. Throughout the text, I tie local conditions to tribal, state, and national interests as a means of analyzing the tensions between local, Indigenous agency and external influence and control. Within that space of tension, contradiction, and possibility, Rough Rock and other Indigenous communities struggle for voice, for a place to be Indigenous *in Indigenous terms*—a "place to be Navajo."

When the writing began, the text that unfolded was largely descriptive. In the process of writing I came to appreciate the profound relevance of the oral testimony and history upon which the book is based for theories of cultural production and resistance (Holland, Lachichotte, Skinner, & Cain, 1998; Levinson, Foley, & Holland, 1996). Rough Rock's biography complicates this theoretical framework, and a treatment of it is gently layered throughout the text.

Rough Rock's story springs from its physical and human landscape, and that is where I begin. I also explain how I came to the story—the history of my involvement with the school and community and my role as researcher, collaborator, interpreter, and framer of the account. Subsequent chapters grow out of the oral histories that form the book's foundation, including elders' narratives of community origins and traditional education practices as well as their accounts and their children's accounts of often horrific experiences in Federal Indian schools. Two parallel themes weave throughout these accounts: on the one hand, the constant pressure of governmental attempts to manage and control Navajo lives, and, on the other, the creative resistance of community members to those colonizing forces.

The demonstration school entered Rough Rock not as a grass roots development, but as part of the apparatus of a then-beneficent state. An offshoot of Federal War on Poverty programs, the demonstration project sought to use the school as a vehicle for developing local leadership and the local economy. Several chapters document the unfolding of this experimental project, and what one school board member would describe as the "life and death struggle" of Indigenous schools. This includes the paradox of "doing" Navajo education within the confines of a historically alien institution, the moments of opportunity seized in the name of self-determination, and the dilemma of how to respond to the forces of linguistic and cultural assimilation emanating from both within and outside the school. The book concludes by returning to a statement by a bilingual teacher at the school, that its writing represents an opportunity to tell "what are the hopes and dreams of Rough Rock." Reflecting on this statement, I suggest historical, theoretical, and advocacy implications of this very local but broadly significant demonstration in Indigenous schooling.

This book is thus part of a larger discourse on minoritized schooling and Indigenous languages and cultures (see, for example, Cajete, 1994; Hornberger, 1996; Kawagley, 1995; Lipka, Mohatt, & The Ciulistet Group, 1998; Lomawaima, 1994; Manuelito, 2001; McLaughlin, 1992; Peshkin, 1997; Philips, 1983; Spring, 1996; Tompkins, 1998; Valdés, 1996; Wax, Wax, & Dumont, 1964; Wolcott, 1967). Informed by critical education theory, the book raises issues of Indigenous identity, voice, and community empowerment. It also raises issues of praxis—that is, of how to apply principles of social justice to build a more just social world.

As one of the few ethnographic accounts of Indigenous schooling, this book is intended, first and foremost, to engage Indigenous educators and parents, at Rough Rock and beyond. I also believe Indigenous issues and perspectives must penetrate the "mainstream" debates on education reform, bilingualism, multiculturalism, literacy learning, and language planning and policy. I have therefore written with a wide audience in mind—educators, anthropologists, sociologists, language and literacy specialists, policy analysts, and scholars in American Indian and Ethnic Studies. Finally and importantly, the book is intended to inform a broader readership of policy makers and citizens who cast votes on such crucial issues as the restriction of minority language rights and access to jobs, education, and social services. This is, in short, social research for social change (Fine, 1996). Rough Rock has much to teach us all, and it is in this spirit that I offer the following account.

—*Teresa L. McCarty*
Tucson, Arizona

Acknowledgments

Every text has a subtext, and this is no exception. *A Place To Be Navajo* has been 20 years in the making, and in that time I have amassed a multitude of authorial debts. I would never have gone to Rough Rock without the support of Robert and Ruth Roessel, two of the most influential people in American Indian education up to the present time. Their mentorship, wisdom, and the passion they hold for Navajo education have inspired me from the beginning of our friendship. In many ways, this book began with them.

I would never have stayed at Rough Rock for so long without the support of colleagues there. Regina Hadley Lynch, Fred Bia, Gene Johnson, and Norman Eck were my first work associates at the Rough Rock School. They welcomed me into the community, challenged me at appropriate moments, and shared their stories with me. Much of what I learned from and with them is recorded here.

Afton Sells, Dan Estell, and Gary Coan gave me the opportunity to return to Rough Rock in 1988 to collaborate with them on the school's bilingual/ bicultural education program. That story is told on these pages, too. For their contributions to that part of the account, I am particularly grateful to bilingual teachers Sally Begay, Lorinda Gray, Emma Lewis, Evelyn Sells, Gloria Sells, Lynda Teller, Lorene Tohe van Pelt, and Rita Wagner.

Two people have been especially important in my recent work and relationships at Rough Rock. Galena Sells Dick has been my co-researcher, teaching partner, advisor, and friend. She and her husband, Ernest W. Dick, have made my family and me feel a part of their family. As president of the Rough Rock School Board in 1995, Ernest Dick was directly responsible for commissioning this book. I thank Galena and Ernest for making this book, and my long-term involvement at Rough Rock, possible.

When it began to look like this would in fact become a book-length manuscript, I began searching for a publisher. One winter day I called Joel Spring and asked if he might be willing to review it for his series on Sociocultural, Political, and Historical Studies in Education. Although I was familiar with his work, I had never met or spoken with Joel before. He surprised me with his first-hand knowledge of Rough Rock and Navajo education. Soon, I had the good fortune to be working with both Joel and Senior Editor Naomi Silverman at Lawrence Erlbaum Associates. This book has benefited greatly from their belief that, in Naomi's words, "books can change the world," and from their editorial and substantive advice. The book also has benefited from the superb production expertise of Linda Eisenberg and the LEA staff.

After Joel Spring and Naomi Silverman, Courtney Cazden, Char Ullman, and Murray Wax read the earliest versions of the book. Char Ullman ultimately read it again ... and again. I thank Courtney, Char, and Murray for their thoughtful feedback and encouragement. Harry Wolcott reviewed a subsequent version as he traveled cross-country by train to the 1999 American Anthropological Association Meeting in Chicago. There, he devoted several evenings to discussing the manuscript with me. I thank Harry for giving so generously of his time, and for his incisive commentary.

Many other colleagues and family members graciously donated their time to read and offer comments on the manuscript. I owe a great debt of gratitude to them all—Galena and Ernest W. Dick, Wayne Holm, Nancy Hornberger, K. Tsianina Lomawaima, John Martin, Susan and Glen Minor, Robert A. Roessel, Jr., Richard Ruiz, Irene Silentman, Bernard Spolsky—and to my father, James McCarty, who applied an English teacher's expertise to make the text more readable. My stepfather, John Doulin, provided invaluable assistance with the final preparation of the photographs.

Special thanks are due to Wayne Holm, another legendary figure in Navajo education, who provided 35 pages of handwritten comments on an earlier draft of the manuscript. This book has been enhanced immeasurably from his insights and extensive knowledge of Navajo/American Indian education and history.

My spring 2000 Qualitative Methods class also evaluated an earlier version of the manuscript. I especially thank María Inés Armenta, María Hilda Bernabei, Stephanie Charging Eagle, Christina Lawson, Joseph Martin, and Mary Ann Stack for their thoughtful feedback.

Most of the oral narratives in this account were originally recorded in Navajo. For their assistance in translating and transcribing these texts, I thank Mildred Walters, Geneva John, Mary Willie, and Irene Silentman. They made the text accessible to a wider readership. To Millie Walters, who labored over the transcriptions and translations for several years, and Irene Silentman, who gave the Navajo spellings and grammar a final inspection, I owe additional thanks. Any remaining linguistic or interpretive errors, of course, are mine alone.

These pages are uniquely graced by the power and beauty of Fred Bia's art, and to Fred, my long-time colleague and friend, I owe extra words of gratitude. Thank you for publicly sharing your work, and for helping me, and readers, glimpse an insider's view of Rough Rock.

To Sanford (Sandy) Kravitz, thank you for sharing—at the penultimate moment of the book's production—your "best Washington story," retold in abbreviated form in chapter 6. I salute your leadership in helping to establish the first Indigenous community-controlled school.

There are many others at Rough Rock and beyond to whom I am indebted: the 1995–1996 Rough Rock School Board; current Executive Director Monty Roessel for continued support of the project and assistance with archival photographs; school registrar Benjamin Bennett for providing access to school records and a 30-year perspective on the Rough Rock School; former Executive Director Carl Levi for tangibly supporting the book project with equipment and interviewee honoraria; Stephen Wallace for tutoring me in the curriculum development project described in chapter 10; the late Susanne M. Shafer for mentoring me throughout my original fieldwork and beyond; W. K. Kellogg National Fellowship Program advisor Hubert Jones for many late nights of valuable advice; Kellogg Fellows Martha Bidez, Lora-Ellen McKinney, and Cathy Raines for writing tips and encouragement; Ray McDermott for steering me to the ethnography of place; Jerry Lipka for supporting and helping to expand the teacher–researcher collaboration examined in chapter 11; Shearon Vaughn for completing the graphics in record time; and Joshua and Gella Fishman for their gentle but firm reminders that the places for Indigenous languages and cultures ultimately must be constructed outside of school.

To all those who agreed to be interviewed for the book, I extend my deep appreciation. I hope you will find authenticity and respect for your words here.

Several grants facilitated the fieldwork and transcription/translation of Navajo oral history texts. I gratefully acknowledge the support of the W. K. Kellogg National Fellowship Program; the University of Arizona College of Education Research Fund; and the University of Arizona Foundation.

Finally, I thank my parents, Virginia Doulin and James McCarty; my step-parents, Mildred McCarty and John Doulin; my sisters, Julie Pitchford and Valerie Mussi and their families; and my niece, Amity Pitchford Roebke, who accompanied me on many of the oral history interviews. I have learned from each of you and have been blessed by your support. To my husband, John Martin, I owe an enormous debt. Your faith in me and this work can never be repaid.

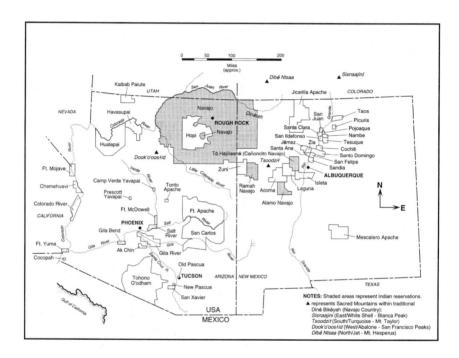

FIG. 1.1. The Navajo Nation and Rough Rock in the U.S. Southwest.

Framing the Story

From its origins in the Pagosa Mountains in Colorado, the San Juan River forms an arch within the Four Corners region of the southwestern United States—that point in the high desert where the borders of the modern states of Arizona, Colorado, New Mexico, and Utah meet. As the arch descends southwestward toward the Colorado River, it is met by Chinle Wash, which winds for nearly 100 miles through a landscape of red rock buttes and mesas, multi-hued canyons thick with cottonwoods, and small family farms. This is the heart of the Navajo Nation. It is the place where people settled with their livestock after leaving Dinétah, the Diné (Navajo) homelands near present-day Farmington, New Mexico. It was also the site of some of the most intense Navajo resistance when, in the autumn of 1863, Colonel Kit Carson led a scorched earth campaign through the Chinle Valley and adjoining Canyon de Chelly, burning fields and homes, slaughtering family sheep, and precipitating the exile and incarceration of 8,000 Navajos at Fort Sumner, New Mexico.

U.S. Highway 191 runs through the Chinle Valley now. Driving north from Chinle, Arizona, a town of about 3,000, one sees, beyond the modern housing and tourist facilities built to accommodate visitors to Canyon de Chelly, the forested mountains of the Defiance Plateau and, nearer the road to the west, a long and narrow red rock ridge, behind which rises the tan and blue-streaked contours of Black Mesa.[1] On each side of the road are traditional hogans (in Navajo, *hooghan)*, or earth and log homes, alongside frame houses, mobile homes, and family fields. In summer, the fields lie green with corn, squash, melon, and alfalfa.

About 15 miles north of Chinle is the smaller settlement of Many Farms and a sign pointing west that reads, "Rough Rock, 15 miles." This is the way I entered the Rough Rock community more than two decades ago as a non-Indian

---

[1]Black Mesa also is known as Black Mountain or *Dziłijiin* (literally, mountain, it extends black, the one; Young & Morgan, 1987, p. 360), but Black Mountain has come to mean the area near the Rough Rock Trading Post, and Black Mesa the area as a whole. Black Mesa is the English term used most frequently by Rough Rock residents.

hired by the Rough Rock School Board to help develop a K–12 Navajo bilin-
gual/bicultural curriculum. I have purposefully introduced the story of the
Rough Rock Demonstration School this way, mapping an outsider's route into
the community and school.

I first took the turn-off to Rough Rock on a crisp, blue-skied March after-
noon in 1980. Dr. Robert A. Roessel, Jr., the school's cofounder and first director, was helping to develop Rough Rock's Navajo Studies program, and he
invited me to assist. Recently relocated from my hometown of Columbus,
Ohio, I was a young graduate student in social-cultural anthropology at Arizona
State University (ASU), where I had been working with Robert Roessel, who
also was serving as a visiting professor at ASU's Center for Indian Education.
Previously, I had worked as a youth counselor, teacher, and educational liaison
for the Fort McDowell Yavapai-Apache community near Phoenix. In the context of that work and my studies, I learned of the ground-breaking initiatives in
Indian education taking place at Rough Rock. Of my first glimpse of this fa-
mous place, I wrote in my field journal:

> Leaving Many Farms, there is a steep, short climb to the top of the ridge. Above
> lies a sweep of blue-green foothills and sandstone bluffs. Rising about 500 feet
> above these bluffs are the dark, steep cliffs of Black Mesa. The school is nestled at
> the base of the cliffs. I immediately recognized the familiar water tower and ele-
> mentary school complex from the many photographs of Rough Rock in books.

Rough Rock School in 1980 had been in operation for 14 years. Founded in
1966, the school grew out of Federal War on Poverty programs. By the time I
moved to Rough Rock in the fall of 1980 it already had been established as an
innovative program in Indigenous education—the first school to have an all-
Navajo governing board and the first to teach Navajo language and cultural
studies. Numerous books and articles had been written about the school, and
Rough Rock's Navajo Curriculum Center, started in 1967, had published dozens of texts and teachers' guides on Navajo language, culture, and history. But
the school board and staff felt the Navajo curriculum was incomplete, and in
1980 they submitted a proposal for a 3-year Federal grant to fill in the gaps. The
grant was funded and I was hired as a curriculum writer for the Materials Development Project which, in addition to my position, funded a Navajo language
and culture specialist, an artist, and a secretary/editorial assistant—all members of the community.

I lived at Rough Rock for the next 3 years. In addition to working on the curriculum, and with the school board's consent, I completed a dissertation on the
school's bilingual/bicultural program (McCarty, 1984; 1987; 1989). In 1987,

FIG. 1.2. Rough Rock Elementary School and dormitories, 1983.
(Photograph by Fred Bia, courtesy of Rough Rock Community School.)

while employed by the Arizona Department of Education's Indian Education Unit, I was invited back to Rough Rock to work as a consultant to bilingual teachers and the elementary school principal on a new bilingual/bicultural program they were developing with the Hawai'i-based Kamehameha Early Education Program (KEEP; see Begay, Dick, Estell, Estell, McCarty, & Sells, 1995; Vogt, Jordan, & Tharp, 1993). Although I currently teach at a university 450 miles away, I have continued to work at and with the people of Rough Rock ever since, traveling there regularly to conduct ethnographic observations of bilingual classrooms and to collaborate with teachers, teacher aides, parents, and administrators on the bilingual/bicultural program.

In the course of this long-term work, my family and I established lifelong friendships with many people at Rough Rock. I long ago stepped "over the line" between researcher–writer and friend—a line that is, I believe, artificial and obstructive to long-term ethnographic and applied research and that, at any rate, would have been impossible to sustain for more than two decades of involvement with this small, kin-centered community (see Valdés, 1996, p. 13).

This is not a disinterested or dispassionate account. The impetus for writing comes from my desire to consolidate my long-term work with the school, and a request from the school board and staff. In 1996, Rough Rock marked its 30th anniversary as the first American Indian community-controlled school. A great deal of enthusiasm preceded this event, and the school board wanted a book that would chronicle the history of the school. I was both humbled and excited to be asked to work on such a book, but from the beginning I believed it should be a collaborative effort. In September 1995, I met with then-school board president Ernest W. Dick and several school staff members to discuss the possibilities. They made it clear that they wanted a balanced account—one that thoughtfully confronted a full range of experiences and processes glossed with the value-laden terms, "success" and "failure" (see, e.g., Varenne & McDermott, 1998). As my colleagues at Rough Rock described it, the goal in this book was to reflect on the school's history. "In 30 years, what were some of the accomplishments and problems? We want to establish a real experience," Ernest Dick said. "The way I look at it, it's how Indian education actually survived."

These words hint at the theory of history that guides this account. This is not a history of universals or absolutes, but an "effective history" in the way Nietzsche (1887/1968) and, a century later, Foucault described: It "deals with events in terms of their most unique characteristics" (Foucault, 1984, p. 88; see also Eisenhart, 1998, p. 395). It is a history that uses local memory to challenge dominant historical narratives, and to re-imagine the possibilities within Indigenous schooling (Lipsitz, 1990; McLaren & Tadeu da Silva, 1993). This is a history concerned not with continuity but with disruption and discontinuity; not with detailing intrinsically knowable events, but with understanding the complicated forces that positioned one community at the center of a movement for Indigenous education control.

From this perspective, Ernest Dick's words in 1995 were prophetic, for, as I discuss below, Rough Rock almost did not survive its 30th year. But in the fall of 1995, hopes were high, and we—a voluntary team of teachers, school board members, administrators, and other school staff who expressed an interest in the project—began to plan the book. The centerpiece would be a series of oral history interviews of community members and people outside Rough Rock who had a role in the school's evolution. High school students would act as videographers for the interviews. "The students think it's wonderful," their teacher reported at an initial meeting of the team. "They're really excited. They've written questions. They want to be part of it. And they say, 'Oh, Rough Rock's important?' 'Yeah, you know, we're talking about it being the first community school.' I think this could be an experience that really could touch them .... It brings the story full circle."

The methodology for the interviews and this study as a whole is discussed more fully in the following chapter. Here, let me briefly summarize the events that preceded the writing. We—the self-identified "book project team"—began the first series of interviews in January 1996. In March I returned to Rough Rock for additional interviews. On April 22, a day before I was scheduled to return for a final series of community interviews, a group of about 100 parents, students, and staff staged a protest at the school, preventing buses from entering the elementary school parking lot and calling for the removal of certain administrators and school board members. The rift within the community growing out of this event has only begun to heal; the causes are enormously difficult and complex, and they relate directly to the issue of self-determination and local education control. I analyze the protest later in the book, recognizing, as Michelle Fine points out, that "the risk lies in romanticizing of narratives" and retreat from analysis (1996, p. 80). Two immediate impacts of the protest were to curtail the interviews and dampen the entire anniversary celebration. Rough Rock marked its 30th year with massive reductions in school enrollment and staff, and with considerable uncertainty about whether it would, in fact, survive.

There was a time when I felt equally uncertain about writing this account. Clearly the events of the spring of 1996 dashed the collaborative efforts originally envisioned for this project, as cooperation among various community members and some school staff became untenable. But I have been fortunate to remain on good terms with all my associates at Rough Rock. All have been adamant in wanting this story to be told. "If you don't do it, Terri," one colleague at the school told me, "no one will."

I have no illusions that this is the case, but I know that the stories told to us by elders and other community members are gifts, intended to be shared. Like others who have written on minoritized education from a position outside the community, I have struggled with how to frame those stories—with, as Guadalupe Valdés writes, "finding a voice with which to write ... respectfully and in friendship" (1996, p. 13). As I present the account that follows, I do so respectfully and in friendship and solidarity, with the hope that this story of Rough Rock will provoke change by illuminating the conditions that enable or constrain Indigenous and other minoritized communities from providing a decent, humane, and uplifting education for their children. "This is an opportunity to recognize the importance of what was started 30 years ago," one school administrator said, "and to rededicate ourselves to that." "This is an opportunity," a bilingual teacher added, "to say what are the hopes and dreams of Rough Rock."

FIG. 2.1. "My parents said there will be life here and people will live here." —Mae Hatathli   (Photograph by Fred Bia, courtesy of Rough Rock Community School.)

People, Place, and Ethnographic Texts

My mother and father came upon this land so many years ago. I don't remember it that well. I think I was about 5 years old. Here we stay on our land that we have had for so many years. Here we have our homes. Our sheep, horses, and cattle—these came here with us. We made life here. My parents said that there will be life here and the people will live here. My father has gone now as well as my mother. Now there are only those of us who are the children. That is how we live.

—*Mae Hatathli, Rough Rock, March 1996*

In her 70s when she gave this account, Mae Hatathli has witnessed great change in the land around Rough Rock and the life it sustains. To a large extent those changes have been wrought by the school. As a starting point for examining those changes and the larger fight for self-determination they both summoned and represent, this chapter sketches Rough Rock's physical and social landscape. I also explain the procedures for data-gathering, the sources of information used to construct this text, and my role in presenting the story that follows.

TSÉ CH'ÍZHÍ

Tsé Ch'ízhí—Rough Rock—is named for the rocks near a spring at the northern base of Black Mesa, which stretches for 60 miles across northern Arizona (see Fig. 2.3).[1] On the southern edge of the mesa lie the 12 Hopi villages where people from Rough Rock traditionally traded mutton and other goods for Hopi peaches and paper-thin *piki* (blue cornmeal) bread. This high, arid, beautiful land supports prickly pear cactus, agave, sage, piñon pine, juniper, and a variety of shrubs and grasses. Above Rough Rock, on Black Mesa, elevations reach over 8,000 feet, and grassy meadows adjoin deep stands of ponderosa and piñon pine.

---

[1] *Tsé Ch'ízhí*, Rough Rock, is used here to describe the place and to introduce the community. Later, I also use "Rough Rock" to refer to the school. The reference to "Rough Rock" as meaning the school and/or the community is clarified by the context in which the reference occurs.

FIG. 2.2.   Rough Rock Springs in winter, c. 1983.
(Photograph by Fred Bia, courtesy of Rough Rock Community School.)

In summer, temperatures on the plateau below the mesa can reach into the 90°s, with periodic torrential rains. Those rains are welcomed for the forage they provide for livestock, and in a good fall season the tawny tufts of wild grasses and a profusion of yellow flowering shrubs and sunflowers line the roadsides. Winters below the mesa are cool but relatively mild, with occasional snowstorms. "On top"—the common reference to settlements on Black Mesa—winter can be isolating and severe. Reverend Vern Ellis, a Quaker missionary who had lived at Rough Rock for almost 30 years when I resided there during the 1980s, recalled the "big snow" of 1973–74, when food and supplies had to be airlifted to families on top. "Lots of people were stranded on top," he said. "It was really critical." With luck, spring brings more rain, and for a month or so, fierce winds. If rain is plentiful, by May the land is carpeted with breathtaking expanses of green grass, golden chamisa or snakeweed, and tiny purple flowers.

At the junction of the Many Farms highway and the road leading into Rough Rock, a sign reads: *"Rough Rock Community School—Diné Bi'ólta."* The road first passes by a cluster of nearly identical stucco employee houses. Beyond this, a water tower imprinted with bold black letters, "Rough Rock," rises against the blue-green face of Black Mesa. Beneath the tower sit the elementary school, dormitories, cafeteria, plant management services building, a clinic, and a large log hogan in which cultural activities take place. Recently, a Navajo Studies Center was established in a double hogan near the entrance to the elementary school campus, with a huge metal identifying sign marking the prominence attached to this program. Surrounding the campus are horseshoe-shaped rows of employee housing and mobile homes. This is the elementary school compound; encircled by wire fence, its physical features resemble those of many small communities across the reservation.

Farther down the road from the junction are the chapter house—the seat of local government for the 1,500 community members—and rodeo grounds. About a quarter-mile further, at the end of the road, are the high school and middle school. Here, where the road forms a T, a graded dirt road leads to the top of Black Mesa. The pavement continues toward an old stone building and another double hogan. From the 1930s to the 1960s, this was a Bureau of Indian Affairs (BIA) day school. Today, these buildings house the school board conference room, school administrative offices, and a school post office. Just west of the administration building is the Friends Mission, and to the east, adjacent to the spring, is the

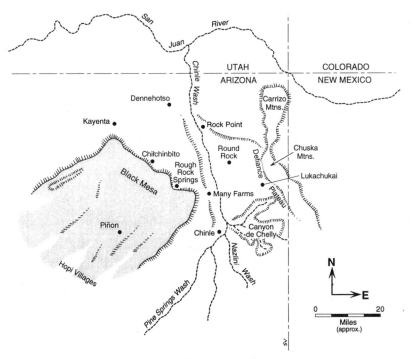

FIG. 2.3. Traditional Rough Rock–Black Mesa land use area.

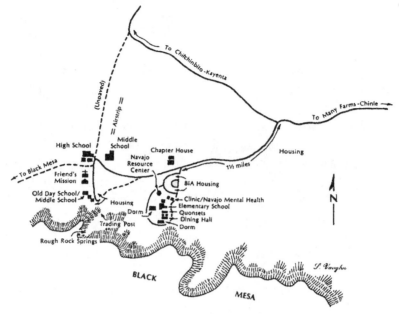

FIG. 2.4.   Rough Rock school complex and surrounding facilities.

Rough Rock Trading Post, also used as the community post office. A third cluster of tribally financed housing is situated across the road (see Fig. 2.4).

Beyond the school, a network of extended family households, locally called camps, dot the land in all directions. Accessible by dirt roads and for the most part not visible from the highway, each household includes one or more frame houses and/or hogans, a ramada or shade house, a stock corral, and often an agricultural field. Many are without running water or electricity. This is "traditional" Rough Rock—the community of matrilineal, extended families in which Navajo remains the dominant language and through which sheep and goat herding, farming, religious life, and mutual aid are organized.[2] Ties of kinship and clanship weave across the network of camps, binding families throughout the area and linking wage earners who live "the modern way," in housing near the school, with relatives who live on and work the land in the traditional Navajo way.

---

[2]The Navajo kinship system has been treated at length by others, and I will not repeat that here. See Kluckhohn and Leighton (1962) for a general account; Witherspoon (1975) provides a more specific analysis based on his fieldwork in the Rough Rock–Black Mesa area. The Rough Rock School also has published a series of student booklets and teachers' guides on kinship and clanship entitled, *K'é Bína'niltin.*

FIG. 2.5. Homestead in the Rough Rock area, at the base of Black Mesa, 1982. (Photograph by Fred Bia, courtesy of Rough Rock Community School.)

COMING TO THE STORY

I made my first survey of this social network in January 1981, when I and my colleagues in the Materials Development Project—Fred Bia, Gene Johnson, and Regina Hadley Lynch—conducted interviews with community members on their views about bilingual/bicultural education. The following summer, we began a 6-month community oral history project in which we interviewed community elders about their lives before and after the coming of the demonstration school. In the course of that work, we constructed extensive genealogies and family histories of people throughout the area. Figure 2.6 shows the network of households in the Rough Rock–Black Mesa area. We interviewed approximately 40 individuals from a cross-section of these households.

Most of these interviews were conducted at peoples' homes and in Navajo by Fred, Gene, or Regina. In a few cases we were able to audiotape the interviews, which Regina translated into English. But many people refused to be recorded by machine. When audiotaping was not possible, our practice was to take copious notes during the interview and, at its conclusion, to drive down the road to a shady

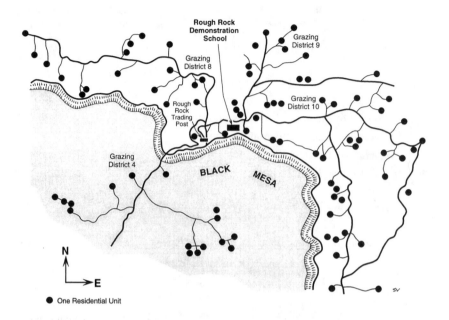

FIG. 2.6. Households in the Rough Rock–Black Mesa area, 1981. (Adapted from Allman, 1978.)

spot where we parked and debriefed in English. I took verbatim notes of the debriefings and shortly thereafter typed them up. (Word processors were not yet in wide use—certainly not on the reservation.) Together, the four of us would then review the debriefings or translated transcriptions to clarify meanings and, as much as possible, render the texts in the interviewees' words. Years later, when we met to plan this book project, Fred Bia recalled our earlier methods:

> The way we've done it before, we've gone out and just talked to them [elders, community people], and come back, and we'll give it to Terri. And I'll just sit down there and talk to her. So you have to have grown up in the traditional way to be the best [the most accurate interpreter/translator]—sometimes you can misinterpret what these people are saying. And after she writes it down, you've got to really check to make sure it makes sense the way you told it to her. And, she can put some fancy words in there, but after awhile it doesn't sound like what you got from the person. So you've got to start going back through it and tone it down some more. It's really important to get it right there from that person [the translator] right at that moment.

Clearly the debriefings alone were an imperfect method! We were able none-theless to use this material to produce a series of attractively illustrated student texts that told a history of Rough Rock from community members' perspectives (Bia, Lynch, McCarty, & Yellowhair, 1982a; 1982b). Several of the people we interviewed in 1981 are now deceased, making their testimony even more pre-cious. I retained copies of the debriefings and transcriptions (the school also has copies), and, with the school board's and interviewees' or their families' per-mission, include some of this material here.

Taking a lesson from that experience, we sought a more systematic and pre-cise method for conducting the more recent interviews. At the school board's request, I developed an overall outline for the book project, which they re-viewed, commented on, and, in revised form, approved. We agreed that if the book were published, royalties would go to a college scholarship fund for Rough Rock graduates. I then generated a preliminary list of questions, a partic-ipant consent form, and an interview protocol; all were subsequently negotiated and revised with the school board and members of the book project team. High school students, who were to act as videographers for the interviews, also de-veloped a list of questions: "How was Rough Rock School 30 years ago?" "How was it like in the old days?" "Do you think this school will continue?" "How old are you?" "What is your clan?" "Did you used to ditch?"[3] "What changes have you seen happen in Rough Rock?" "What would make this school fun for us students after 30 years?" "Who runs this school?" We incorporated these questions into a final list, while still endeavoring to leave the interview process open-ended.

We also generated a list of potential interviewees. Bilingual program direc-tor Galena Sells Dick and community liaison Ray Ann Terry went out into the community to discuss the project with interviewees, obtain consent, and sched-ule the interviews. While this established a more formal tone than we would have liked, we felt it was necessary, both as a courtesy to those who agreed to give their time and stories, and as a way to avoid labor-intensive trips to distant camps only to find no one at home.

When the time came to conduct the interviews, I accompanied Galena, Ray Ann, and the other school staff members and high school students who periodi-cally joined us. For the most part, Galena and Ray Ann conducted the inter-views in Navajo. Interviews typically lasted 1 to 2 hours. Some lasted longer, and on a few occasions we returned for a second interview. All were audiotaped

---

[3]The student's reference here is to unauthorized (by school personnel) absence from school, also known as "skipping" school.

and the students also videotaped several interviews. We took notes, and, as soon as possible after the interviews, debriefed in English, this time with the aid of a laptop computer. Between January and March 1996, we interviewed 15 elders. Between 1996 and 2000, I also interviewed several bilingual teachers and other school staff members, former school board president Ernest Dick, the school registrar, people outside the community who had been involved in the school's early development, and Rough Rock graduates. Although there were more people on our list, including school board members, teachers, and school administrators, the events of the spring of 1996 made interviewing them impossible.

The most difficult problem at this stage was getting the Navajo interviews transcribed and translated. We arranged for this beforehand and several school employees generously offered to help, but the time involved proved, quite simply, to be too much. To complete the translations, I obtained a small grant through my college to hire Geneva John, a native speaker who had grown up at Rock Point, about 40 miles from Rough Rock. Once again, time and limited funds proved to be obstacles. Geneva and I decided that the only way to complete the task was to temporarily bypass transcribing the tapes in Navajo, and to translate them directly into English. Geneva completed all the translations. The process took over a year.

More than a year later, I received a university grant to transcribe and refine the translations of the Navajo oral texts. Mildred Walters, a graduate student in my department at the University of Arizona and a native Navajo speaker from Torreon, New Mexico, completed the transcriptions and revised the translations. Dr. Mary Willie of the University of Arizona Linguistics Department also reviewed and helped refine some of the translations. When the manuscript was nearly complete, Irene Silentman, a linguist with the Navajo Nation Language Project, made final corrections of the Navajo translations. Throughout this process, I conducted "member-checks" with colleagues at Rough Rock; that is, I checked back with them periodically to confirm the accuracy and authenticity of the translated texts and the manuscript in general. In addition to the excerpted narratives presented here in English, the original oral histories and translations will be archived at Rough Rock and the University of Arizona.

All ethnographic texts are filtered through the recorder's perspective and experience, and in this sense are translated texts. Whenever two or more languages are involved, especially languages as typologically different as Navajo and English, the problems of translation are magnified. I present the English translations here knowing that, despite the labors of those who worked so long and so well to make them accessible to a wider audience, they fail to capture the richness and texture of the original accounts. I nonetheless hope that Navajo and non-Navajo readers will find meaning in the translated words.

The oral histories collected from 1996 and those gathered during my earlier work at the school constitute primary resources for this account. I also draw upon 20 years of broader ethnographic fieldwork at Rough Rock and my work in Indigenous education at the state and national levels. As a Rough Rock school employee and community resident during 3 of those years, I was participant, observer, and witness during Rough Rock's "middle years." I saw the school from the inside out and from the outside in, as I participated in weddings, funerals, traditional ceremonies, and the affairs of everyday life. Both formally and informally, I studied and worked with the Navajo language, although I never became proficient. With my colleagues, neighbors, and friends, I shared joys and deep satisfactions as well as sorrows, disappointments, frustrations, and hurts. Throughout this time I kept a field journal and, with the school board's permission and assistance from the school registrar, collected 17 years of school board minutes, student achievement records, newsletters, and other official documents.

By virtue of distance, my more recent work at Rough Rock has been less intense and less rich. But in some respects it has been more collaborative. With Navajo teachers at the elementary school, I have been a co-researcher since 1987 on the school's bilingual/bicultural program and the development of children's literacy in Navajo and English. In this work we have compiled a corpus of data on children's experiences in the community and school today. These data and the teacher research they represent form the foundation for the later chapters of this book, providing a point of comparison to my earlier work and the oral histories.

In the context of this recent work we have observed an alarming shift in children's use of and proficiency in Navajo. More and more children come to school each year with only passive knowledge of the community language. Yet, even as their knowledge of English increases, they are still stigmatized as "limited English proficient," and they experience considerable difficulty in school. Language shift is a reservation-wide phenomenon and, indeed, is a crisis engulfing virtually all Native North American communities today. It is a topic raised poignantly and frequently in the oral history interviews. Perhaps more than any other single experience, language loss sums up the struggle to protect Indigenous identities, lifeways, and rights. I return to these issues in the final chapter of the book.

PHOTOGRAPHY AS A WAY OF KNOWING AND TELLING

This story is told primarily through written text, but also through photographic images. "Much like someone relating a complex story," psychologist and photographer Victoria Muñoz (1995) writes, "a group of photographs strives for cohesion, consistency, and continuity, an overall feeling and tone" (p. 67). Viewing photographs "as if listening to a story," she continues, "offers insights into an understanding of identity as told through images" (p. 67).

With some exceptions, the photographs here are the work of Fred Bia. Most were taken as part of our collaboration on the Materials Development Project from 1980 to 1983. In the course of that work, Fred, a native of Rough Rock who attended the Institute of American Indian Arts in Santa Fe, New Mexico, and who teaches art at Rough Rock, studied with photographers Ansel Adams and Cole Weston. Fred became increasingly active as a photographer, pushing Adams' "zone system" to create the bold black-and-white images that appear on these pages. Fred had always been drawn to photography, he said, because photographs provided a rich resource for his realistic oil and watercolor landscapes.

Fred Bia's photographs offer another pathway into the story, a way of seeing, knowing, and telling through the lens of one who has lived and continues to live the story. The faces and places, captured as moments in time, help make visible a living, breathing experience. They offer another way to read this account and the oral testimony it contains, drawing us into the community and the school in ways that words alone cannot.

ON REPRESENTATION AND WRITING
WITHOUT ANONYMITY

This discussion would be incomplete without acknowledging the issues of representation and anonymity. Those who requested that this book be written did not foresee, nor did they desire, an anonymous case study. This book is about Rough Rock. Because of Rough Rock's status as the first American Indian community-controlled school, it would be disingenuous and impossible to disguise its identity. There is only one.

Historians have been writing life histories of people and places undisguised by pseudonyms for some time. But in the social sciences, particularly in the field of anthropology and education, anonymity remains the rule rather than the exception. In this sense, this *is* an exceptional account. Anonymity and its lack are both problematic. The absence of anonymity entails a special obligation that is both ethical and interpretive, and that spotlights thorny issues of representation in ethnography (see, for example, Fine, 1996; Van Maanen, 1995).

I do not intend to speak "for" Rough Rock. Instead, by highlighting the voices of Rough Rock community members, I have tried to speak *with* and *to* them. Yet, as K. Tsianina Lomawaima (1994) points out in her history of Chilocco Indian School, I am the one who records, edits, analyzes, organizes, constructs, and ultimately, *writes* the account (pp. xvii, xvi). My response is to tell the story as transparently as possible—that is, to make clear, in language that is at once accessible to a broad audience and attempts to do justice to the complex issues at hand, the many perspectives that frame the account. Still, there is no mirror-like relationship "between the word and the world" (Lather, 1999, p. 527). This account is filtered through my position as a White female who grew up in urban working-class circumstances very different from those about which I write.

It goes without saying that I have kept confidential that information entrusted to me in confidence. To the best of my knowledge, no information is revealed here that might compromise those individuals whose words or experiences appear on these pages. This means that some important information has been omitted; I take responsibility for this. No account is ever complete. This account, like others, is partial.

PARTICIPATION, AUTHENTICITY, AND SOCIAL ACTION

"Real participation," Margaret LeCompte (1993) observes, "may even mean a lifetime of collaboration" (p. 15). My involvement at Rough Rock does not span a lifetime, but 20 years is a *long* time. While I think I know the community well, I recognize there is very much I do not know and never will. My reading of Rough Rock's history and implications is open to critique and debate (Tate, 1997).

At the same time, basic tenets of researcher responsibility and concerns for social change demand close attention to authenticity and credibility in the account. I hope that this account will "ring true" to people at Rough Rock and those who know of their work (see Lomawaima, 1994, p. 15). Along with the community members who originally envisioned this book, I also hope this story contains critical lessons for other Indigenous and minoritized communities—and those who study or create policy with and for them—about the possibilities and the struggles in Indigenous education. I hope, in short, that understanding will animate social action and fulfillment of the vision of social justice for which Rough Rock stands.

Rough Rock has much to teach us about how to create more just and democratic education systems in which children and their communities grow and thrive because of, not despite, who they are. At the same time, Rough Rock's history illustrates Joshua Fishman's (1984) argument that by their very nature, schools represent a dual-edged sword; even when they are under community control, schools lead out of and away from the community they serve. The increasing intrusion of English into the most intimate family and community domains at Rough Rock, despite the school's long history of bilingual/bicultural education, is evidence of this, and of just how powerful and insidious the levers of assimilation can be.

Can school really be "a place to be Navajo," a place to be Indigenous, a place where children learn, grow, and question from a position that values and builds upon who they are? These are extremely difficult questions, and they weave throughout the school's biography. I proceed on the assumption that schooling constructed by and through Indigenous communities *can* be a counter-force to the myriad forces that seek to marginalize and erase Indigenous voices and identities. Finding ways to achieve these goals is what Rough Rock is all about, and the story this account seeks to tell.

FIG. 3.1. "The land, if you learn it, will be your livelihood."—Frank X. Begay (Photograph by Fred Bia, courtesy of Rough Rock Community School.)

3

"How It Was"

One of the defining characteristics of colonial schooling for Indigenous children was its intentional disregard for the community "funds of knowledge" children bring to school (González, Moll, Floyd-Tenery, Rivera, Rendón, González, & Amanti, 1995). "Back then," Galena Dick recalls of her early school experiences, "we easily distinguished between the home and school cultures.... When we returned to school, we identified ourselves as a different person" (Dick & McCarty, 1996, p. 75). These conflicts are nearly universal in Indigenous accounts of going to school (see, e.g., Grant, 1996; Ilutsik, 1994; Lipka et al., 1998; Sekaquaptewa, 1969; Watahomigie, 1998; cf. Horne & McBeth, 1998). The conflicts and their material consequences influence both the responses of Indigenous communities to contemporary education programs, and the linguistic and cultural resources available to implement those programs.

To understand these issues at Rough Rock and their broader implications, we must examine "the historical spaces of the past and present" in which the issues reside (Popkewitz, 1998, p. 535). What events, relationships, and life routines have molded collective identities at *Tsé Ch'ízhí* ? What processes have helped construct individual senses of self? This chapter explores those processes—what Holland, Lachicotte, Skinner, and Cain (1998, p. 18) call the "sediment of past experiences"—primarily through the words of community elders.

BECOMING AWARE

We were small when our mother died and our grandmother took us in. At that time, the homes were so far apart. People were only talked about as being far away. Right here, there were no children at the time we were small. We didn't know each other or even see each other. I don't know why it was like that. There were no hospitals, either. When the children caught a cold or got sick, they would be cared for at home. This was how it was. We only had a trading post with no other buildings. That is how I became aware of it.

—Dorothy Begay, Rough Rock, January 1996

People speak of "becoming aware" of their surroundings—*háni' hazlį́į́'*, "when one becomes aware"—and *ádaa' áhozhniidzį́į́*, "when one becomes self-aware." According to Navajo theories of child development, this is the period between the ages of 2 and 6, when personal histories begin (Begay, Clinton-Tullie, & Yellowhair, 1983, p. 15; Begishe, 1981).

For elders at Rough Rock, those histories are rooted in memories of the land, and of life in the camp with parents, aunts, uncles, siblings, grandparents, and other kin. "I became aware of things when I turned 6 years old," 74-year-old Frank X. Begay said in 1996. Sitting in a room off the kitchen in his tidy home on top of Black Mesa, he continued: "There was rain and the land was wet ... we lived off the land .... Back then, we made our living from planting and livestock."

Written records place Navajo settlement of these lands in the 1600s, although oral historical and archaeological evidence suggest even earlier Navajo habitation here (Goodman, 1982, pp. 54–55). Rough Rock elders start their accounts at or shortly after the Navajos' military surrender to U.S. troops at Fort Defiance, Arizona, and their subsequent 300-mile Long Walk to Fort Sumner, New Mexico, in the winter of 1864. Stories abound of the miserable trek across wintry plains and three rivers, and of the murders by soldiers of elderly people and pregnant women too weak to carry on. "When this anguish and heartache [are] combined with the unequaled physical suffering experienced at Fort Sumner," Robert Roessel (1983) writes, "a faint glimpse of the impact this tragedy had, and continues to have ... may be realized" (pp. 518–519).

Fort Sumner, also called Bosque Redondo by Mexicans, was situated on the east bank of the Pecos River, about 165 miles southeast of Santa Fe, New Mexico. To Diné, the place is known as *Hwéeldi*. To speak of it still brings tears to peoples' eyes.[1] According to tribal historian Martin Link (1968), Hwéeldi symbolizes "death, hardship, suffering, inadequate food and lack of clothing" (p. 1). The government's goal was to transform Navajos into villager-farmers and thereby to dispossess them of their identities and lands. But repeated crop failures, raids by other tribes whose territories the military post occupied, the corruption of the Indian agents in charge, and a smallpox epidemic that took over 2,300 Navajo lives finally led to a government investigation and an end to this

---

[1]Young and Morgan (1987) state that *Hwéeldi* is derived from the Spanish *fuerte,* fort or stronghold (p. 463). For Navajo testimonials on the Long Walk and Hwéeldi, see Broderick H. Johnson and Ruth Roessel's (1973) edited volume, *Navajo Stories of the Long Walk Period.*

genocidal "experiment" (Bailey, 1978; Spicer, 1962). In 1868, 29 Navajo leaders signed *Naaltsoos Sání,* the Old Paper or treaty that returned 3.5 million acres of Navajo lands. The treaty also promised that for every 30 Navajo children between the ages of 6 and 16, a schoolhouse and teacher "competent to teach the elementary branches of an English education shall be furnished" (Article VI, reprinted in Link, 1968, p. 7).

Bit'ahnii Yéé Be'esdzáán provided the earliest local account of that time. It was a warm June day in 1981 when Fred Bia and I drove to her camp. She was sitting outside, on a bed under a shade house, a gray kitten curled near her lap. Bit'ahnii Yéé Be'esdzáán was perhaps 90 years old at the time. Her mother had been born in captivity at Fort Sumner.

> My mother's name was K'é Hoonibah. When my mother was being born, a group of soldiers came up over the hill carrying swords. My mother's grandmother was afraid. "What are they going to do to us this time?" my grandmother thought. But all this time, the soldiers had only come to discuss peace with the *naat'áanii* (Navajo leaders) at Fort Sumner. Then all of sudden, there were a lot of people talking up there over the hill. There was peace *[k'é].*

Over a century later, we can only imagine the terror 'Bit'ahnii Yéé Be'esdzáán's grandmother felt at the time, having witnessed the murderous acts of soldiers on the Long Walk. Surely there was relief and hope in the naming of her newborn daughter: K'é Hoonibah means "Peace Finally Found You," "Peace Arrived," or "Peace Caught Up With You." "After my mother was born," Bit'ahnii Yéé Be'esdzáán told us, "they moved back near Rough Rock. My grandmother used to tell me this story."

That time of resettlement and the reunion of families also is marked by the story of a massive rock slide *(Hodeezhoozhí),* the vestiges of which still can be seen on the face of Black Mesa (see Fig. 3.2). The rock slide is a monument to tragedy, a silent witness to genocide. We interviewed Fred Bia's father, Joe Bia, in our office in the fall of 1981. He recalled:

> It happened a little before the people were taken to Fort Sumner. That's the story that's been handed down. The rock slide was a foretelling that something big was going to happen, something that would really change people's lives. Medicine men had visions that there would be trouble. At first there was a little bit of dust rising up, but it kept increasing. The slide kept coming down for 4 or 5 days. That slide, and the event it forecasted, mean a lot to Navajos. They shed tears even to think of it today, and what happened afterward—the anguish and turmoil they went through.

FIG. 3.2. *Hodeezhoozhí*, Rock Slide, a sacred site on Black Mesa.
(Photograph by Fred Bia, courtesy of Rough Rock Community School.)

Adult survivors of Hwéeldi were each to receive a few head of government-issued sheep or goats. According to Link (1968), when people returned to their lands, "they brought back with them only 1,500 horses and mules and 2,000 sheep and goats" (p. 11). The government subsequently distributed seeds, farm tools, hoes, and wagons. These supplies entered the Rough Rock area only sporadically and in meager amounts. Blair Tsosie, a World War II veteran who gave his age in 1996 as 74 or 75, remembered this story of those times:

> This is what my late grandmother said: "When a rock slide occurs, it will bring enemies." ... She said the mountain rumbled for exactly 4 days .... And then the rock slide happened, ... horses neighed, the sheep bleated .... Four years later, enemies came.

> ... It is said that livestock existed in great abundance. All those were taken away. Along came hunger and everything else, until there was nothing. Somehow the people managed to survive.

> My late maternal grandfather had just turned 4 months old, when he and my [great] grandmother went to *Hwéeldi* .... They had no livestock—they had all been taken away. [When the people were released], they were [each] given two goats. They herded them back from *Hwéeldi* .... After [my relatives] had all come back, they settled here .... We still live in the same place.

LAND, LIVESTOCK, AND LIFESTYLE

As Blair Tsosie's account reveals, with their small government-issued rations, people returned to what was left of their lands and began rebuilding their lives. Roessel (1983) observes that confusion surely existed regarding the new reservation boundaries; "the Navajos felt they were returning to the land they lived on prior to Fort Sumner but in reality the 1868 reservation contained no more than 10 percent of the land they earlier owned and used" (pp. 519–520). The 1868 reservation included only parts of the traditional use areas in the Rough Rock–Black Mesa region. In 1878, the U.S. government restored some additional lands to the west. Through subsequent reservation expansions, the reservation grew to encompass 25,000 square miles. Today, the Navajo reservation spreads over parts of northern Arizona and New Mexico and the southern part of the state of Utah, an area roughly the size of the state of West Virginia or the country of Austria. It is the largest and most populous reservation in the United States (see Fig. 1.1).

"It Rained and Snowed a Lot"

The children and grandchildren of Hwéeldi survivors describe a rich and verdant landscape during their youth, one nurtured by abundant snow and rain. As she held her young grandson on her lap, Dorothy Begay continued her story (begun in the epigraph to the previous section):

At the time, we had a lot of rain. *Níłtsá nidi ba'át'é ádin íídą́ą́'*—only female rain.[2] There were plants everywhere then. During the spring, there would be all different flowers making up the earth. When it would get dark, you could see a highlight of plants against the sky. There were yucca plants all over. That is how different flowers made up the place. And that is how we lived with them.

FIG. 3.3.   "Different flowers made up the place, and that is how we lived with them."—Dorothy Begay
(Photograph by Fred Bia, courtesy of Rough Rock Community School.)

---

[2]The literal translation of this is, "Even the rains were gentle then" (Irene Silentman, personal communication, April 26, 2000). Dorothy Begay's words reference female rain; gentle and nourishing, it feeds the soil, allowing vegetation to flourish. Male rain is torrential, running off and eroding the surface soil (Bia, et al., 1982a; Kluckhohn & Leighton, 1962). This conception reflects a gendered duality in Navajo worldview: Life is said to exist between Mother Earth and Father Sky; male and female hogans have distinct architectural styles and purposes; landforms and other aspects of the natural world are similarly gendered (see, e.g., Kluckhohn & Leighton, 1962, pp. 311–312).

Margaret Dalton, 73 when we interviewed her on the first day of spring in 1996, also recalled the rain. Seated at the kitchen table in her mobile home "on top," she shared these images:

> In past winters, at the end of winter, the earth would be frozen .... During this month [March], it would start to thaw. Water would trickle very slowly and the ground would soften ... [until] the ground would rise like bread. The plants and flowers would then sprout up nicely everywhere .... It made a beautiful sight. Those things I became aware of.

FIG. 3.4. John Dick (Táchii'nii/Red Streak clan), 1983.[3]

FIG. 3.5. Thomas James ('Áshįįhí/Salt clan), 1983.

(Photographs by Fred Bia, courtesy of Rough Rock Community School.)

---

[3] As is traditional in Navajo society when introducing oneself, photo captions here include an identification of individuals' maternal clans, with an English translation of the clan name. There are problems, however, with translating clan names, as some have multiple or uncertain meanings. Wayne Holm, director of the Navajo Nation Language Project, notes as a case in point that Táchii'nii, often translated as Red Streak Clan, may have to do with water (personal communication, February 21, 2000), a point supported by Young and Morgan (1987), who translate Táchii'nii as "the red running into the water people" (p. 352 [the noun, water, is *tó*; "into the water" is *taah*; Young & Morgan, 1987, p. 1061]). Holm further points out that the –*nii* affix, referencing clan, more accurately means "those [people] who are X." "One does not somehow participate in 'red-streakness,'" he observes; "one is Táchii'nii" (personal communication, February 21, 2000). To assist non-Navajo readers, I nonetheless include the translated clan names with the photographic identifications. The important point is the local, social meaning attached to clan affiliation (see also Kluckhohn & Leighton, 1962).

The plants, the flowers, the berries of bushes and trees—all these "made up the place," providing food for people and forage for livestock. "Here, there was an abundance of a plant this big," Mrs. Dalton said, gesturing with her hands raised above the floor. It was called *waa'* [wild spinach or "bee weed"]—

> Their flowering tips made a beautiful sight. They were also a source of food. When they grew tall they would be picked and boiled. Some would be stored. Some would [be taken] to the Hopis. They greatly appreciated it. That's how it used to be.

People also harvested piñon nuts, wild onions, yucca seeds and fruit, and red sumac berries. "Upon this Mother Earth, there used to be a great variety of vegetation," John Dick, the first president of the Rough Rock School Board, reminisced. When we interviewed him in the living room of Ernest and Galena Dick's home in 1996, John Dick was unclear of his exact age; he was born "before the papers [census records or cards, both of which preceded the issuing of birth certificates] started." Ernest Dick estimated his father's age at 89. John Dick remembered, "And rain, there was rain! So many different plants used to grow .... People used to gather them."

But the staples of life were corn and the meat and other by-products of sheep, goats, cattle, and horses. These resources organized daily and seasonal routines. "We used to plant over there in Chinle," long-time school board secretary Thomas James reported. In his 80s and legally blind when we interviewed him in his hogan in 1996, he told this story of his younger years:

> Yes, we used to plant corn and squash, watermelon and cantaloupes .... We used to plant in Chinle. When you needed to, you went out to gather plants .... On very rare occasions, there would be flour. That's how it was.
>
> … We had goats. In the morning, you would go out and milk the goats. There were these thin bowls that would be filled [with goat milk] every day. Then you boil [the milk]. Then you add cornmeal .... That's how we ate .... That's what I made my daily job.

The oral histories depict a pattern of fluid family movements governed by seasonal needs for pasture, timber, and water, and by widely recognized rights to customary land use areas. "A Navajo may live wherever his mother has the right to live," Gary Witherspoon reports (1983, p. 526). An anthropologist who directed Rough Rock's Community Services department during the school's early years, Witherspoon adds that "a Navajo may live wherever his or her spouse has the right to live" (p. 526).[4] At Rough Rock, many families maintained winter camps "on top," where they could be assured of adequate supplies of timber for fuel. Others established winter camps below the mesa, returning to the top during summer months to pasture their livestock. As Thomas James indicates, families also maintained summer camps near their fields in the Chinle Valley. All of this is consistent with a diffuse and flexible sense of community and place. There seemed to be land enough for all, and people respected the use rights of others. Blair Tsosie recalled:

> The people moved into the mountains during the summer, then they would move back down .... People drank melted snow during the snow season. They also drank rain water. Sheep and horses drank it as well [and] people used it without fear when preparing food .... That is how it began, granddaughter.

While families moved "from one area to another," as Mae Hatathli told us, they generally returned to the same homesites and use areas year after year.

FIG. 3.6. Hasbah Charley (Bit'ahnii/Under His Cover clan), 1983. (Photograph by Fred Bia, courtesy of Rough Rock Community School.)

---

[4]In their exceptional text, *Between Sacred Mountains: Stories and Lessons from the Land,* Bingham and Bingham (1982) present personal narratives of traditional land use from people living in and around Rock Point, Arizona, about 40 miles northeast of Rough Rock (see Fig. 2.2). For additional discussions of Navajo land use, see also Williams (1970) and Kluckhohn and Leighton (1962).

"There was no concern about land boundaries," Mae Hatathli added. "No one spoke about such things then. People moved from one area to another ... even into the rocky areas. We would spend the summer there. We'd also move into the mountains."

Elders also speak of a web of cooperative relationships that extended from camp to camp. "Back then, people used to help each other out a lot," John Dick said. Hasbah Charley, a great-grandmother when we interviewed her in 1996, recalled her childhood as a time when people "really looked after one another .... People [never] said bad things to each other. They all lived peacefully .... That's how we've come this far."

In his account of Navajo social organization, Witherspoon (1983) refers to this as the principle of communalism. "Communalism operates not only in the placing of individually owned sheep into a common herd, but also in the sharing of the products of the herd. Food from the herd is shared among everyone in the residence group" (p. 535). Oral histories from Rough Rock detail how the sharing of sheep products and other resources provided clothing as well as food. According to Hasbah Charley, "We didn't even have shoes. When it snowed," she explained, "people would go where a horse had been killed. Each person would get a piece [of hide] and bring it back. Boots were made for everyone, and that's what you wore throughout the winter."

Of girls' attire, Hasbah said, "that was only a small part." Smiling, she told of her clothes made from cotton flour bags: "Those flour sacks, remember? They had *dahyiitá* [crescent or quarter-moon shapes] printed on them. When the flour sacks emptied out, they'd be sewn together to make skirts. We walked around with quarter-moon prints! That's what people wore."

During those times, people traveled by horse and on foot; as late as the 1940s, only a few people had wagons. "Whenever we made a move anywhere," Hasbah Charley said, "there were only horses packed with our belongings. There were also many donkeys used as pack animals .... No one knew anything about vehicles."

Hasbah Charley and others described the arrival of the first automobiles—"the strange black thing that crept across the clearing" where the sheep grazed. "'What is it?' people asked. 'Let's all go over and see what it is.' ... It was a small black strange thing with four wheels that Béésh Biwoo'ii [a man named Gold Tooth] was driving around. That's when cars made their appearance."

Thomas James made us all laugh as he related his first encounters with the black thing:

FIG. 3.7. Original stone and adobe structure that was once part of the Rough Rock Trading Post.
(Photograph by Fred Bia, courtesy of Rough Rock Community School.)

One day while I was out herding sheep in the clearing, there was a black car .... I was terrified of it. There was a road through the clearing to Tsélání [a settlement south of Rough Rock on Black Mesa]. There it was, on the road, in the clearing .... I ran for the nearby ditch and out from there .... My mother told me, "Don't cross its path. It will run over you." That's why I was so scared of it!

Automobiles heralded other developments: The black Ford that frightened young Thomas James brought supplies for a new trading post at Tsélání, south of Rough Rock. In 1926, a White trader set up a tent-store near Rough Rock Springs. This became the Rough Rock Trading Post. "It came close enough for us," John Dick recalled, "even for people who lived high in the mesa. They used to lead their horses there with packs."

Traders bought and sold Navajo livestock, served as conduits for temporary wage work off the reservation, expanded the market for Navajo rugs and silverwork, and influenced diet, clothing, and other aspects of daily life. When the Rough Rock Trading Post opened, "people then started going over there and bringing back things like coffee and flour," Thomas James said. He recalled the subsequent transformation in his everyday attire:

> I did not have any of the clothes I am wearing now. There were no shoes. I had no pants, no shirt. I wore only a white cloth sewn into pants and a shirt. I wore moccasins. That was how I went after the sheep …. After the store opened, I got pants, shoes, and even a shirt. I was even given a wide-brimmed hat.

Education in the Community and Home

As in other Indigenous communities during this time, education was not an experience divorced from daily life, but was integral to children's socialization and to everyday affairs. Learning was participation in the social world—involvement in communities of social practice (Lave & Wenger, 1991). "What were girls taught at home?" we asked Mae Hatathli in 1996. "Just to walk the right path and to live a good life," she replied. She went on to provide this description of her upbringing:

> They [parents and elders] always told you how to care for sheep. This is what you were told as a girl …. If someone else should go after the sheep, then [you were told] to prepare some food …. There was also carding wool, spinning, and weaving …. You followed instructions. Though you didn't know how to weave, … you learned by helping to finish a rug …. You could also try to do one yourself if you wanted to. You set up a loom and weave. It might come out lopsided at first, but eventually you got better …. This is how we were taught.

Boys and girls shared the tasks of herding sheep, caring for and handling horses, and grinding corn (see, e.g., Bennett, 1964; Dyk, 1938, p. 9). As Mae Hatathli's account indicates, girls also learned to weave and care for the home. Dorothy Secody, a weaver in her 70s when we interviewed her in 1996, remembered: "Our mother told us the different ways we could prepare food using cornmeal. As I grew up, my mother taught me to weave, and to dye the yarn using different plants."

All the elders speak of parental discipline, which taught important life lessons. In their discussion of Navajo child-rearing, Leighton and Kluckhohn (1974) refer to this as "hardiness training;" it was not intended as punishment, they say, but was for the children's own good (p. 56). Awakening their children in the pre-dawn hours, parents urged the children out of the hogan, instructing them to run toward the east and, in winter, to roll in the snow.[5] "I would be thrown into the snow," Thomas James recounted. "The snow was this deep," he said, raising his hand almost to the seat of his chair, "when my mother took me out, tore off my clothes, and threw me into the snow"—

> Then she would rub snow on me before I could finally come inside, where there was a big fire. I would be dripping with snow and she'd say, "Go back out and take another dip in the snow." I'd go out and take another dip. I would be dripping and full of snow. That is how I was raised.

"It's a good thing my mother did all those things to me," Thomas James concluded. "She talked to me about it .... "Make yourself strong. Test yourself." This is how I was taught and how children were taught then."

Blair Tsosie also noted that, "What I've described seems all rather harsh, but I've lived it"—

> With holes at the knees, without shoes, one would be up and about in the early morning, at dawn. During lambing season, you'd go out with a blanket belted around your waist so when the sheep or goats had [lambs or kids], you'd tuck them in your blanket and bring them home. It was a lot of work and very difficult. They were tough, these men and women, and that's how they were able to survive.

"That's how we all survived," Hasbah Charley insisted. "When it snowed, we were told, 'Go strip and take a dip in the snow' .... We'd come back in all shivering and cold. All young boys and girls were required to do that .... I think that's probably what gave me strength and made me physically strong." "As much as you can handle," Mae Hatathli said, "you were told to do things. Even farming in the cornfields, irrigating, planting—that is what we were told."

Livestock and their importance anchored these teachings. In a 1981 interview, Dorothy Begay described her experiences this way:

> Once we awoke in the morning, the first thing that came to our minds was herding sheep, taking out the sheep, what are the sheep going to eat. Once we had our breakfast, ... there was always someone who was going to tend the sheep. You didn't wait for someone else to do it (cited in Bia, McCarty, & Lynch, 1983, p. 12).

As they reached the age of 6 to 9, "when one begins to think and do things on one's own"—*nitsídzíkees dzizlíí'*—children typically received a lamb or two

---

[5] According to some, where this practice occurred, it was often done only with the first snow (Wayne Holm, personal communication, February 21, 2000).

from parents. Marked with an ear notch associated with the child, the lamb symbolized the beginning of the child's personal herd and the acceptance of adult obligations. "The lambs are placed in the child's care to teach her the importance of livestock in the family economy and to instill in her a sense of responsibility," Navajo educator Shirley Begay writes (Begay et al., 1983, p. 21). Products from the animals, such as wool, were recycled into the family economy. In our 1981 interview with her, Dorothy Begay[6] continued:

> [W]e were taught to weave all day and even at night, carding and spinning the wool for the next rug. Once the rug was completed and sold, you would be ready to begin another one. Young girls and women did this into the late hours of the night. Even so, we were able to get up before the sun rose, when it was still dark, and herd sheep. We were always told that herding sheep and weaving rugs were the ways we would survive [economically] in this world (cited in Bia, McCarty, & Lynch, 1983, p. 12).

Through lectures and stories, parents and elders reminded their children to "Let the livestock which were given to you be your thought …. Let all that has been given to you be your thought" (Begay et al. 1983, p. 37). Parents stressed that livestock would provide children with a living and enable them to survive to old age. Daily observation and experience verified and reinforced those lessons. "I did everything I was told by my parents, especially about the livestock," Hasbah Charley said, recalling these words of her parents and grandparents:

> "We are teaching you here. This fire [home/hearth] that we've built for you, you will make that your school …. You should remember this land that we have given you," they told me …. *Yáa!* Mother, father, I am thankful for what you've taught me. I will remember it always and live by it.

Life lessons from the land, livestock, and home developed children's moral behavior and values. "Sheep are the means of incorporating children into the life and communal economy of the residence group," Witherspoon (1983) writes; in this corporate enterprise, "the child learns the meaning, necessity, and nature of group or communal life" (p. 529). Caring for the herd during the day, working with the products of sheep and goats in rug weaving and food preparation, and listening to instruction regarding proper behavior related to livestock

---

[6]Begay, also spelled Begaye, is an Anglicization of *biye'*, his son, and is a common Navajo surname, not to be taken literally when used in this way. In this case, Shirley Begay and Dorothy Begay are not related.

and land were the contexts in which children internalized communal values. "My maternal grandfather used to say, 'People have survived on sheep and goats, and if you do for yourself and aren't lazy, then it will be worth your while to have them also,'" Frank X. Begay recalled. He elaborated on his grandfather's lessons:

> "Sheep, livestock are a means of survival. If handled right, they will help you survive .... The land, if you learn it, ... will be your livelihood." My grandfather used to say this to me. And it is true .... It is like that today. That is how it is.

As children reached the age of 10 to 12 "when one's thought begins existing"—*honitsékees nilíinii hazlį́į́'*—they participated more fully in adult activities, including learning songs and prayers for earth, home, and livestock, and participating in ceremonies. "There is a song for horses and sheep," Blair Tsosie said, recalling what his elders had told him:

> Mother Earth has a song also. There are prayers [and] you take corn pollen with you whenever you go. With it, you have long life, you progress; it is a way of doing things; it is self-respect .... That which is called caring for oneself, walking in beauty.

> "Some day, at some hour," [I was told], "although you're poor, you will be asked to do something ... a man will have come to you. There is a reason for his coming, an emergency ... there might be an illness ... he might be in search of a medicine man. If you are competent, you will continue his quest .... You will lend your horse. You will be a means of survival." They [the elders] taught in this manner.

For girls, a puberty ceremony still common today—*kinaaldá*—acknowledges and celebrates this time of life. "As a young girl," Dorothy Secody remembers, "my mother told me, when I get my puberty [first menses], please do not hide it, because that is very sacred." The 4-day *kinaaldá* focuses on the girl's physical and mental endurance. She runs in the morning and noon on all but the fourth day, when she runs only in the morning, each time increasing the length of her course. Throughout the ceremony she grinds corn, prepares food, and serves guests. These "will be her tasks as a woman and mother," Shirley Begay et al. (1983) observe; "undertaking them during the four days of her puberty ceremony will prepare her to be helpful and dependable" (p. 71).

Traditional education, then, involved observation and involvement in family activities related to the home, the herd, and the fields, and the gradual assumption of adult responsibilities. Through formal and informal processes, children learned physical and intellectual endurance; in lectures, storytelling, and participation in the social world, they learned the roles, relationships, and ideals of a good and full life. They learned, in short, what it meant *to be Navajo*. In recurring contexts of social interaction, they personalized the cultural resources, language, and symbols that constituted a Diné identity and way of life (Holland et al., 1998, p. 100).

Together, these teachings reinforced a central value, *k'é,* meaning kinship, clanship, peace, love, and "right and respectful relations with others and with nature" (Bia et al., 1983, p. 3; Witherspoon 1983, p. 524). *K'é* embodies the ideals of cooperation, sharing, and respect and responsibility for oneself, one's family, the livestock, and the land. "'You will have visitors continually,'" John Dick remembers being told. "'Someone traveling from afar will spend the night at your home. You will feed him, and he will be on his way. He will be thankful to you.' You must have heard some of these teachings yourselves. Well, this is the way it was."

FIG. 4.1. "We stayed at school all the time. I was very lonely."—Dorothy Secody. (Photograph of Navajo school children courtesy of Arizona State Museum, University of Arizona.)

4

"We Were Going to School Being Taught Only by Anglos"

Interviewer: How old were you when you went off to school for the first time?

Thomas James: Sixteen, it is said .... Yes, that's when I left for school [in 1925]. That was when the policeman [the Indian police responsible for enrolling children in school] came to visit. I left with my late grandfather, Tsinaajinii Hastiin .... I rode double with him on his horse as we went to the school [in Chinle]. I wore a hair bun .... There, they cut off and threw away my hair bun. That is how I started school. There were a lot of older and taller [over-age] students in school.

Interviewer: Tell us about that. What was it like when you first entered school, and what was being taught? Who were your teachers? Were they Navajos or Anglos?[1]

Thomas James: They were all Anglos. There were no Navajos. There were no [Native] teacher aides either. We were going to school being taught only by Anglos. But they were good teachers. They taught us well. [But] if you caused trouble, there was a ruler this size [demonstrating a few feet with his hands] that would be used to slap your palms. That's how it was then.

—*Rough Rock,* January 1996

---

[1]"Anglo" is a common reference for persons who self-identify and/or who are identified by others as White; the term has little or nothing to do with English ancestry. Like other identifiers (e.g., Black, Native American, American Indian, etc.), both "White" and "Anglo" serve to position rather than indelibly define identities. The term in Navajo is *bilagáana*, "White man" (or White person; see Young & Morgan, 1987, p. 221).

In 1887, Congress passed the General Allotment and Compulsory Education Acts, a two-fisted policy of forced assimilation intended to transform Native people into yeomen farmers by dividing their lands, while schooling their children in the trades and domestic service. The effect of the Allotment Act was to dispossess tribes of millions of additional acres of their lands, parceling out allotments to individual tribal members and thereby opening so-called "surplus" lands to Anglo-American settlement. At the same time, compulsory education sought to recast Indigenous identities and, as Lomawaima (1995) points out, prepare Indian people as a working class "amenable to Federal control" (p. 332). Central to this human experiment was the eradication of Indigenous languages. In the words of then-Commissioner of Indian Affairs J. D. C. Atkins (1887/1992):

> The object of greatest solicitude should be to break down the prejudices of tribe among the Indians; to blot the boundary lines which divide them into distinct nations, and fuse them into one homogeneous mass. Uniformity of language will do this—nothing else will (p. 48).

This chapter examines the implementation of these policies within the Navajo Nation and the community of Rough Rock. As will be seen, schooling intruded unevenly into peoples' lives. For many, the initial response was resistance or indifference. Later, the Navajo tribal leadership engaged in a prolonged struggle for more and better schools.

"IT WAS LIKE BEING IN PRISON"/
"IT MADE ME STRONG TO A LOT OF THINGS"

In one of the first (unsuccessful) attempts to live up to the 1868 Navajo Treaty provisions for education, the Indian Bureau in 1882 opened a boarding school run by missionaries at Fort Defiance, the place where Navajo people had been incarcerated prior to the Long Walk. "Navajos were either uninterested or directly antagonistic to the boarding school," anthropologist Edward Spicer (1962) states (p. 223). Disciplinary methods at Fort Defiance resembled those at other Federal Indian schools, and included solitary confinement and chaining students to their beds (see Fig. 4.2).

These practices precipitated violence at Round Rock, about 35 miles northeast of Rough Rock, where, in 1893, community members rose up against Indian agent Dana Shipley as he attempted to kidnap Navajo children and haul them off to Fort Defiance (Roessel, 1983). Shipley was nearly killed

FIG. 4.2. Indian school at Fort Defiance, Arizona, late 19th century. (Photograph from RRCS archives, courtesy of Rough Rock Community School.)

by Bilį́į́lizhinii, Black Horse, a regional leader. The incident reflected wide-spread hostility toward compulsory education at the time.

School stories such as these are now firmly implanted in Rough Rock's oral tradition. After the first BIA school opened at Fort Defiance, eight additional boarding schools were established on the Navajo reservation, including the one at Chinle attended by young Thomas James. Additional boarding schools opened at Fort Apache in eastern Arizona, Fort Wingate in western New Mexico, Phoenix, Albuquerque, and Santa Fe, as well as in California, Kansas, Oklahoma, Nevada, and the state of Washington. These schools were attended by children from many different tribes. The schools were notorious for their English-only curriculum, militaristic discipline, inadequate food, overcrowded conditions, and a manual labor system that required students to work half-days in the kitchens, boiler rooms, and fields, and allowed the government to operate the schools on a budget of 11 cents per pupil per day (Meriam et al., 1928). Of his years at Fort Apache, Thomas James remembered:

> You couldn't expect a great meal before you .... All we had to eat at noon were beans and a piece of bread. It was like being in jail. There wasn't even coffee, only water. That is all we ate. The boys I came with began to feel homesick. We were starving.

Many children fled these conditions on foot, some perishing from exposure on the long trek home. Others succumbed to the brutality of the *siláo,* or police sent to round them up and return them to school.[2] When we interviewed him in 1996, Thomas James told this story of the peril young boys faced at the hands of the *siláo*:

> I had just gotten to school [at Chinle]. I hadn't been there a month, maybe about two weeks, when some boys asked me to run away during the night. There was me, a boy from Many Farms named Marshall, another one from here named Ashkii Łitsoií [Yellow Boy] ... and his brother. So there were four of us .... We went straight to the road down the hill, a place called Ma'iitóhí [Coyote Wash], in between the rocks. Just as we started toward it, a horse appeared behind us on the hill. It was a man named Kenneth. He had a whip with him.

---

[2]According to Young and Morgan (1987), *siláo* derives from the Spanish *soldado* (soldier). It may mean soldier, policeman, or army (Young & Morgan, 1987, p. 687). Wayne Holm (personal communication, February 21, 2000) states that with the advent of World War II, Navajos came to call soldiers *siláo łitsoií* (yellow police), "presumably referring to their khaki uniforms."

... Just as the horse appeared, there was a deep arroyo. Marshall and I started down, then we ran up to some hills and hid. As we stood there scrunched down, Kenneth rode by on his horse. The other boys ran on toward a side hill. As they descended, he caught up with them.

We continued on up ... to the top of the hill and stayed there, watching the boys scrambling around for rocks and hitting [the policeman] with them. The two of us started off and ran as fast as we could straight back to school.

Interviewer: [laughing] Having gotten scared of him?

Thomas James: Yes, we got scared .... I guess while he was chasing the boys on his horse, he ran over one of them. The boy died.

A month later, Thomas James and his friend Marshall ran away from school again. This time they made it to Thomas's uncle's home several miles from the school. Finding no one at home, the boys entered through a small window, built a fire, and roasted some corn they had discovered in a box near the stove. Waking at dawn, they crawled out the window and began running toward Rough Rock, knowing the *siláo* was on horseback and not far behind. Finally, they arrived at Marshall's home. Marshall's father chided the boys: "Why do you run away? Tomorrow I will have you ride double and take you back to school." Thomas James finished his story:

We spent the night there. When I went outside, I saw it was almost dawn. I started out [toward Rough Rock] ... and arrived where my family was living at the time. After I had been home for a week, Siláo Yázhí [Little Policeman] came by on his horse. I was out herding sheep. When I brought back the sheep, I noticed the horse. He rode a brown horse, and there it was. I almost ran off again. But my mother called to me ... and told me to come back in. I came in and ate. "We will go back now," he said to me. That was it. I did not say no again.

Later in his school career, along with his peers from Rough Rock, Thomas James was sent from Chinle Boarding School to Fort Apache. It was there, he said, that he was told never to speak Navajo: "They told us only to speak to each other in English."[3] David Begay, whom Fred Bia and I interviewed at Rough

---

[3]Thomas James' words here seem to imply that children were not told to speak only English at Chinle Boarding School, which other accounts and policy documents indicate was not the case. It is likely that the distinction Thomas James makes between language use at Chinle Boarding School and Fort Apache is based on the fact that there were Native dormitory personnel at Chinle who may have used Navajo with students, despite the Bureau of Indian Affairs' policy forbidding it.

Rock in 1981, also attended Fort Apache Boarding School. He described the 200-mile trip to Fort Apache in 1924, and the strict military system that greeted students on their arrival there:

> They took us to Keams Canyon [on the south side of Black Mesa, within the Hopi reservation] on horseback.[4] We stayed there for about a week. Then they took us to Fort Apache in a Model T Ford. We stayed there at school all summer. Our relatives would come in wagons or on horseback to visit us. Then at the end of the spring, they would come to take us home. It used to take us 7 days to get home.
>
> Fort Apache was an army post turned into a school. It just seemed like we had military style at Fort Apache. Every Sunday we had to parade for our superintendent. They had a band, and then we were in the band and marching like the army. Even the little kids had uniforms. During the school year they wouldn't let us speak Navajo.

FIG. 4.3. Dorothy Secody (Táchii'nii/Red Streak clan), 1983.

FIG. 4.4. Simon Secody (Ma'ii Deeshgiizhnii/Coyote Pass clan), 1983.[5]

(Photographs by Fred Bia, courtesy of Rough Rock Community School.)

---

[4]For a moving personal account of a Hopi girl's experience at Keams Canyon Boarding School, see Helen Sekaquaptewa's (1969) autobiography, *Me and Mine*.

[5]Presumably the clan name translated as "Coyote Pass" identifies people who trace ancestry to Jémez Pueblo, in New Mexico. Wayne Holm (personal communication, February 21, 2000) notes that this is another example of why clan names should not (cannot) be translated; the name "has nothing to do with coyotes or passes," he says, but rather with social identity rooted in membership within a named kin group.

Simon Secody, a member of the Rough Rock School Board for 4 years, remembered similar experiences at Phoenix Indian School: "Every Sunday, we went to church. We wore gray uniforms." His wife Dorothy, who spent 5 years at Chinle and a half-year each at Fort Defiance and Fort Wingate, could not remember anyone having long hair. "All the students looked the same," she said, referring to their army-issue uniforms and the bowl-shaped hair cuts all students received. "We didn't get to go home …. We stayed at school all the time, even on weekends. I was very lonely there," Dorothy said. "We weren't allowed to speak Navajo."

Children who could not or would not speak only English, or who "reverted" to Navajo with their peers, faced penalties that left emotional as well as physical scars. Such practices lasted well into the latter part of the 20th century. A generation after Dorothy and Simon Secody attended school, Galena Dick, who attended Chinle Boarding School during the 1950s, found little had changed. She states:

> We were forced and pressured to learn English. We had to struggle. It was confusing and difficult …. Students were punished and abused for speaking their native language. This punishment was inflicted even by Navajo matrons in the dorm. If we were caught speaking Navajo, the matrons gave us chores like scrubbing and waxing the floors, or they slapped our hands with rulers. Some students had their mouths "washed" with yellow bar soap …. This shows that even for Navajo adults like the dorm matrons, school was not a place for Navajos to be Navajos (Dick & McCarty, 1996, pp. 72–73).

Fred Bia attended the Chinle Boarding School at roughly the same time as Galena Dick. He remembers punishments that were "to a point where it was ridiculous"—

> You know, if you were just laying there, you were not bothering anybody, there was no way it was going to keep *anybody* awake if you have your eyes open and aren't sleeping …. People are going to be snoring away. But they'll throw you out of there just for having your eyes open. They'll make you stand in the living room … and you'd be holding like four or five dictionaries over your head just for doing that. Or … they make you scrub the whole living room with a toothbrush ….

"It was really ridiculous," Fred reiterated, "some of the things that they used to do"—

> … they would hit, too, with boards … if you were talking there [in the dormitory], whispering. Or they would sneak up on you and go and lay a big old two-by-four

.... This is not a ruler, this is—you know what rebars are? [a metal bar used to re-inforce concrete]—and they would lay that across your back there. And [you] just roll over and just lay there and don't even make a sound, but you just hold it in there until that [pain] barely goes away ....

Despite the violence to their bodies and psyches, people at Rough Rock do not speak of their school experiences only in disparaging terms. Thomas James went as far as the ninth grade when, at age 26, school officials "told me to just go back home." He characterized the schools he attended as both "really good" and "like being in jail." Fred Bia said his school experience, although "not the proper way to educate *anybody*," "made me strong to a lot of things." And Agnes Begay, who served as a councilwoman for the Rough Rock-Many Farms Chapter, cited the school's gifts of Christmas toys that, in her memory, softened the experience of leaving home. When Regina Lynch and I interviewed Agnes Begay at her home in Many Farms in 1981, she told us in English:

My mom said, "No, you're not going to go to school. We'd rather put boys in school than girls" [a reference to the crucial role of girls in the home]. But I just made myself enroll .... So I went to Chinle in 1921. I remember my grandma and grandpa took me on horseback to school. They stayed overnight. And that night—Christmas Eve—I received a big doll [from the school staff]. That was something great. I just loved it, and I was really glad I went to school.

But most elders we interviewed attended school for only a few years, or did not attend at all. Frank X. Begay said he "desperately wanted to go to school," but when the time came, he literally missed the bus:

The horses were saddled. The children were to gather at Smokestack where they would then board a bus. I was told I would be going there with them .... Four of us left on horseback. Once we got to the top of the hill, the bus left. Darn! They said the bus was full, so it left. I was so disappointed. We just came back.

"If I had gone to school," Frank X. Begay mused, "what would I be doing here?" Smiling, he speculated, "Maybe I would have been among those cussed at in Window Rock" (i.e., a tribal politician). As we laughed at this image, he continued: "Maybe I would have been a school teacher somewhere. I always say that I might have been a school principal. What would it have been like to have gone to school?"

Unlike Frank X. Begay's family, many parents were adamantly opposed to sending their children to distant schools from which they might not return for months or years. "Education was looked upon as a threat and a foe to the Navajo way of life as well as a threat to the Navajo family," Robert Roessel (1983) writes (p. 522). Like other parents, Hasbah Charley's mother and father saw little purpose in their children learning a foreign language and alien ways, so they hid their daughter when the *siláo* came around:

> I said I wanted to go to school but my parents and grandparents said no. "What will you do with school? You can't make a living from it. We are teaching you here .... Sometime in the future when we've grown old and no one cares for us anymore, you will only want to run away and abandon the land." ... No, I never went to school.

Chuckling, former school board president John Dick told this story of how his mother resisted the school police (who were her clan relatives), even as they tried to intimidate her with visions of a host of social ills that would befall her unschooled son:

> There was a person by the name of Curly Hair and several [other] men ... who used to come down from Chinle. "Put your children in school," they said. They came to our house. "I see you have two boys, my daughter .... Your children will go to school—go enroll them."
>
> "No, my father, he looks after the goats."
>
> "That's all right—now *you* can look after them," they tried to persuade her. They pleaded.
>
> So she brought a goat and butchered it for them and roasted meat for them and they ate. "He will start causing you all sorts of trouble," [they said]. "You are hanging on to him for nothing .... He will gamble. He will start chasing girls. There [in school], he will be taken care of, ... and when he grows up, *then* you can have him do chores for you."
>
> These were some of the things they said to her. "No, my father, please don't say those things to me. He is the only one. There is no one else, no one."
>
> That was it. So that is why I didn't go to school—not even one term.

THE NEXT GENERATION

While families at Rough Rock struggled with these realities, in Washington, D.C., Secretary of the Interior Hubert Work convened a series of meetings between his staff and the privately funded Institute for Government Research about the desirability of an independent survey of "general conditions" among Indian people (Meriam et al., 1928, p. 56). Two years later, the study's technical director, Lewis Meriam, published the survey team's findings in what is commonly referred to as the *Meriam Report*. It is a scathing indictment of Federally controlled Indian education. "The survey staff finds itself obliged to say frankly and unequivocally," Meriam and his associates declared, "that the provisions for the care of the Indian children in boarding schools are grossly inadequate" (Meriam et al., 1928, p. 11). The report went on to list an array of deficiencies, including inadequate diet and medical services for pupils, overcrowded dormitories, unprepared and inadequately compensated teachers, restrictive discipline, a curriculum that prepared students for employment neither off the reservation nor at home, and the fact that "boarding schools are frankly supported ... by the labor of the students" (Meriam et al., 1928, pp. 12–14).

The *Meriam Report* presaged the educational reforms launched under President Franklin D. Roosevelt and his Commissioner of Indian Affairs, John Collier, who served in his post from 1933 to 1945. His "Indian New Deal," according to historian Margaret Szasz (1974), included economic development, tribal self-government, and "civil and cultural freedom" for Indian tribes (p. 41). The Indian New Deal shaped the next half-century of Indian policy.

At Rough Rock, the immediate impact of the Collier-era reforms was the construction of a road and a community day school. In 1933, Roosevelt established the Civilian Conservation Corps (CCC), which placed nearly 6 million dollars at the disposal of the Indian Office for a separate Indian CCC (Szasz, 1974). The CCC provided funds to build a graded road from Rough Rock Springs to the top of Black Mesa. The road enabled men to haul timbers down from the mesa with which to build a small school near the springs.

Community day schools, Szasz (1974) says, grew out of Collier's "conviction that Indian education should be rooted in the community and should, in turn, stress the values of native culture" (p. 46). With its two adjoining stone hogans that served as the girls' dormitory, the Rough Rock Day School seemed to reflect these ideals, at least architecturally. A 1961 article in the *Navajo Times* captured this scene from inside the classroom walls: "The Rough Rock School was to be a 'native,' barefoot setting. There was no furniture; the children brought sheepskins to sit upon. Miss McClure [the first teacher] brought her own bench" (quoted in Boyce, 1974, p. 111).

However, those who attended the day school testify that, in practice, it differed little from BIA boarding schools. Ernest Dick began his school career at the day school at age 5. He recalled the inadequate food and being forced to scrub floors and do laundry. "That was one of the things I hated about being in a BIA school—they were forcing you and making you do this," he said. Although day schools in theory were to be just that—schools in which children would return to their families at the end of the day—the day school concept flew in the face of inadequate roads and funds to maintain buses, as well as the assumptions of White educators that family influences "interfered" with students' educational progress. "I think we were only allowed to go home twice a year or twice a semester," Ernest Dick reported, Then, he said—

> After we came back from home, they would shave your head, shave your hair off again and make sure you take a shower, all of that, you know. But these attendants were all Navajos. They were trained by BIA to have this type of a treatment. And we weren't allowed to talk Navajo .... And our visitation from our parents was very limited—maybe 5 or 10 minutes, that was it.

Ernest Dick's older sister, Lynda Teller, a bilingual teacher at the modern Rough Rock School, concurs: "Every once in awhile, maybe within a month or 2 months, either my grandfather or my mother would come for just a little while. You could only spend about 10 minutes out of the classroom to see them, and then the teacher would chase you back into the classroom." When I interviewed Lynda Teller in her Navajo Studies classroom at Rough Rock Elementary School in 1996, she spoke of the wrenching emotions she felt upon entering this "community" school:

> When I first entered school at Rough Rock, I was scared and I saw a bunch of kids crying after their parents. I didn't know what to do, whether to cry or not. But I know for sure I didn't cry. But my little brother Ernest was crying. I felt so bad because he was crying. We were enrolled at the same time.
>
> … My paternal grandfather, *shicheii*—Etsitty Begay—is the one who took us in to the school. My mother was there too. We were taken there in a wagon. Ernest had a little bitty suitcase, and I had a suitcase too. When we were enrolled, I remember my grandfather and my mom, they had to go with their thumb print for signatures. And they took our suitcases, and when my grandfather was going to leave, he was telling those dormitory assistants, "I don't want you cutting my granddaughter's hair. I don't want you people chopping her hair off to make her look like a Hopi." And then one of the dormitory staff was explaining that the only time they would do it was when we had head lice or bugs. He said, "I don't care, I don't want you people cutting her hair off. When she gets to her puberty, I want her hair long for *kinaaldá*." He kept saying that.
>
> So he left, and when they left, that's when I started crying.

Lynda Teller recalled the institutional atmosphere of the day school which, despite its architecture, imparted little sense of Navajoness: "It was nothing—it was just that hogan with that pink wall, brown wall—it wasn't even homey-like. It was just those high bunk beds." She too remembered the chores—doing laundry and cleaning the dorm—and the spoiled food. To enforce a "clean plate" policy, older students were enlisted as disciplinarians:

> They assigned this one boy ... and if we're not finished with our milk, he would hit us with a long stick and say, "Drink it!" Sometimes the milk would be sour and we still had to drink it. Before school time, we would go way off behind the girls' dorm, and ... throw up there. And we would cover it with sand, and come back into the building and start school at 8.

MISSIONARIES AND NAVAJO LITERACY

During Lynda Teller's 3rd-grade year, the Friends Evangelical Mission opened a church and school next to the day school. In 1981, Regina Lynch and I interviewed missionaries Vern and Ross Ellis at the parsonage; they had built the mission and had lived there for 27 years. "We didn't duplicate the old BIA school," Vern Ellis told us; the mission school ran from grades 3 through 8. "We had dormitories there, and we had the capacity for 20 children, and we lived more like a big family."[6]

Graduates of the mission school speak fondly of its family-like atmosphere, which stood in stark contrast to the day school. "We were treated much differently there," Ernest Dick said. "People were friendlier .... It was a lot of individual attention." And Lynda Teller recalled:

> When I got to the mission, ... it was *a lot* different. We were like a family, with only 14 students. We had a couple that were our dormitory parents, and then there were the missionaries, Vern and Ross Ellis. We had a *bilagáana* [Anglo or White] teacher.
>
> ... When I got there, I felt so comfortable—I don't know why, I guess because the people were so nice to us. They were like our own parents. Every day we had home-cooked meals .... The people that funded the mission would bring us a lot

---

[6]In the same interview, Reverend Ellis explained how he and his wife came to settle at Rough Rock: "Our home had been in Colorado. Our church felt like they would like to have a mission work among the Navajos. They did some exploratory work to determine where there were needs for missionary work. They finally found there *was* no mission work being done at Rough Rock, and it seemed like it was an open door and like there was a real need." After obtaining the tribally-required 100 signatures from local residents, the Friends Mission was granted a lease to the site. "Then I came down with the work crew and we built the church," Reverend Ellis said.

of foods, and hand-me-down clothes. And we were the first ones to pick out what we wanted. Some of them were still brand new.

That the provision of decent meals, humane treatment, and hand-me-down clothes provokes fond memories is testimony to the grace and resilience of those who lived these education histories—and the naturalization of conspiring systems that sought to recast Indigenous students' identities according to Anglo-European/Christian ideals. But there was an additional and more potent instrument of conversion: literacy in Navajo.

By the 1950s, Navajo had been written for almost a century through the efforts of Franciscan and Protestant missionaries, academic linguists, and Federal officials (Young, 1972). The most durable orthography had been developed in the 1930s and 1940s by William Morgan, a Navajo, and Robert Young, an Anglo ("YounganMorgan," one word, as they are still known), under the auspices of John Collier's Indian Education Office (Holm, 1996). During the 1940s and 1950s the Bureau also published a monthly newsletter, *Ádahooníłígíí* ("Events"), and a series of bilingual primers composed in English and translated into Navajo (Emerson, 1983; Lomawaima & McCarty, 2002; Spicer, 1962). In addition to Biblical tracts, a corpus of literature had been created and, according to Spicer (1962), by the middle of the 20th century "possibly several hundred Navajos were writing and reading ... the language" (p. 457). As these numbers attest, Navajo literacy was by no means widespread (Holm, 1996, p. 4).[7]

When we spoke in 1996, Lynda Teller described the revelation she felt at first experiencing her language in print:

> What I remember about the language was that I was so amazed that our *bilagáana* teacher could read something out of the Bible and it sounded very familiar. It was in Navajo. She would read it for us, and then we would follow, repeating it after her again .... Every day in class we took 30 minutes to go through the Navajo vowel sounds, the consonants. She had a lot of things on an easel chart. And then I thought to myself, "Oh, this is the English letters" ... and she was reading it, but it was coming out as Navajo words. That's what amazed me. And I guess that's how I got interested in it. I thought, "This is *my* language, and this is how *I* can talk."

Lynda Teller's literacy experiences at the mission school led eventually to a career as a bilingual educator. Although the initial focus of her native language

---

[7]A special issue of the *Journal of Navajo Education* guest-edited by Irene Silentman (Winter, 1996) chronicles the 150-year evolution of Navajo literacy, including reports in Navajo. See also Daniel McLaughlin's (1992) excellent ethnography, *When Literacy Empowers: Navajo Language in Print.*

literacy was reading the Bible, as it was for many Indigenous people, Lynda Teller and others reappropriated their literacies for Indigenous ends (see, e.g., Lockard, 1996). She and other mission school graduates describe their initial literacy experiences at the mission school as a "plus."

Lorinda Gray, a bilingual teacher at the modern elementary school, also attended the Friends Mission School. "At the mission school," she said, "we were taught in English, but there was a time when we did written Navajo, and we read in Navajo. Like, we probably read the whole New Testament in Navajo!" she joked. At the same time, Lorinda observed, "We didn't really learn anything about the traditional [Navajo] ways of doing things, because it seems like the mission people were really against our religion."

Lorinda Gray, Lynda Teller, Ernest Dick, and others in their generation went on to complete their high school education at places such as Fort Wingate, Chilocco Indian School in Oklahoma, Albuquerque Indian School, and the church-run Indian school in Haviland, Kansas. Their experiences in these larger institutions connected them with a wide network of Indigenous students, many of whom would become lifelong friends and professional allies. (See also Esther Horne's account of this, in Horne & McBeth, 1998.) But even as going away to school had these positive consequences, it took young people away from their families for even longer periods of time.

Still, all of the individuals we interviewed speak of the powerful attachment they maintained to their language and culture. "I was pretty much taught in the traditional way," Ernest Dick reflected—

> But when you go back to school, it's a totally different life again. Well, actually to a degree I think it's conflicting because in the Navajo way, this is the way it's done, but the White man's way, this is it, this is the only way according to Christianity—what they teach you and all of that. But I am a strong believer in my way—the Navajo way—because I learned that through my dad, and through my mother and my grandfather and my uncles.

CONFLICTING IDENTITIES

Ernest Dick's words seem to bring full circle the personal and collective educational histories sketched here. By the late 19th century, schooling had replaced the military as the hammer of Federal hegemony—the means by which Indigenous languages, cultures, and identities were to be pounded out and reshaped. The relentlessness of this system is manifest most perversely in its normalization of physical abuse, and in the ways schooling turned Navajo against Navajo, kin against kin. How much more powerful and internalized the English-only message, how much more intimidating and demeaning the punishments, when they are inflicted by Native school personnel and peers? In some cases, schooling literally made children sick to their stomachs, yet they felt compelled, as Lynda Teller relates, to hide the evidence of their bodies' violent rejection of school "and come back into the building and start school at 8." Or, as Fred Bia says, to bury their pain in stifled screams.

It may be, as Fred Bia's testimony suggests, that such criminal treatment morally steeled children against the intended erasure of their identities. Their resistance and fortitude were emblematic of their agency and control. For the boarding school system did not succeed in "blotting out" Indigenous languages and cultures. For Diné, not only did this system impact only a portion of the school-aged population, it could not overcome the powerful pull of kinship on children's lives and loyalties, or the resources they found in family, community, and *k'é*. These were the salient cognitive and affective resources with which most children continued to identify.

"Formal education did change my behaviors and attitudes," Galena Dick writes in her language autobiography (Dick, 1998, p. 24). "At the same time," she continues, "I maintained a strong belief in my language and culture." This latter sentiment, widely shared among the generation coming of age in the 1960s, formed the ideological reservoir from which a new, Indigenized form of schooling would be constructed.

FIG. 5.1. "It was an enormous transition in a very few years." —Wayne Holm (Photograph of mother and children c. 1939 courtesy of Arizona State Museum, University of Arizona.)

A Portrait of Change

Back in the old days, there just wasn't much education, and people didn't want too much of it, partly because the schools around here just went up to certain grade levels, and that's where your education ended.

… But my grandfather after awhile finally started asking people to put their children in school to get educated. He finally told people that the responsible people with livestock …, they're not sending them [their children] to school, so they're going to have a leadership that's not going to be of a quality they want—a good, responsible leadership. So he was concerned about that, and so he really asked people to put their kids in school.

—*Agnes Holm, Window Rock, January 1996*

On a snowy evening in January 1996, Galena Dick, my niece Amity Pitchford Roebke, and I visited Agnes and Wayne Holm at their home in Window Rock, Arizona, the seat of Navajo tribal government. Agnes is Navajo; her husband Wayne is Anglo. For over 30 years they had been among the staunchest and most effective advocates for education in and through the Navajo language and culture (see, e.g., Holm & Holm 1990; 1995). Because of their long-term involvement in Navajo education, including developing the acclaimed bilingual/bicultural program at Rock Point, Arizona, we hoped they would provide a perspective from outside the Rough Rock community on the demonstration school and its impacts.

Agnes Holm's grandfather was Chee Dodge, a prominent rancher, interpreter, and tribal leader. In the late 19th century, he worked with Washington Matthews, the Anglo post surgeon at Fort Wingate, to produce one of the first Navajo orthographies (Lockard, 1996). Chee Dodge went on to become the first chairman of the Navajo Nation and a leading activist for more and better Navajo schools.

Wayne Holm picked up his wife's story, describing those times:

Up 'til World War II, you couldn't fill Navajo schools, partly because you couldn't see what good going to school would do. It didn't lead to any kind of worthwhile work at all.

… During World War II, a lot of people went into the services, but even more people worked off-reservation and saw that, for better or worse, you were at a real disadvantage without an education. So there was a real *demand* for schools. Of course, it took 6 or 8 years—but in '54 the government finally began to respond to this, and there was a massive expansion of Bureau of Indian Affairs schools, and also massive construction of public schools at that time.

And so you went from a time when, in 1948, less than half the Navajo kids who could be in school were in school, [until], by the middle '50s, you had 90% of the kids that were in school. So it was an enormous transition in just a very few years.

It is difficult to pinpoint the moment when circumstances began to change in ways that precipitated the transition to which Agnes and Wayne Holm refer. I approach such a discussion with caution. But this account would be incomplete without an exploration of those years before and after the war, for the events of that time, along with the events and educational histories described in the previous chapter, laid the foundation for the demonstration at Rough Rock—and for sweeping transformations in Indigenous schooling.

"WHEN THEY TOOK THE SHEEP, WE USED TO CRY"

The 1930s were times of tremendous privation on the Navajo reservation, the effects of a national economic depression exacerbated by rampant sickness and a devastating Federal livestock reduction program. In the years following the Navajos' imprisonment and return from Fort Sumner, they had been remarkably successful at rebuilding their herds—so much so that the rangeland vegetation became depleted and the topsoil it held in place was washed and blown away (Reno, 1981). The tribe's solution was to increase Navajo rangeland. As Philip Reno (1981), former economics professor at Navajo Community College (now Diné College) points out, "the public domain in these years was open for stockmen (White stockmen as a rule) to graze as many animals as they could" (p. 28).

But White politicians in the newly created states of Arizona and New Mexico resisted returning "public" (more accurately, publicly seized) lands to Navajos, voting instead to construct one of the largest dams in the world about 300 miles west of the Navajo reservation. Boulder Dam, later renamed Hoover Dam for the U.S. president who authorized its construction, would provide electricity, flood control, and irrigation to the rapidly developing U.S. Southwest. But the long-term efficiency of the dam was threatened by silt run-off from Navajo range lands (Iverson, 1990).

And so began another protracted struggle between Diné and the Federal government. In 1935 the Federal government declared the Navajo reservation "100 percent overgrazed," and, under Commissioner Collier, instituted a program of voluntary, and subsequently forced, herd reduction that resulted in the slaughter or removal of over half the sheep and goats on the reservation (Roessel & Johnson, 1974).[1] Individuals who refused to comply with the program were subject to imprisonment without due process; some remained incarcerated for months at locations unknown to family members (Roessel & Johnson, 1974). The program also divided Navajo and adjacent Hopi lands into range management districts, within which people were required to keep their reduced herds. The traditional land use area around Rough Rock was carved into three of those districts: District 10, the area surrounding the trading post and springs east to Many Farms (designated the Chinle District); District 4, directly above the springs on Black Mesa (the Piñon District); and District 8, northwest of Rough Rock Springs (the Dennehotso District; see Fig. 2.5).[2] Within each district, household heads were issued grazing permits that limited the number of "sheep units" they could hold.[3] This meant an abrupt change in land use for people who had moved more or less freely among the new land use areas, responding to climate cycles and family needs, and guided by the principle that one respected the use rights of those who were already there.

People recall these times with great sadness and bitterness. Agnes Begay, a young girl during that time, told us: "We used to cry, my sister and I—when they took the sheep, we used to cry." And, in the fall of 1981, Regina Lynch and I interviewed Sally Woody in her hogan near the demonstration school. She gave this account of the government seizure and destruction of her livestock:

> About the time I was 20 years old, about 1930, was when I heard of livestock reduction. I would be out herding sheep and would be told to take my herd over to a certain location. People wondered what for, but if you didn't take them over there,

---

[1]Between 1933 and 1947, stock reduction dispossessed people of 122,000 goats (reducing herds from 173,000 to 56,000); 220,400 sheep (reducing herds from 570,000 to 358,600); 9,000 horses (reducing ownership from 44,000 to 35,000); and 10,000 cattle (reducing ownership from 21,000 to 11,000; see Iverson, 1981, p. 54).

[2]Districts were formed of aggregated communities; the districts were then aggregated into agencies (Goodman, 1982).

[3]A "sheep unit" counted as one mature sheep or goat. Each mature cow counted as four sheep units, and each mature horse, five sheep units (Boyce, 1974, p. 254).

these policemen would just come around and round up your livestock and herd them off. [A Navajo man] was one of the first policemen to be sent to round up live-stock. We were told he worked closely with John Collier, whoever he was. We cried for our livestock, but even if we cried they were hauled off and put in corrals where the trading post is located. Maybe if you were lucky and got there on time, they paid you $1.00 a head for the sheep they were taking. It was too late to find out how many they took.

This was the same time as the districts were marked. Before that, people were able to move up on top and back down here freely. No one said anything about, "You're on my land."[4]

Stock reduction permeated all aspects of family and community life. Live-stock constituted the primary currency for paying ritual specialists, and herding the chief context for child socialization. "Without sheep, who will teach the children?" one elder pointed out. Given families' reliance on stock raising and agriculture for subsistence, the program devastated family economies as well. In 1939, the U.S. Soil Conservation Corps surveyed annual per capita incomes in the Rough Rock area, estimating those incomes at just $122. At least a third

FIG. 5.2. "When they took the sheep, we used to cry." —Agnes Begay (Photograph by Fred Bia, courtesy of Rough Rock Community School.)

---

[4]See Ruth Roessel and Broderick Johnson's (1974) edited volume, *Navajo Livestock Reduction: A National Disgrace,* for additional personal narratives on the hardships experienced during this time.

of that derived from livestock (Soil Conservation Service, 1939, Table III). Livestock reduction removed a way of living without providing an alternative. While sheep were being slaughtered to conform to Federal carrying capacity quotas, people starved. Nowhere in the United States was the economic depression more painful or acute.[5]

At the same time, according to the published diary of then-Director of Navajo Education George Boyce (1974), an epidemic of diarrhea, measles, influenza, and tuberculosis swept across the reservation. At Rough Rock, the day school personnel supplied the only local health care. In her weekly report of May 9, 1941, the school's White, female teacher described this situation:

> When Monday morning came, the roads were reported as drying. It was decided to spend the day calling through the valley. So we started, with a thermometer, some aspirin and a goodly supply of oranges.
>
> We traveled 86 miles, visited nine hogans, found 17 sick, 16 with measles …
>
> On Tuesday, we were informed that a former school boy had died and his two little sisters, formerly school girls, were very sick. Would we please see them? But school was in session. A missionary in this area called at four other hogans and brought back to the school six very sick children. That afternoon, our school dining room was like a hospital without equipment (Boyce, 1974, p. 103).

"WE NEED SCHOOLS"

These conditions led many people, mostly men, to seek employment on the railroads, in the mines, in seasonal agriculture and service industries—wherever they could find work in larger reservation towns and in border towns and cities. With the outbreak of World War II, 3,700 Navajos joined the armed services; another 10,000–12,000 took war-related jobs (Young, 1961). Many Rough Rock

---

[5]Livestock reduction had more far-reaching ramifications. Local chapters were responsible for enforcing herd reduction, and chapter officials were instructed on the total number of sheep units allowed within their jurisdiction. This resulted in a grossly unequal distribution of loss. The vast majority of people owned only a few head of sheep—less than 100—while a small minority, including many chapter officials, owned 12,000 or more (Young, 1968, p. 66). It was chapter officials, therefore, who in general made the least sacrifice. Not surprisingly, this created animosity and resistance among small stock holders, which was exacerbated by the fact that those who refused to give up their livestock were kidnapped and incarcerated in off-reservation jails (Bingham & Bingham, 1976). This eventually destroyed the Rough Rock Chapter; it was not restored for 30 years. Stock reduction also drove a wedge between the tribe and the Federal government, and was a major reason for the Navajos' rejection of other Collier-era reforms, including the 1934 Indian Reorganization Act which provided for constitutionally-based tribal governments (Iverson, 1981; 1990). As a consequence, the Navajo Nation has never had a tribal constitution.

men and women found work with the ammunition depots at Fort Wingate and at Bellemont, near Flagstaff, Arizona.[6] Blair Tsosie spoke proudly of his service in the Army Air Corps, which took him to California, Texas, Italy, and Australia. He remembered the day he was inducted at a military base in Los Angeles:

> There were so many of us [Diné] there. Some had entered wearing hair buns .... [The men] had their hair shorn while they still wore their hair buns .... They were bagged and stacked much like wool during shearing time.

The war years are significant not only for the Navajos' contributions to the war effort, which included the famed Code Talkers who used Navajo to develop an unbreakable military code and thereby help assure an Allied victory in the Pacific, but also for the change in attitudes toward schooling that peoples' war and work experiences produced. "Navajo servicemen and former war workers alike returned to the Reservation with a new understanding of the role of [formal] education in the life training of their children," Robert Young, then assistant to the Navajo agency superintendent, wrote in 1961 (Young, 1961, p. 13). In her history of Navajo education, Gloria Emerson (1983) put it this way: "Although only a fledgling interest, it was a change from the anger and resistance of the 1800s and the apathy of the 1900s" (p. 659).

The situation was this: Federal stock reduction had so destroyed families' means of livelihood that the opportunities for which children were prepared through traditional socialization no longer existed. Yet schooling—sporadic, irrelevant, and child-negating as it was—offered few viable alternatives. Moreover, parents' refusal to send their children to school was one of the few ways people could resist coercive policies such as stock reduction. In the more than half-century since the first Navajo boarding school opened at Fort Defiance, the Federal government had been unable or unwilling to keep its 1868 treaty promise of a school and a teacher for every 30 school-aged children. Aside from the deplorable conditions and abuse in the schools, there simply were not enough of them to accommodate all Navajo school-aged children.

World War II "brought the Navajo school system to its knees," then-BIA Superintendent of Education Hildegard Thompson wrote many years later (1975, p. 79). With Congressional interests focused on the war, funds for Indian education dwindled. Gas, rubber, and money shortages forced the closing of bus routes, and Navajo schools idled and deteriorated. In 1941, the annual per pupil

---

[6]So many Navajos worked at Bellemont during the war that it became known by other Native people as "Navajo Depot" (John F. Martin, personal communication, June 15, 1998).

allotment in Navajo schools was an astonishing $300 per year, half of which went for heat, light, and emergency school repairs (Boyce, 1974, p. 109). Four Navajo boarding schools, including Chinle, had to be closed. Congress further reduced Navajo school funding in 1945. One year later, Chee Dodge led a tribal delegation to Washington, D.C. In Congressional testimony, he explained the choices his people faced:

> We have been told that our ranges are overstocked and that we must reduce our livestock to prevent total destruction of our range .... We therefore ask that ... means be provided for people without sufficient livestock to make their living in some other manner .... We need the schools so that our children can compete with other children (Boyce, 1974, p. 217).

About this time, George Sanchez, a consultant to the Bureau of Indian Affairs and professor of psychology at the University of Texas, and Navajo Education Director George Boyce, released two reports on Navajo education. Sanchez called for more on-reservation school construction, while Boyce urged placing Navajo students in BIA bordertown dormitories where they could attend off-reservation public schools. Then, during the winter and early spring of 1947–1948, a blizzard hit the reservation, isolating thousands of people living at and near Rough Rock and Black Mesa. The drama of this event turned the eyes and ears of the national media on the Navajo Nation. *Time* magazine dispatched a reporter to Window Rock, who subsequently published an article on reservation conditions and the lack of school facilities. One week before the article appeared in print, the new Commissioner of Indian Affairs, William Brophy, secured the funds with which to reopen 18 Navajo schools (Iverson, 1981).[7]

Along with the return of thousands of people from war-time employment, these events marked a watershed in the history of Navajo education. Informed by the Sanchez and Boyce reports, Congress in 1950 approved Public Law 81–474, a long-range development plan for Navajos and Hopis that ended stock reduction, provided $25 million for Navajo school construction, and created an

---

[7]When she read this account, Galena Dick was reminded of a personal story of the blizzard of 1947. It was April 23, the night of her birth. Although it was spring, the snow was still deep. Just past midnight, Galena's mother awoke and asked her husband to bring her parents; "I think I'm going to have a baby," she said. Galena's father went outside to hitch the wagon. The moon was full, "like bright daylight," he would tell Galena years later. Galena's father left to get her grandparents, then went to Dorothy Secody's home. All would return to help Galena's mother through her first labor. As he waited outside the hogan, Galena's father heard a baby cry. Then, according to Galena, he went back into the house and was greeted with the exclamation: "It's a girl—a girl is born!" This is but one example of the ways in which personal and institutional histories at Rough Rock intertwine and adhere.

elementary and vocational education program for Navajo children aged 12 to 18 who had not previously attended school. Congress also urged the rapid transfer of responsibility for Navajo and Hopi education to public schools (Roessel, 1977). To expedite the plan, the Navajo Tribal Council authorized the Navajo Emergency Education Program, a "crash" program that turned BIA school dining rooms into classrooms, erected quonset huts for on-reservation dormitories, acquired makeshift dormitories in reservation border communities as part of Boyce's bordertown program, and accommodated additional children at 37 trailer schools, including schools at Black Mesa and the Chinle Valley (Young, 1961, pp. 17–18).[8] Reflecting on those times, Agnes Holm observed that even with all these expansions, there still were not enough on-reservation schools. "It was off-reservation again," she said.[9]

PUBLIC BUT SEPARATE

P.L. 81–474's emphasis on public education ran headlong into an entrenched system of racial segregation. The 1954 Supreme Court case of *Brown v. Topeka, Kansas Board of Education* unmasked widespread school segregation and discrimination against African Americans in U.S. schools. School-based discrimination against African Americans did not (and does not) change quickly, but changes occurred even more slowly for Indigenous peoples. On the Navajo reservation, the blatant school segregation condemned in *Brown* continued to be rationalized as accepted educational practice for many years (see, e.g., Thompson, 1975).

Under John Collier, reservation public schools had been authorized by the Johnson–O'Malley Act of 1934. Within the Navajo Nation, however, those schools were hardly public: They served only the children of non-Indian BIA employees and those Navajo students who were able to get to the school daily and whom teachers considered able to "keep up," socially and academically, with their Anglo peers (Emerson, 1983). "It was a real definite colonial school,"

---

[8]The Black Mesa trailer school closed after the first year due to a shortage of water (Thompson, 1975, p. 207).

[9]According to Wayne Holm (personal communication, February 21, 2000), eventually the Bureau's plans for Navajo students called for use of off-reservation schools and the hospital at Intermountain Indian School in Nevada; construction of bordertown dormitories; enlargement of some BIA schools as boarding schools; and massive construction of public schools. "I started teaching 26 beginners in the living room of my apartment. In 1954, there was an attempt to open up three classrooms in every school where two had been the spring before," Wayne Holm said.

Agnes Holm said. In our interview with them, Agnes and Wayne Holm illuminated how the system worked:

Wayne Holm (WH): What was the public school called?

Agnes Holm (AH): *Bilagáana yázhi bi'ólta'* (little Anglo school).[10]

WH: The public school [meant], in effect, going to school with little Anglos. That word is no longer used now .... But at that time it stood out, because that's where the Anglos went to school, and the Navajos went to BIA school.

AH: And the only ones that went to that school also were [the children of] Federal workers.

WH: Missionaries, and traders, and some Navajos who could get their kids in.

AH: So that you have a group of people now that went to those original schools … and the rest of us went to boarding school .... And it went on like that for a long time, these "little public schools" and the big boarding schools.

"I guess that's why they were always side-by-side," Agnes Holm said with irony. "We always wondered why schools were side-by-side, but they had reasons for their separation."

Circumstances rather than social enlightenment eventually brought this multiply segregated school system down. In the 1950s, Congress passed Public Laws 874 and 815, commonly called Impact Aid. Originally intended to supplement the budgets of public schools on tax-exempt military lands, political pressure by reservation educators resulted in amendments to Impact Aid that provided for schools on or near reservation and other Federal trust lands. By providing funds for public school construction and improvement, Impact Aid created Indian-majority public school systems on and near reservations nationwide.[11]

But on the Navajo reservation, the new public schools only cloaked other subtle and insidious forms of discrimination. Benjamin Bennett, Rough Rock's

---

[10]Literally, "Anglos little their school."

[11]Agnes Holm remembers a public school at Fort Defiance in the late 1930s; Wayne Holm suspects there may have been such schools in most agency towns at the time. The historical documents I consulted indicate that the first public schools established under P.L. 815 and 874 were the "little Anglo school" at Fort Defiance and a public school at Ganado, about 30 miles west. Between 1950 and 1960, public schools were established at Crownpoint, Kayenta, Shiprock, Tohatchi, Tuba City, and Chinle. The latter four included secondary schools, but for the most part, Navajo students still had to go off the reservation to attend high school (Iverson, 1981).

school registrar from the day the school opened in 1966, taught at both BIA and public schools prior to coming to Rough Rock. When Galena Dick and I interviewed him at the elementary school in 1996, he remembered the attitudes and practices prevalent when he began his teaching career:

> [I]n those days of course, there was a pecking order, because the first years I taught school were in public schools. You looked down your nose at the BIA. And the first year I taught [on the Navajo reservation] was in an old BIA school building ... [which] had just gone to a public school. I can remember seeing literally, ... just pages and pages of children whom the public school wouldn't take.
>
> ... Public schools then were considered the elite type of thing. If you went to the public school you were really something. If you went to the BIA school, you were looked down upon.... And this was one of the incentives [for teachers]: You won't have to take children who were 1 or 2 years behind grade level.[12]

Within a few years, the Rough Rock Demonstration School would forever change this situation. But in the 1950s and early 1960s, the government's goal was simply to enroll more Indigenous children in school. By 1960–1961, 30,000 Navajo students had been enrolled—13,000 in reservation boarding schools and bordertown programs, 6,000 in off-reservation boarding schools, 7,500 in reservation public schools, and the rest in trailer, mission, and day schools (Young, 1961, pp. 60–61, 65). This was six times the number of students enrolled in 1939, and twice the number of Navajo students in school only a decade before. "And so finally," Agnes Holm summed up, "people started putting their children in school."

"WE GREW UP CONFUSED"

The oral histories make it clear that school and community at Rough Rock were experienced differently by people of different generations. When asked what they remember about growing up, Rough Rock elders consistently begin their accounts with word pictures of family, home, livestock, and land. Education was, for them, quite literally "learning the land." The elders' accounts can be seen as what Holland et al. (1998) call "narrativized identities"—stories that

---

[12]Wayne Holm notes that this practice continues to this day, and that its effects may in fact be salutory. "In recent years," he states, "BIA schools have come to serve, at least partially, as a safety net for kids the public schools can't or won't take" (personal communication, February 21, 2000).

tell of the continuity and importance of people, place, and community that construct their cultural world.

Their children, on the other hand, begin their personal histories—the time "when one becomes aware"—with accounts of separation, conflict, and confusion associated with being "put" in school. Their stories are of "positional identities" shaped by their positions within coercive structures of power (Holland et al., 1998). "My parents put us all in school," Lorinda Gray remembers, "and I went over there [to] the old BIA boarding [day] school." Lorinda then attended Shiprock Boarding School ("That place was *so* big, I used to get lost"), and the Friends Mission, and "then they sent us off to another mission school in Haviland, Kansas." Speaking of her children, Margaret Dalton recalled that after they graduated from the Friends Mission, they attended Chinle Boarding School. "That is where they [school officials] put them," Margaret said; "I did not take them there."

For the elders, formal education constituted a minimal, if painful, part of growing up. For their children, Anglo-American schooling begins, frames, and textures remembrances of childhood and youth. Their early life stories lead out of and away from the community, sometimes through the efforts of parents convinced that Anglo-American schooling would provide their children with opportunities and a better life, but more often through the agency of school and church officials.

The life stories of this latter generation speak of the separation of young and old, and of the difference between home and alien places. Ernest Dick describes this when he says, "When you go back to school, it's a totally different life." Galena Dick, who participated in the Bordertown program, tells this story of the social worlds she negotiated as a child (Dick & McCarty, 1996):

> When school let out in May, I came home and my parents and grandparents would ask if I got promoted .... I think they were just happy my siblings and I were promoted to the next grade; they knew we weren't flunking. At the same time, because my parents and grandparents really didn't know what my life at school was like or what we had to go through, I grew less interested in school. Still, my father verbally encouraged me to gain knowledge. I grew up confused.
>
> Back then we easily distinguished between the home and school cultures. When we went home, we were immersed in Navajo and another way of living .... When we returned to school, we identified ourselves as a different person with a different language. Unlike my learning at home, education at school was strictly an individual learning process of training in basic academic skills (p. 75).

And so a tension existed: While many parents viewed Anglo-American schooling as necessary, it separated children emotionally, intellectually, and physically from their homes, draining families and the community of their youth. The demonstration school would ultimately bring these young people back home, both in the sense of affirming their Diné identities and by creating an opportunity structure that explicitly valued those identities. But in the meantime, what kind of place *was* Rough Rock in the years just prior to the demonstration school? What human and material resources existed there prior to the school's founding?

"THE SHEEP ARE THE ONES THAT KEEP ME GOING"

In the oral history interviews, people had little to say about their community during this time. With young people away at school, those parents who could, found work outside Rough Rock. Fred Bia, who began school at age 7, was a young boy growing up during this time. He remembers his male relatives "always working somewhere in the mine, so I ended up taking care of their livestock. Everyone was working somewhere else." Transportation was still by horse and wagon. "Even going to the trading post," Fred said, "I would ride a horse. This was in the early '50s, and I would hardly see any vehicles."

Health conditions at Rough Rock had improved little since the epidemic of diarrhea reported by the White headmistress at Rough Rock Day School in 1941. Reverend Vern Ellis, who founded the Rough Rock Mission in 1954, remembered that:

> … diarrhea was by far the largest cause of death. Sanitation was poor, there was no water … and no way to haul water. What little bit [people] had they had to haul by team and wagon …. Especially in children, they went fast [i.e., they became ill from diarrhea and soon died], and when people lived several miles up on the mountain—there were no pickups at all—by the time they got in to help and got us, and we got them in [to the hospital 60 miles away], it was often too late.

In 1955, Cornell University and the U.S. Public Health Service began a long-term project in the Rough Rock–Many Farms area designed to address these problems by developing a locally acceptable health service delivery system (Young, 1961). Part of that project involved a demographic and socioeconomic assessment of the service area. In the remainder of this chapter, I rely on the published accounts of the Navajo–Cornell Project to sketch a picture of the community just prior to the opening of the demonstration school.

Codirected by anthropologist John Adair, who had worked on the reservation for 20 years, the Navajo–Cornell Field Health Research Project had the assistance of the Navajo Tribe and the BIA, as well as Native specialists such as linguist William Morgan (Sasaki, 1961, p. 103). In a report published in 1961, the project identified a population in the Rough Rock–Many Farms–Black Mesa area of 2,292, including "406 family hogans" and 148 camps, defined as a "closely knit, family group" (Loughlin & Dennison, 1961, p. 113). The most densely populated area, the researchers say, was along the highway running through the Chinle Valley, with 12 to 13 people per square mile—"an admittedly rural area" (Loughlin & Dennison, 1961, p. 113). Least populated were the lands at and around Rough Rock, with less than one person per square mile. "The remainder of the population," the project report continues, "is scattered with perhaps the most inaccessible section being, particularly during periods of snowfall and rains, Black Mountain [Black Mesa]" (Sasaki, 1961, p. 104).

The project also surveyed English-speaking abilities, although the methods for this were admittedly crude.[13] Of 809 people surveyed, "37 percent (296) were able to speak and understand communications in English," one project report states; this included 165 men and 131 women (Sasaki, 1961, p. 105). Although many men had no formal education, "they had acquired the speech skill in their work situations with non-Navajos and thus were placed in the category of English speakers" (Sasaki, 1961, p. 106). English speaking ability correlated directly with age: Of young people aged 14–19, 105 girls and young women (80%) and 103 boys and young men (62%), were identified as speakers of English. Of adults aged 30 to 64, only 26 women (20%) and 62 men (38%) were so identified (Sasaki, 1961, p. 106).

The Navajo–Cornell Project cites sheep, cattle, agriculture, weaving, wage work, tribal and BIA assistance, and earnings from ritual practice as the primary economic resources at the time (Sasaki, 1961). A drought in the 1950s had reduced income from some of these sources, limiting both herd size and farming operations. Livestock, Sasaki (1961) states, accounted for only 7% of total earned income, and farming income was "meager and of little significance," although both were essential to subsistence (pp. 108–109). Income from wage labor also had dropped due to railroad layoffs and the completion of several Federal and tribal construction projects.

---

[13]The chief criterion for listing individuals as English-speaking was the extent of their schooling, "or whether or not the Health Visitor from the clinic had indicated that [s/he] did or did not speak English" (Sasaki, 1961, pp. 105–106).

All of this reduced earned income at Rough Rock to $586 per family per year, or $85.00 per capita—an incredible level of poverty that stands out even more starkly in comparison to the $2,335 per family reported for the reservation as a whole (Sasaki, 1961, p. 103). Summarizing the Navajo–Cornell Project economic data, researcher Tom T. Sasaki (1961) observes that "the income level of the vast majority of the residents ... is extremely low, lower than that for the Navajo population as a whole" (p. 112). The single largest source of income was earned by but 3% of the adult population: salaried employees of the Navajo–Cornell Project and the BIA (p. 112).

This social and economic portrait indicates that in the years directly preceding the advent of the demonstration school, families at Rough Rock still had not recovered from the economic blows inflicted by Federal stock reduction and exacerbated by drought, nor had they begun to benefit from promised new opportunities associated with increased Federal spending on schools. With many children away at school, parents and grandparents shouldered much of this economic burden alone. Those who could found off-reservation employment in the mines, on the railroad, and in short-term government projects and agricultural labor. But those who remained at Rough Rock lived as they always had, relying on the lessons of their elders who, as Hasbah Charley reminisced so eloquently, "built a fire" for them. Land, livestock, and kinship would provide the bases of life.

Those lessons of what it means to be Navajo have not been forgotten. "My sheep are here," Hasbah Charley said in 1996, "and I think of them as my parents .... They are the ones that keep me going day after day."

FIG. 6.1. "Rough Rock is the most exciting thing in Indian education anywhere in the country."—Robert A. Roessel, Jr. (Photograph by Paul Conklin from RRCS archives, of ESL teacher Joyce Robinson with Rough Rock students and old BIA day school in background, 1966, courtesy of Rough Rock Community School.)

6
Origin Stories

At the beginning there was a place called the Black World, where only spirit people and Holy People lived. It had four corners, and over these four corners appeared four cloud columns which were white, blue, yellow and black. The east
column was called Folding Dawn; the south column was Folding Sky Blue; the
west one was Folding Twilight, and the north one was Folding Darkness ....
(Yazzie, 1971, p. 9).

One of the first published accounts of Indigenous origins by Indigenous people
is Ethelou Yazzie's edited volume, *Navajo History,* released in 1971 by Rough
Rock's Navajo Curriculum Center. The book tells of the Diné emergence
through three underworlds to the present Glittering World, the creation of the
sacred mountains that anchor Navajo country in each of four directions, the
placing of sun, moon, and stars, and the odyssey of the revered deity, Asdzą́ą́
Nádleehé (Changing Woman), and her twin sons, Naayéé' Neezghání (Monster
Slayer) and Tóbájíshchíní (Child Born of Water). Stunningly illustrated by re-
nowned Rough Rock artist Andy Tsihnahjinnie, *Navajo History* recounts the
significant events, landmarks, people, and cultural practices that constitute collective memory and reinforce a Diné worldview.

In introducing this text to its readers, Dillon Platero, former chair of the Navajo Education Committee and then-director of the demonstration school, wrote
that the book's significance lay not only in its content, but in the fact that it was
"a labor brought forth by Navajo people for Navajo people" (Yazzie, 1971, p.
6). Some doubted, he added, that such a book could be produced and that if it
could, "Navajo people could not do it." He offered *Navajo History* as refutation
of these paternalistic attitudes.

Dillon Platero might have been speaking for the demonstration school itself
and of the larger struggle for Indigenous self-determination. In the context of
more than two centuries of colonial education, placing school governance in the
hands of Indigenous communities was more than a radical concept. "This is
why Rough Rock is the most exciting thing going on in Indian education any-

where in the country," Robert Roessel told a reporter in 1967. "This is why our program has ramifications far outside the Indian world" (Conklin, 1967, p. 9).

This chapter recounts the stories of how this experiment originated—the significant events, people, and struggles that made possible the first American Indian community-controlled school. It is a story of remarkable perseverence and historical accident, as internal-community and external-bureaucratic interests found themselves, for a moment at least, fortuitously aligned.

"WE ARE FOLLOWING THE FOOTPRINTS"

The origin of the Rough Rock Demonstration School, Robert Roessel (1977) writes, "goes back to a Navajo sweat house located in a steep canyon at the base of Black Mountain"—

> There a group of Navajo men, while taking sweat baths, planned that some day there would be a school. The remains of that sweat house still remain as a reminder of the vision of this group ... (p. 1).

"Now we are following the footprints," Frank X. Begay reflected when we spoke with him in 1996. Those footprints do perhaps lead back to the vision in the sweat house. But by the early 1960s, the Bureau was well into its drive to increase the number of Navajo schools. And here, the story of Rough Rock takes a detour to Rock Point, Arizona, where, for some years, the local education committee had petitioned the Bureau of Indian Affairs for an expanded school. In 1963, the BIA finally agreed, but subsequently offered to "sweeten the deal" if Rough Rock community members could be persuaded to send their children to Rock Point as well. "And the next part of the story is one that Rough Rock doesn't know anything about," Wayne Holm grinned when we interviewed him in 1996. Just as the BIA prepared to build a seven-teacher school for 210 students—

> ... they told the education committee, "If you guys will wait a year, we'll build a 660-pupil school, and we'll have all the kids from Rock Point and Rough Rock at this new school at Rock Point." And boy, the committee just about salivated at the thought of all those new jobs with 660 pupils. And they talked about it for a couple of weeks, and apparently they made a trip over to Rough Rock. And I don't know who they talked to, but they came back and ended up saying, "We wouldn't want our kids to have to go to school at Rough Rock, and go get them out of the dormitories and all that, and it really isn't right for the Rough Rock kids to go here. So you tell those [BIA] people that we would rather have the little school for now, and then we'll go after a bigger one as soon as we get that one. We don't think it's right to build a school here for the Rough Rock and Rock Point kids."

John Dick was one of the community members consulted about the proposal to send Rough Rock children to the Rock Point School. He remembered Rock Point's altruism and Rough Rock's refusal to buckle under BIA pressure. "They [BIA officials] were telling us to join Rock Point," John Dick said in 1996, "because there were so few of us [i.e., there were a relatively few school-age children]. But the men [local leaders] disagreed."

And so the BIA built two elementary school facilities, one at Rough Rock and one 40 miles away at Rock Point. But even as the Rough Rock School was under construction, other events transpired to transform its mission. To understand those events, we must trace other "footprints" leading to the nearby communities of Round Rock and Lukachukai, Arizona, to Arizona State University 350 miles south of Rough Rock, and to Federal offices in Washington, D.C.

ANTECEDENTS

In 1964, as part of the Johnson Administration's War on Poverty, Congress passed the Economic Opportunity Act (EOA), designed to involve "the poor ... in planning, policy making, and operation" of local economic development programs (Bennett, Pearson, & Plummer, 1967, p. 188). Organized through the Office of Economic Opportunity, the EOA provided funds for Community Action Programs (CAPs) intended to develop local economic and human resources in urban and rural areas throughout the United States. On the Navajo reservation, these were called Local Community Development Programs (LCDPs). Overseen by the Navajo Office of Economic Opportunity, LCDPs built and improved roads and established adult education programs, community stores, preschool centers, and chapter houses across the reservation.

Linked to the LCDPs were three Indian Community Action Centers, including one at Arizona State University in Tempe. Robert Roessel, a member of the Office of Economic Opportunity (OEO) Task Force on Indian Affairs, served simultaneously as the director of that program and the founding head of the Center for Indian Education there.

The biographies of Robert Roessel and his wife, Ruth Wheeler Roessel, intertwine so closely with that of Rough Rock that I must pause briefly to introduce them here. Their influence on Navajo and American Indian education is legendary. I met them both in the spring of 1980, while Robert (known to all as Bob) Roessel was visiting professor at Arizona State University and while he and Ruth also worked in Rough Rock's Navajo Studies program. One chilly March evening, I visited their home at Round Rock, near the Arizona–Utah border. As we sat in front of the fireplace, I asked Bob what had brought him to Rough Rock.

As a boy growing up in St. Louis, Missouri, he said, he read every account he could find on American Indian people. After serving 18 months in the Pacific during World War II, Roessel decided to pursue his early interests in Indigenous peoples by studying anthropology under Robert Redfield at the University of Chicago. Roessel became disenchanted with anthropology, however, because, he said, anthropologists "weren't really interested in Indians as people." After completing his master's degree, he returned to the university to earn the education credits he needed to join the BIA as a teacher.

After a year at the BIA school in Crownpoint, New Mexico, Roessel came to Round Rock where Ruth Wheeler's uncle had built a makeshift schoolhouse from a tar paper-covered storage building. My field notes, taken during our March 1980 visit, provide some idea of Roessel's guiding philosophy and his reception by Round Rock community members. Even as a young teacher, Roessel worked collaboratively with the community to involve parents in the school. He began an adult education program that boasted a class of 60 to 70. He personally bused his pupils in his truck. He recalled one meeting of the Round Rock School Board in which a hat was passed around, and everyone donated whatever they could—Roessel included. Some chuckles went through the gathering at this, much to Roessel's bewilderment. After the hat had gone full circle, a parent gave it to him—to buy gasoline for his truck. This was one of the most memorable events of his teaching career, he said.

FIG. 6.2.   Ruth Roessel, 1981.
(Photograph from RRCS archives, courtesy of Rough Rock Community School.)

FIG. 6.3.   Robert A. Roessel, Jr., c. 1980.
(Photograph from RRCS archives, courtesy
of Rough Rock Community School.)

Ruth Wheeler grew up in a traditional Navajo home, the daughter of a medicine man and a prominent Round Rock family. She met Bob Roessel when she was 19, and the two soon married. When I met her in 1980, Ruth said this of the philosophy of education she developed over the years: "Our book is the Mother Earth and the Father Sky." Education should be "based on experience," she continued, with the development of children's language embedded in Navajo culture—"like a weaving, where everything is interwoven and forms a pattern."

This holistic philosophy and the conviction that Navajo communities should determine their own forms of schooling guided Ruth and Bob Roessel's subsequent work at Low Mountain, Arizona. There, working in a trailer school, they led a grass roots movement to elect a Navajo school board and initiate numerous community development projects. The Roessels estimated that over a 3-year period, more than 25,000 volunteer hours were invested in clearing roads and trails to accommodate school buses, and in building a community canteen, basketball court, sewing room, and rodeo grounds (Roessel, 1967, p. 104). But when the BIA failed to permit volunteer workers to eat school food purchased with Federal funds, the Roessels became disillusioned. Bob Roessel (1967) writes:

> … what we did at Low Mountain is proof of what can be accomplished when the Indian Service and the Indian people work together toward common objectives.

If the Bureau is really sincere in wanting [Indian control], then some such project
as that at Low Mountain will provide proof that this is possible (p. 110).

In the Low Mountain experience lay the seeds of the Rough Rock Demonstration School. While at Arizona State University, Bob Roessel presented
those ideas to OEO Director Sargent Shriver and to Sanford (Sandy) Kravitz,
Director of the CAP's Office of Research, Demonstration, Training and Technical Assistance. Both men knew the Roessels well, having recently visited
Round Rock and discussed with them and Tribal Chairman Raymond Nakai the
possibilities for War on Poverty programs on the Navajo reservation. In 1965,
Bob Roessel, Raymond Nakai, Chinle Councilman Guy Gorman, and Allen
Yazzie, then chairman of the tribal education committee and a former teacher–
principal at Round Rock, submitted a proposal to OEO. It called for an experimental program at the Lukachukai Boarding School about 45 miles northeast of
Rough Rock. The program would be jointly funded by the BIA and OEO, with
OEO providing funds for school-based community development activities and
an innovative English-as-a-second-language and Navajo cultural studies curriculum.

This was to be a school like no other, with its primary mission the cultivation
of local leadership, economic development, and the promotion of Navajo language and culture. A locally elected, all-Navajo school board would, for the
first time, establish policy for and oversee the school.[1]

"WHO KNOWS IN WHAT CASUAL WAYS THE MATTERS OF THE WORLD ARE DECIDED?"

The Lukachukai project lasted only a year, undermined by jurisdictional disputes inherent in a two-layered system of existing BIA employees and new
OEO staff. Still, BIA and OEO officials felt pressed to complete the planned
3-year project. What happened next was seemingly fortuitous. In our 1996 interview, Wayne Holm picked up the story. As a young principal at Rock Point,
he had been present at a BIA meeting when the Lukachukai school principal
"made that comment about, 'Hey, they're building that school over at Rough

---

[1]An Indian-controlled school board had already been established at Blackwater BIA School,
on the Gila River reservation in central Arizona. But this was a much different model than that
proposed for Lukachukai. As Wayne Holm described it when we interviewed him in 1996, "It
was a way of doing education cheaper by contracting with the local people and giving them less
money than what they had before." Other Navajo schools, including Rock Point, had local school
boards, but they had no formal budgetary, planning, or policy-setting control.

Rock—why don't those [OEO] people go over there and get out of my hair?'"
Wayne continued:

> I passed this on to [BIA Assistant Area Director for Education, William
> "Buck"] Benham at a meeting, simply saying—because, you know, you had
> mixed feelings about it. I didn't like what was going on at Lukachukai, but you
> thought the idea was a good idea .... Saying if you set a school up like this *at*
> Rough Rock, and saying, *if* people succeed, then their success is all their own.
> But if it fails, you can't blame it on the Bureau .... Benham was so struck by that
> he said, "Let's get in the car and go see [BIA Navajo Area Director] Graham
> Holmes. He's at a meeting out at Ganado."

"So before you know it," Wayne laughed, "we were tearing up to Ganado
[about 70 miles by car to the south] to talk this over with Graham Holmes, and
he really liked this idea."

As it turns out, there is much more to the story. In the spring of 2000, following up on a tip from Wayne Holm, I interviewed Thomas R. Hopkins by
telephone. Hopkins had been the BIA's chief of curriculum when the demonstration project began. He remembered the political pressure on Commissioner of Indian Affairs William Bennett to ensure that the demonstration
project went forward despite the problems at Lukachukai. "The message to
Bennett was clear," Hopkins said: "'This demonstration project is not going to
fail—you see to it.'" Bennett called in his Area Director for Education, Graham Holmes, who called in his assistant, William Benham.

At the time, Hopkins was on the Navajo reservation to evaluate an ESL program there. Benham told Hopkins the substance of his conversation with
Wayne Holm, as well as the message from Bennett that the project would not
be allowed to fail. Discussing these ideas with Hopkins, Benham laid out this
scenario: "You've got a new school at Rough Rock. Why not give the project
to Bob Roessel—lock, stock, and barrel? What do you think, Tom?"

Hopkins replied that it sounded like a good idea, and Benham then contacted
Roessel. "He didn't buy off immediately," Hopkins recalled. Instead, Roessel
told Benham he needed to consult with his colleagues on the project and the
people at Rough Rock. Years later, Bob Roessel would tell me what a difficult
decision he and his family faced. At the time of Benham's call, the Roessels
were living in Tempe, Arizona, where Bob Roessel was directing the Center for
Indian Education at Arizona State University. He was the youngest full professor on the faculty, he served on the presidential task force on Indian Affairs, and

his work was receiving national recognition. The Roessel children were attending good schools, and Bob Roessel's parents, who were in fragile health, lived nearby. Weighing these circumstances and Benham's invitation to come to Rough Rock for a year, the family ultimately decided to leave Tempe. "It really moved me, when they asked me to come back here," Roessel told me.

But there is another twist to this story. Just days before this book went to press, I received a call from Sanford Kravitz, who learned of my work at Rough Rock. He offered this testimony on the behind-the-scenes political muscle—his own—that propelled the demonstration project forward:

> I went to the BIA people and said, "You promised support, and we didn't get that support [at Lukachukai], and I'm going to the Secretary of the Interior and tell him what you've done" …. I was fairly high up at OEO, so the next day I got a call from the head of Indian education and of community development, who said, "How would you feel if we gave you a completely new school?" So the three of us got on a plane, flew to Gallup, and we stop at Lukachukai, where everybody's waiting for the big Feds to arrive. And this caravan takes off. I don't know where we're going, but we drive to Rough Rock and there is a brand new school …. And [the BIA officials] said, "If you don't go to the Secretary, we'll give you this school for the demonstration" …. I remember this as vividly as if it were yesterday.

In 1996, reflecting on the demonstration school's founding, Wayne Holm recalled the words of a 17th century Swedish bishop: "Who knows in what casual ways the matters of the world are decided?" Wayne Holm continued: "I've always thought this thing of [moving the Lukachukai demonstration] to Rough Rock was … decided in a very casual way." Looking back, the apparent casualness of the decision masked very intentional relations of power.

"WE DECIDED TO STAND UP FOR IT"

Here, the story's trail again returns to Rough Rock, for the proposal to establish the demonstration project there clearly needed the community's input, approval, and support. The Rough Rock school plant had been completed but was as yet unstaffed; would community members want to make it the Rough Rock Demonstration School? Frank X. Begay remembered the chapter meetings at which the demonstration project was proposed:

> It was this Anglo person by the name of Bob Roessel who stood up for it and began it. They talked about it, his wife and him. At that time they didn't have community-controlled school boards. [The proposal was that] maybe these community members can be put into office who will run the school in Navajo. These are the things they discussed and that's what happened.

John Dick also attended those meetings. He recalled the message that Ruth and Bob Roessel, Councilman Guy Gorman, and Director of Tribal Resources Ned Hatathli presented to the community:

> We were first given the reasons behind [the demonstration project]. "Your culture has brought you this far for countless years. It has been your prayers and livelihood .... You will not lose it. It will be taught in school .... Now all our children will progress into the future [with knowledge of] our strong livelihood." ... This is what they said to us.

At the third meeting, John Dick told us, "There were many women and men gathered. I was among them sitting by the door." It was John Dick who finally threw his influence behind the project:

> People went up to speak, and then another .... "What should we do?" they asked. "This is an experiment, so let's see how it turns out," I said, and made a motion and created quite a stir. We decided to vote for it—*bee nídidiijah*—stand up for it. And everyone was in favor of it. Yes, this is truly what happened.

FIG. 6.4. *From left to right:* Todecheenie Singer, with original school board members Ada Agnes Singer, John Dick, BIA Assistant Area Director for Education William "Buck" Benham, and original school board member Teddy McCurtain, 1966. (Photograph from RRCS archives, courtesy of Rough Rock Community School.)

At a subsequent chapter meeting, community members elected a five-member school board: weaver Ada Agnes Singer, and chapter leaders John Dick, Teddy McCurtain, 'Áshįįhí Tsosie, and Yellowhair Begay. All represented District 10. A short time later, Thomas James joined the board as the representative from District 8; Whitehair's Son was elected to represent Black Mesa, District 4. "Including me," Thomas James said, "there were seven of us, and they called us the Seven Members. These [other] men did not understand English." Thus, Thomas James, who had attended school from his 16th to his 25th year, was elected board secretary. John Dick became the first board president and Teddy McCurtain, vice president—positions they would hold for many years. Bob Roessel left his position at Arizona State University to assume the school directorship.

"THE ONLY PEOPLE IN AMERICA THAT *REALLY* BELIEVED IN INDIAN CONTROL"

Meanwhile, in Window Rock, Graham Holmes and William Benham prepared contracts for the tribal council's signature so the tribal education committee

FIG. 6.5. Rough Rock Demonstration School cofounder Allen Yazzie with Dillon Platero, second director of the school, 1967. (Photograph from RRCS archives, courtesy of Rough Rock Community School.)

could receive school funds and channel them to the Rough Rock School Board. The BIA would contribute the school plant and $307,000 in operational funds; OEO would contribute $335,000 for an innovative cultural identification and TESL (Teaching English-as-a-Second-Language) curriculum, and for community development projects. Just as Holmes and Benham left to deliver the papers, the tribal council adjourned its annual session, leaving the project without a fiscal agent. With only a few days remaining before the fiscal year deadline, Allen Yazzie, Guy Gorman, and Ned Hatathli formed a private, non-profit organization to contract with OEO and the BIA for school operating funds (Johnson, 1968, p. 22). The corporation was called DINÉ, Inc., signifying "The People" in Navajo and the English acronym for Demonstration in Navajo Education (Johnson, 1968).

"To a lot of people, they couldn't understand it," Wayne Holm said. "They had this DINÉ, Inc., and it always looked strange because they weren't Rough Rock people." But the project needed an incorporated entity, and quickly. Wayne Holm continued:

> … the impression I got was that Bob [Roessel] was presented with this idea with very little time. In fact, you had to organize as a group to receive the money, and it was done with just *days* or weeks … that's why you ended up with this awkward situation where you had DINÉ, Inc. to receive the money and then pass it on. In the same way, Rough Rock got asked, "Would you like to do something that nobody's ever heard of before, on very short notice?" And the board had to be organized and it had to agree to do something that was really pretty frightening and pretty innovative at the time.

With the demonstration project in place, the footprints Frank X. Begay spoke of headed straight toward the national spotlight. "Whatever OEO did, for good or for bad," Wayne Holm observed, "for the first time, OEO put Navajos in *administrative* roles." Prior to Rough Rock and Lukachukai, "there were just a *handful* of Indians, and particularly Navajos, that had been in administrative roles," he added; the demonstration project "must have been just shocking to people at the time." The people who founded and funded the project, and especially the community who stood up for it, "were probably the only people in America that *really* believed in the fact that Indians could administer their own school programs."

FIG. 7.1. "People were enthused about the school. 'How wonderful!' it was said."—John Dick (Photograph from RRCS archives, courtesy of Rough Rock Community School.)

Community and Classroom

On September 12, 1966, the first American Indian community-controlled school opened its doors to 220 students, from beginners (6-year-olds) through sixth grade. Only one child in the two beginners classes, which had a total enrollment of 38, was reported as speaking English (Roessel, 1966b).

"And it was just like, if you're having a dream and you're trying to go someplace and you can't get there," school registrar Benjamin Bennett remembers of those first days of school. A White educator who had taught on the reservation and worked with Robert Roessel at Arizona State University, Ben Bennett arrived at 2:30 p.m. on the school's opening day. He remains school registrar to the time of this writing. When we began gathering oral history data in 1996, we were especially interested in his long-range view. "It was interesting," Ben said, "the attitude of the Bureau .... We kept hearing things like, 'Rough Rock won't last for 6 months'"—

> There were just so many things to do. Finally on September 12, "We're starting whether you're ready or not." Then, the students were all boarding students, with the exception of [one family]—they brought their children in.

"THE WHOLE THING WAS OPEN"

"What was it like, those first days and months?" we wondered as we talked with community members 30 years later. John Dick began—

> People were enthused about the school—those who lived in the area and others from afar. "*Dooládó'da!* (How wonderful!)" it was said .... When the school first opened, people thought it was great work that was being accomplished. The school was created to learn everything possible. A great amount of [income] was distributed.

Ben Bennett concurred: "The main thing for the first day and several weeks after," he said, "people wanted jobs. The whole thing was open. People were in and out ... they wanted to apply for jobs."[1]

To understand the demonstration at Rough Rock requires shedding notions of what "doing school" is about. This was not to be a school in the conventional, classroom-focused sense. The whole thing *was*, in fact, open. "This is a community-oriented school, rather than child-oriented," Robert Roessel told a journalist who visited Rough Rock in 1967. "In the past, Indian schools have taken little interest in their communities, but here, we want to involve adults and teenagers, dropouts, people who have never been to school" (Conklin, 1967, p. 8).

And so, those who read or hear about Rough Rock years after its inaugural days must imagine a completely different kind of school. Imagine, for example, a school whose goal was education in the broadest sense—of cultivating the talents and resources of an entire community, fostering a sense of shared purpose and hope, and *creating* a community around the school. In a community with annual per capita cash incomes of $85.00, school jobs and economic development projects were key to this, and an entire school division, Community Services, was devoted to community outreach (see Fig. 7.2). "It was *all* a Navajo program," Robert Roessel reflected when I spoke with him years later—

> We brought the entire community into the school. Many projects were developed to do this—a greenhouse ... poultry farm, a furniture factory. This was the Navajo Emphasis program, and Navajos were involved in all aspects of it. This was what the school was all about.

The greenhouse Roessel mentions began with the assistance of dormitory students, who planted and tended the seedlings, then sold them to Rough Rock residents. The poultry farm, financed through a Farm Home Administration loan, operated out of the old day school and sold eggs and chicks to community members and school staff. The toy and furniture factory, financed by OEO, employed three local men; the Navajo Office of Economic Opportunity purchased their products and distributed them to Headstart preschools on the reservation. An adobe home project provided training in adobe brick construction. Local workers completed an adobe building to house the Community Services office

---

[1]Between July and the end of September, the school board hired 91 full-time employees, including 45 Navajos, 38 from the local area. In addition, eight parents served as dormitory aides on a 6-week rotating basis, and two community members were hired as part-time management trainees in the dormitories and administration services. Through an arrangement with the Navajo Nation and the University of Utah, 15 Volunteers in Service to America (VISTA) workers came to Rough Rock to assist in the classrooms and dorms (Roessel, 1966b, pp. 1–2).

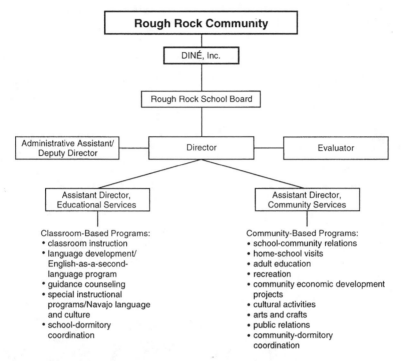

FIG. 7.2. Early school organization.

and built a science building and several model homes that later were occupied by Rough Rock residents.

The school also sponsored an OEO-funded arts and crafts project, which hired Navajo instructors to teach rug weaving, basket and moccasin making, silversmithing, leather work, pottery making, and dress and sash belt weaving to adults. Participants enrolled in the program for 4 to 9 weeks and received a small stipend. Often, the school purchased participants' finished products, selling them to school staff, visitors, or off-reservation vendors. The goals of this program were to revitalize traditional Navajo arts and crafts, cultivate a cadre of local artisans, and establish new market outlets for their work. Remembered fondly by its participants, the arts and crafts program also nurtured a sense of comradery and communal pride. Hasbah Charley, who continued to work as a weaver for many years, recalled the goodwill the program generated:

> The work we did was good …. We learned rug weaving and basket weaving. We also learned to weave sash belts. [The school] asked me to become really in-

volved, and that's what I did. And that was good. To this day, [these activities] are still my teachings and what I talk about.

Now, imagine a school organized around principles of kinship, family, and communalism. Communalism was most evident in the dormitory parent program. Dormitory assistants acted as surrogate parents, watching over the children, providing counseling and moral support, and sharing their knowledge of oral traditions during evening storytelling sessions (Roessel, 1977, p. 2). Lynda Teller explained, "The community parents would stay in the dorm Monday through Friday, helping. Some would work nights .... They were doing a lot of crafts in the dorm, and also in the classroom." Dorm parents received a small stipend for their work. To maximize community participation and the distribution of income, they rotated on an 8-week basis.

Mae Hatathli worked as a dormitory aide for many years. She remembered how she cared for the children, patching their worn clothes and instructing them on traditional values and behaviors.

FIG. 7.3. Community members building an adobe house, one of the school's economic development initiatives, late 1960s. (Photograph by Marguerite Swift from RRCS archives, courtesy of Rough Rock Community School.)

We helped watch over the children there. I did things like make their beds, and I sewed their clothes where they were torn. They [the school board] asked me to talk to them and I did that. I told them to do their best .... That's how the school started.

There were other, more subtle applications of the kinship principle. Imagine a school where the informal knowledge residing within extended family households was valued as much or more than that formalized by certificates or degrees. Central to the feeling of "openness," this quality was remarked upon by many people we interviewed. "A lot of these people who worked at the school didn't really have that formal education to be specialized in certain areas," Lorinda Gray pointed out, "but they had jobs. I think that broadened a lot of community interest at the school." Frank X. Begay, who served as a dormitory aide for many years, remembered this about the day he was hired:

I was asked if I wanted a job. "I didn't go to school—what could I possibly do?" I said.

"Children are starting at the school and we want you to work there," I was told.

"I didn't go to school, what could I do there? I don't know how to write," I said.

"Stop saying that," I was told. "You are going to help us. This is a school run by the community. It is not a BIA school."[2]

The kinship principle extended to other, less formal school functions designed simply to bring people together in what historically had been an alien institution. Hasbah Charley reminisced—

When the school began, we used to hold meetings and potlucks for the community, and everyone donated meat [sheep]. It was a lot of fun. We had people from all over—men, women, and teenagers. That's how it was then.

Besides sponsoring community meetings and dinners, the school functioned almost like a branch of the extended family, assisting community members in times of need. During a severe snowstorm in 1967, school personnel helped

---

[2]As part of the goal of opening the school to the community, the school board decided to half the salaries of dormitory and other community aides in order to hire twice as many people. Years later, Robert Roessel explained that he had opposed this policy: "We had to attract good people since we were *demonstrating*," he said, referencing the high stakes attached to a Federally funded experimental program. The board prevailed, however, and many community members obtained jobs and thus participated directly in the school. "The board was right. I was wrong," Roessel acknowledged.

open roads, get hay to marooned livestock, and assist Air Force helicopters in bringing food to isolated camps. During spring lambing season, the school purchased lamb starter milk, selling it to community members at discounted rates. The school purchased butane and sold it to community members at cost, rechanneling the proceeds to school projects. During an especially hard winter, the school bought coal from a regional construction company and distributed it free to the community. The school water supply provided stock and domestic water, and the school board and Community Services helped bring a U.S. Public Health Service clinic to Rough Rock in 1969. In the school's second year, the board petitioned the Bureau to reinstate the Rough Rock Chapter, and that year, a chapter house was constructed near the school. Aside from the new facility itself, construction work on it provided more jobs and wages. "There was a lot of work and the school helped in so many ways," John Dick recalled.

Finally, imagine a school committed to promoting the community's mental health and spiritual life. This was the purpose of the Navajo Mental Health Project, which began in 1967 with funds personally donated by Ruth Roessel. For more than 20 years, the project continued with support from the National Institute of Mental Health. To prepare more Native healers, the Navajo Mental Health Project funded months- and years-long apprenticeships during which aspiring healers trained under locally recognized ritual specialists. Most instruction occurred in the specialist's home or during ceremonies conducted by him.

The Mental Health Project helped prepare one of the few local female healers, Mae Hatathli. Mae's father was a well-known medicine man who taught for many years as part of the Mental Health Project. Mae wanted very much to learn the Blessing Way (*Hózhǫ́ǫ́jí*) ceremony, the core of Navajo religious thought and practice. She recalls her father being selected to study this ceremony. "Then I began to wonder if a woman along with her husband could join the program," Mae said—

> … so I asked my uncle, John Dick. "Yes," he said, "It is allowed." So I told him that I wanted to join the men. He said it was acceptable .… I joined the group with my father .… We [my husband and I] went with him whenever he was asked to do a ceremony. We did that for several years.

THE IMPACTS OF EARLY COMMUNITY-BASED PROGRAMS

Of all the early community development programs at Rough Rock, the Navajo Mental Health Project was the most long-lived, and by community standards, the most significant and successful. This is perhaps because the project tapped into deeply held beliefs that were and are pervasive within the local culture, but also because this project received continuous funding from a single source over many years. Other projects supported by discretionary funds lapsed within a few months or years, and few had economic benefits beyond the provision of short-term wages.

All of these programs cultivated the community's *human* resources, even as they promoted a collective view that Rough Rock was, in fact, the people's school. Virtually all the oral history testimony about the school at this time reiterates the themes of openness, inclusivity, and a sense of belonging and being needed and appreciated by the school. The demonstration project explicitly depended and drew upon the cultural capital of community members—what Norma González, Luis Moll and their associates call the informal, everyday "funds of knowledge" in households and families (González, 1995; González et al., 1995). For many people, the school provided their first wage employment. Local knowledge was rewarded financially and by the social status conferred by school jobs.

As much or more than anything that transpired in the classroom, the validation and use of community-based knowledge held the promise of building a genuinely bilingual and bicultural school culture. I turn now to consider how that promise unfolded in classrooms and the school curriculum.

INDIGENOUS BILINGUAL/BICULTURAL EDUCATION: "WE HAD A LOT OF ACTIVITIES GEARED TO NAVAJO"

In the spring of 1996 I asked Lorinda Gray, a bilingual teacher at Rough Rock Elementary School, how she would describe the school and community in 1966. At that time, Lorinda had just graduated from Chinle High School. "I always wanted to be a clerk-typist," she explained, but she took a job as a bilingual teacher assistant at the new demonstration school. "I think the community really supported the idea of a bilingual school," Lorinda said, "because it seems like the school was open to the community." Parents and grandparents not only worked in the classrooms, dormitories, and school support services, they often visited the classrooms and "they were participating in the arts and crafts and various other activities," Lorinda recalled. "The administration and the school board and that regional board [DINÉ, Inc.]—they were in there as a whole team to support bilingual education," she added. Lorinda laughed that at annual school orientations, there was so much enthusiasm for bilingual education "you could just taste it!"

FIG. 7.4. Guy Blackburn's and Lorinda Gray's elementary students painting the metal structure that housed their classroom, c. 1967. (Photograph from RRCS archives, courtesy of Rough Rock Community School.)

Bilingual/bicultural education naturally complemented Rough Rock's community development emphasis. "Often in the past," Robert Roessel wrote in the school's first monthly report, "education has been looked upon by Indian parents as a threat"—an either-or proposition that required a choice between two languages and lifeways (Roessel, 1966a, p. 102). In contrast, Rough Rock advocated an additive, "both-and" approach in which students were exposed "to important values and customs of *both* Navajo culture *and* the dominant society" (Roessel, 1977, p. 10).

What did this approach look like in practice? Who were the teachers? How was instruction organized?

FIG. 7.5.   Cultural presentation at Rough Rock by Billy Sam of Many Farms, c. 1967. (Photograph from RRCS archives, courtesy of Rough Rock Community School.)

FIG. 7.6. Elementary students performing a traditional dance as participants in the Navajo Mental Health project observe, c. 1966. *In foreground from left to right*: Project participants John Woody, Jim Hatathli, Mae Hatathli, and Little Laughter. (Photograph from RRCS archives, courtesy of Rough Rock Community School.)

In 1966, the number of certified Navajo teachers could be counted on a few hands. Rough Rock hired three of them, all women, to teach the beginner's classes. Although none came from the community, the six teacher assistants hired (also women) had been born and raised at Rough Rock. Lynda Teller, who had recently graduated from high school and was planning to study nursing in Dallas, remembers receiving a letter in the summer of 1966 from her father, John Dick. "My parents wrote to me and told me there was a school that was going to open here in Rough Rock," she said. "And they said, 'Can you come home? We have a job for you here.'"

Lynda Teller became one of those six bilingual teaching assistants. Her mission school literacy in Navajo had never left her, she said, "even though I was away from home a lot. Eventually, word got around that I could read and write Navajo"—

And so they said, "Well, you're going to teach Navajo to the teachers who don't know how to read or write," and there I was. Anita Pfeiffer [the school's first Educational Services director and a respected leader in Navajo education], said, "I want you to help all these teachers, even the *bilagáanas*, read and write Navajo." I said, "Me? Teach the teachers?" And she said, "Yes!"

In addition to the evening language classes she offered, Lynda Teller rotated between different classrooms as the Navajo language specialist. By the school's second year, four new specialists had been hired to teach Navajo language and social living. Anita Pfeiffer's report of September 1968 gives some idea of how instruction was organized: "Instruction is entirely in Navajo in Phase I where there are bilingual teachers, except for the daily ... oral English program" (Pfeiffer, 1968, p. 10)[3]

Lynda Teller recalled that the school administration encouraged the Navajo staff to use Navajo as much as possible and "to pick up Navajo [literacy] as much as they can." Non-Navajo teachers also participated in periodic live-ins, residing with local families for 2 or 3 days as a way of learning about their students' lives and home experiences. "We had a lot of activities geared to Navajo," Lynda said—

> We had an arts and crafts program in one of the classrooms. Groups of students were taken there, just to watch how everything was done. When they were in the seventh and eighth grades, they could take weaving, silversmithing, sash belt weaving, and leather craft. Then that OEO program [the adult arts and crafts program] would come have workshops with parents, students, and staff ....

Accounts such as these provide some sense of the ways in which the demonstration school attempted to blur the lines between classroom and community. With a core staff of teachers, teaching assistants, and parent assistants, classrooms were hubs of activity and personnel. Lynda Teller's recollections help bring those classrooms to life:

> We had a lot of teachers in the classroom. We had VISTA workers here, and student teachers paid under the Ford Foundation. We had a student teacher in about every classroom then. We had exchange students from foreign countries, and they would show us the way they make their clothes, and do their cooking. So we had a lot of people in the classroom really helping.

---

[3]By the end of the first year, after teachers expressed dissatisfaction with a graded school system, the school board approved an ungraded system designed to remove "the stigma of promotion and non-promotion while giving importance to individualized instruction" (Pfeiffer, 1967, p. 14). Students were grouped into preschool, beginners, and 15 classes of approximately 11 pupils each in "Phase I" and "Phase II." Phase I students remained in self-contained classrooms throughout the day, receiving instruction from both their classroom teacher and specialists who rotated from class to class. Phase II students moved from a base classroom to specialized classes in Navajo language and social living, physical education, science, industrial arts, and home economics, a class specifically requested by board members who asked that adults also be allowed to take it.

"WE WANTED THE NAVAJO LANGUAGE TO BE WRITTEN"

One of the major obstacles to implementing Rough Rock's "both-and" approach was a lack of bilingual/bicultural teaching materials. Navajo literacy materials at the time consisted of those produced by the BIA in the 1940s and 1950s (including some primers and a dictionary), books for teaching beginning Navajo to non-speakers, translated Biblical works, and scholarly accounts written for an adult, non-Navajo audience (Spolsky, Holm, & Murphy, 1970). Navajo teachers had to improvise, and they complained in their monthly reports that students became bored with the duplication of material. As one teacher reported, the question most often asked by the students was, "What are we going to do next?" (Norris, 1968, pp. 85–86).

With a grant from Title I of the Elementary and Secondary Education Act (ESEA) in 1967, the school established the Navajo Curriculum Center, the first enterprise in the United States to be devoted to the production of Indigenous children's literature. "We said we wanted the Navajo language to be learned. It will be written and there will be books on it," former school board secretary Thomas James maintained. "We wanted books in Navajo and on ceremonial subjects. That is how many books came out."

At first, the Curriculum Center was no more than a workroom off a hallway. "That room was an office for Navajo culture," Lorinda Gray remembered, gesturing to a room adjacent to the bilingual program office in the present elementary school. "We had all these people that told traditional stories," Lorinda went on, "and we had people transcribing, and we had people illustrating .... I think that was one of the best highlights of the school."

In its first 4 years, the Curriculum Center produced over a dozen texts, most of them professionally published and beautifully illustrated by local artists. Ethelou Yazzie's (1971) *Navajo History* and Robert Roessel and Dillon Platero's (1968) *Coyote Stories* remain the most popular; they have been reprinted many times and continue to sell briskly around the world. In light of the need for Navajo literacy materials, however, these texts were inadequate; reflecting the priorities of Title I, a compensatory program for English reading and mathematics, nearly all the books were written in English.

In later chapters, I revisit the dilemma of Federal funding and its effects on local education control. Here, it should be noted that while Rough Rock's bilingual/bicultural program was born amidst great enthusiasm and promise, the resources to support it in the classroom were slim indeed. Thus, Navajo language instructor and linguist Paul Platero wrote that "the need for adequate instructional materials was constant" (P. Platero, 1968, p. 81). And Dillon Platero, who assumed the school directorship in 1969, agreed: "One of the main difficulties … faced in the early days was a lack of suitable texts to teach Navajo language and culture" (Platero, 1969a, p. 5).

TESL

In contrast to the relatively unstructured Navajo language and culture curriculum, the TESL (Teaching English-as-a-Second-Language) program appears, in retrospect, positively rigid. Developed by UCLA English Professor Robert D. Wilson and approved by the Bureau for all its Navajo schools, the program's aims, on the surface, seem to have complemented Rough Rock's "both-and" philosophy. TESL would "sensitize" students to two cultures, Wilson said, helping them view both Navajo and English as useful "tools of thought" (Wilson, 1969, p. 65). In practice, however, the TESL program at Rough Rock was skills-driven, remedial, and explicitly unconcerned with natural language experiences. "The constant objective," the program director observed in a monthly report, "is the children's creation of syntactically correct, phonologically well-informed, meaningful sentences" (Hoffman, 1968, p. 10).

Daily "core" and "transfer" lessons involved question-answer drills and practice of grammar rules. A school report (Hoffman, 1968, p. 23) contains this illustration of a beginners core lesson intended to teach the difference between the articles "a" and "an":

What do you have?

I have a _____.

I have an ____.

And from a monthly report (Hoffman, 1968) is this example of a transfer lesson:

A walking trip through the school to see what people were doing encouraged "She's baking a cake. She's typing. They're scrubbing the floor." Many other samples of the present continuous form with third person singular and plural pronouns were easily incorporated into this activity (p. 32).

Other staff reports portray practices that today would draw sharp criticism. The cafeteria, for instance, was viewed as a "specific Anglo experience," with dining behavior modeled after "family type dining in an Anglo dining room" (Hoffman, 1966, p. 9). Prior to lunch, the TESL staff played the lunch menu over the school intercom. Using pictures of featured items, teachers and students practiced the menu vocabulary and, in the lunch line, students "transferred" this vo-cabulary by requesting food items from the kitchen staff (Hoffman, 1968, p. 20). What makes this picture so disconcerting is the fact that most of the kitchen staff were Navajo monolinguals who also were students' kin.

The most marked examples of TESL's behavioristic emphases were its "Madison Avenue" campaigns. Intended to correct pronunciation and gram-matical errors, campaigns lasted 1 to 3 weeks. Before a campaign began, TESL staff and teachers informed students of its purpose; in class, children practiced campaign "dialogues." They then were expected to initiate similar "dialogues" with adults outside class, who dispensed trinkets and other re-wards for correct performances. One campaign (Hoffman, 1968) focused on the elongation of vowel articulation:

> The question practiced by the children—who stretched out vowel sounds—was, "Do you have a balloon in your shoe (in your pocket, in your sleeve, etc.?"). Adults, supplied with hundreds of balloons to hide, soon parted with these prizes as the children guessed correctly and demonstrated that they could stretch out the vowels rather than articulate them with typical Navaho tenseness (p. 32).

In fairness to Rough Rock and to provide a larger context for these prac-tices, it should be remembered that audiolingual approaches were quite com-mon at the time. Indeed, the Bureau had recommended Wilson's ESL program to all its Navajo schools. "It was a different problem then," Wayne Holm pointed out. "The problem ... was finding or creating situations in which the students *needed* English." In addition, he said, when the teacher is the only speaker of the language, "you have to get organized .... Whatever the excesses of ... ESL were, it was an improvement over the largely silent classes that preceded it" (personal communication, February 14, 2000).

In retrospect, the most obvious problem with the TESL program as it was implemented at Rough Rock was the focus on pronunciation and grammatical accuracy at the expense of communication and fluency. This emphasis tended to create contrived linguistic environments—the "Anglo dining experience" and "Madison Avenue" campaigns, for example—none of which were likely to be encountered by children outside of school. The program also assumed that teaching and learning are unidirectional processes—that what is "taught" is re-ceived, assimilated, and thereby "learned." This assumption mirrors what Paulo Freire (1970) calls the "banking" concept of education, in which children are characterized as empty vessels waiting to be filled by more knowledgeable (and powerful) others.

In these respects, the demonstration school was unable to escape its own structural constraints. Now to a deeper consideration of these issues.

DINÉ EDUCATION AND WESTERN INSTITUTIONS

Looking back, Rough Rock's early academic program seems to have been full of both imaginative, Indigenized experiences and remedial, scripted routines. On the one hand, the school privileged the local language and culture, opened classrooms to the community, and carried principles of kinship into the dormitories and other school services. Navajo culture instruction, Robert Roessel claims, was highly successful (personal communication, February 11, 2000). The oral histories and early school documents are full of reports by enthusiastic and dedicated Navajo and Anglo teachers willing to take risks to enhance instruction—to try, for instance, a then-new manipulative mathematics program based on Cuisenaire rods; to develop culturally relevant social studies and English reading units; to participate in home live-ins; and to help colleagues better serve their students by providing after-school classes in Navajo.

On the other hand, the problems inherent in the school's academic program cannot be ignored: the dearth of Navajo print materials, the presence of Anglo-centric texts and transmission-oriented pedagogies, the reduction of children's language and learning potentials to cue-response drills. Nor can we ignore the voices of Navajo and non-Navajo staff members who, in report after report, call for some overarching guidelines to help them articulate the Navajo and English components of the curriculum and bring greater consistency between grades and content areas.

What are we to make of these difficulties and inconsistencies? How do they relate to broader issues in Indigenous and minoritized schooling? A study of Rough Rock classrooms in 1972 sheds some light.

In the spring of that year, visual anthropologist John Collier, Jr. (the son of the former Commissioner of Indian Affairs) went to Rough Rock to conduct a film study of the flow of communication and interaction in school classrooms. With his associates Marilyn Laatsch, a former elementary teacher, and Pat Ferrero, an artist and teacher, Collier produced and analyzed 10 hours of film from preschool to secondary classrooms. The film team was aided by teachers of diverse backgrounds working in San Francisco's multiethnic schools, including an experienced Native American teacher, all of whom provided feedback on the film. While limited by the amount of time spent in the classrooms and the analysts' admittedly outsider positions, the final report, a description of three elementary classrooms, suggests the struggle Rough Rock educators faced in balancing Navajo and Western, school-based ways of teaching and learning.

The report (Collier, Laatsch, & Ferrero, 1972) begins with this description of the Headstart preschool:

> The physical equipment ... contains nothing of traditional Navajo style. The quarters are of wood, aluminum, and plastic with the appearance of a deluxe mobile home. Inside is an immaculate and spacious room, bright, cheerful and efficient. The shared view of the San Francisco teachers who have looked at this film is that the style of the room is typically White middle-class including most of the learning equipment and decorations. The exceptions ... are color prints of traditional Navajo mothers and Navajo words here and there identifying objects and directing room functions. There are also mounted card cut-outs of family members also identified by Navajo words. But the family is a White family dressed in clothes reminiscent of illustrations in the "Dick and Jane" readers (p. 10).

In the course of the morning's activity, photographic frames of which appear in Collier et al.'s (1972) report, the Navajo teacher, a parent assistant, and students move from lively, spontaneous, and affectionate interaction—tooth brushing, hair combing, and play—to a programmed ESL lesson.

> [The teacher] now changes ... to the teacher role, of giving orders to the children in English as an ESL lesson. "Touch your nose," "touch your ear," "touch your leg," she says as she simultaneously acts out these orders .... The children's behavior also changes from a flowing pace with lively involvement, to jerky disorganized body movements as they obey the teacher's intensely acted-out orders in English. Their responses become mechanical and distracted ... (p. 15).

The presence of the camera no doubt influenced these interactions. Yet visitors and cameras were commonplace at Rough Rock (in fact, Collier filmed *another* visitor taking pictures while he was there), and the patterns noted in the preschool were witnessed in other classrooms as well. In the kindergarten class, for instance, the decor ranged "from a Native effort to make a room divider look like a log dwelling [a hogan] to stereotypic decorations of the White classroom type" (Collier et al., 1972, p. 64). In the ESL lesson for the day—

> The teacher holds out a plastic toy sheep in a confrontation with English words. There is no visible response. One little girl clutches another plastic sheep, stares at the camera and then puts the sheep in her mouth. Students rock, lean backwards, grappling for unidentified objects on the floor ... this example of ESL is a confrontation, face to face assault. The student must hear in English a question

which too often takes the form of an intimidating command, rather than an empa-thetic inquiry, and the student must respond to it on the spot—in English. Even in the most relaxed circumstances this can be stressful (p. 70).

In hindsight, I believe we see in these scenes educators attempting to negotiate a complex and risky new social-political terrain. There was the school—not only *not* an Indigenous institution but a historically repressive one, now positioned as an agent of community empowerment. There were Native teachers, graduates of those repressive institutions and conventional teacher education programs, now expected to enact radical pedagogical change. There were the parents, most of whom had little or no schooling or for whom it had been a punitive experience. And there were the students, for whom this was an induction into the culture of schooling. Pressed into all of this, deeply rubbed into every scene, was a long-es-tablished colonial educational system and a set of expectations firmly entrenched in paternalistic and assimilative aims. Finally, there was the fact that all of this was being worked out under the magnifying lens of a national experiment, of which Collier's camera offered but a momentary, if revelatory, glimpse.

In short, no blueprints existed for "doing" school in the way Rough Rock proposed—there were not even any Native teaching materials (or very few). The demonstration project called upon teachers, parents, the school board, ad-ministrators, and students to chart completely new ground—but *within* the structural confines of an existing, non-Indigenous social-educational system. Even 30 years later, it is difficult and dangerous to pass judgment on such a pro-cess. Yet that is exactly what happened when, in 1968, the Office of Economic Opportunity commissioned an external evaluation of the school.

FIG. 8.1. "Rough Rock does matter; it will not be shrugged off." —Dillon Platero (Photograph by Fred Bia, courtesy of Rough Rock Community School.)

8

The Problems and Politics of Program Evaluation

One of the more protracted struggles surrounding bilingual/bicultural education in the United States centers on program evaluation. Many researchers have documented the inappropriateness of standardized testing as a measure of program and student "success" (see, e.g., Cummins, 1984, 1989; Deyhle, 1986; Edelsky, 1991; Gipps, 1999; Lessow-Hurley, 2000; Stefanakis, 1998; Troike, 1984; Valdés & Figueroa, 1994). Researchers also have shown the assumptions of neutrality and objectivity attached to such tests to be both fallacious and pernicious. Yet the pressures for standardization continue, fueled by political expediency, public complicity and naiveté, and expositions on the alleged inheritability of intelligence (see, e.g., Hernstein & Murray, 1994; Rushton, 1999).

Bernard Spolsky and his associates in the Navajo Reading Study wrote in 1974 that, "One of the results of the renewed interest in bilingual education in the United States has been a demand for accurate evaluation of the effects of these programs" (Spolsky, Green, & Read, 1974, p. 1). Spolsky et al. went on to raise several critical questions about how these programs should be assessed: what data are relevant (only standardized test scores?), which outcomes should be measured and how, and how non-pedagogical outcomes such as community empowerment might be "weighed along with all the others" (Spolsky et al., 1974, pp. 1–3). The latter effects, Spolsky et al. suggested, may in fact be the most significant.

This chapter presents a case study of bilingual education program evaluation, illustrating the ways in which power relations intersect, in complex and far-reaching ways, with allegedly neutral evaluative processes. In contrast to claims of neutrality and objectivity, this case study exposes the ways in which evaluation is ideologically saturated, and how competing interpretive frameworks inevitably produce radically different results.

SETTING THE STAGE

In the fall of 1968, Dillon Platero, along with Navajo Area Assistant Education Director William Benham and two tribal representatives, met in Chicago with a group of scholars from the fields of anthropology, education, psychiatry, social psychology, and public health. Among the latter was Donald Erickson, a professor at the University of Chicago and a specialist in nonpublic, parochial education, who had been hired by OEO to evaluate the Rough Rock Demonstration School. At the Chicago meeting, Erickson (Erickson & Schwartz, 1969) outlined his proposed methods for a 6-month study, including interviews of Rough Rock students, parents, and school staff, a stratified sample of board minutes and other school documents, analysis of standardized test scores, staff questionnaires, and an "anxiety scale" to be administered to students (p. 1.7). In addition, the evaluation would compare Rough Rock with three other schools: Rock Point, a BIA school identified as similar to Rough Rock in terms of its demographics and history of experimentation with ESL and bilingual education; Chinle Boarding School, "a fairly typical BIA school;" and Chinle Public Elementary School, "just across the street from Chinle Boarding" (p. 1.7). The evaluation also would involve an "anthropological live-in" by research assistant Henrietta Schwartz, who would spend 30 days in residence at the Rough Rock dormitory, 11 days at Rock Point, 14 at Chinle, and 4 at an annual tribal fair, talking with students and school personnel, observing, "and making voluminous observational notes" (p. 1.12). The conferees in Chicago agreed to Erickson's plan, requesting only that Rough Rock be assessed in terms of its own objectives (p. 1.2).

In the spring of 1969, Erickson and Schwartz submitted their report to OEO. In the fall of that year, the University of Chicago released a public statement excerpting the evaluation and asserting that "Erickson found that 'Rough Rock failed to demonstrate any superiority to other schools in the study'" (Kiyaani, 1969, p. 76). The *Navajo Times* picked up the story, calling the report a "blanket indictment" of the demonstration project (*Navajo Times*, December 4, 1969, p. 27). The following year, a group of articles on what was called simply the "Erickson Report" appeared in a special issue of *School Review* as a feature titled, "Skirmish at Rough Rock." The entire episode resulted in a counter-evaluation by those who had consulted with Erickson in the fall 1968 Chicago meeting, followed by a third, school-commissioned (and generally favorable) reassessment of Rough Rock by a team of Navajo evaluators.

According to school registrar Benjamin Bennett, people at Rough Rock "got very hot under the collar with this evaluation"—

> We had only one copy, and I honestly sat up all night and read that thing through the night. I had to give it back to someone the next day .... What [Erickson] was evaluating and what the school staff thought was important were just not meshing.

What did this report say and why was it so contentious? The report is massive, including nine chapters and four appendices. It would be impossible and unproductive to fully consider all of it here. Instead, I will examine the report's major claims, what they might mean in the life of the community and school, and their implications for Indigenous self-determination.

THE ERICKSON REPORT

As a measure of educational outcomes, Erickson and Schwartz utilized comparative California Achievement Test (CAT) scores for students in grades 1 through 4 at Rough Rock, Rock Point, and two other BIA schools. The scores were reported in grade-equivalents, which, as others have pointed out, provide an illusion of simplicity but, because they are not based on an interval scale, are nearly impossible to interpret.[1] Nonetheless, Erickson and Schwartz say the scores from all four grades show Rock Point "as superior."

Taking for the moment the scores at face value, it can be seen that they fail to prove the evaluators' point (see Fig. 8.2). First, the differences between Rough Rock and Rock Point are negligible in all but grade 4 and it is not known whether students received all their prior instruction at the school for which their scores are reported. Clearly older students at Rough Rock had not, since the school had been operating for only 2 years. Further, such critical factors as the amount of English spoken at home were not controlled. If the scores have any meaning it was for 2nd- and 3rd-year Rough Rock students who had received all their schooling at Rough Rock. When this was taken into account in a second

---

[1]Grade-equivalent scores are an uneven and distorted measure of student achievement for several reasons. A "grade-equivalent score of seven attained by a fifth grader on a math test does not mean that he [sic] knows sixth- and seventh-grade math. It is more accurate to say that he can do fifth-grade math as well as an average seventh grader can do fifth-grade math," Baca (1984) states (p. B1). In addition, fall to spring gains can appear to suggest dramatic improvements, "when the gains were exactly what would have been expected under normal classroom conditions" (Baca, 1984, p. B1). Even those opposed to bilingual/bicultural education have cautioned that grade-equivalent scores "should never be used by anyone for any purpose whatsoever" (Pérez & Horst, cited in Baker & de Kanter, 1983, p. 40).

CAT administration by Erickson and Schwartz, 2nd- and 3rd-year Rough Rock students did not lag behind—in fact, the scores of 3rd-year pupils at Rough Rock and Rock Point were exactly the same (see Table 8.1).[2]

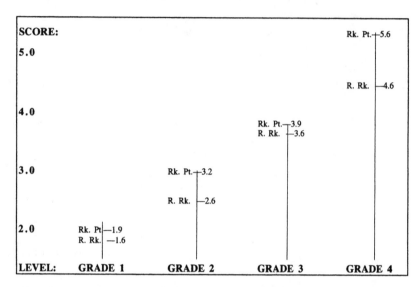

FIG. 8.2.   Mean grade-equivalent scores on May 1968 California Achievement Tests, Rough Rock and Rock Point, as reported by Erickson & Schwartz (1969, adapted from Figure 7.2 [no page number]).

TABLE 8.1

Total California Achievement Test battery grade-equivalent mean scores, Rough Rock and Rock Point, as reported by Erickson & Schwartz (1969, p. 7.26)

Year 2		Year 3		Year 4		Year 5	
R. Rk.	Rk. Pt.	R. Rk.	Rk. Pt.	R.Rk.	Rk. Pt.	R. Rk.	Rk. Pt.
1.7	2.1	2.7	2.7	3.2	3.5	3.5	4.6

---

[2]In January 1969, Erickson re-administered the CAT to students at Rough Rock, Rock Point, and Chinle Boarding Schools. This included a Rough Rock sample of 19 3rd-year pupils, 7 4th-year pupils, 11 5th-year pupils, 14 6th-year pupils, and 11 7th-year pupils, all of whom had attended Rough Rock consecutively for a little over 2 years. Despite the small sample size (the tests were administered the week after Christmas break and many students at all three sites had not returned to school), Erickson and Schwartz infer that the demonstration school "is no better than Chinle," and "inferior to Rock Point academically" (1969, p. 7.38).

Other "indicators" of student outcomes in the evaluation include an "anxiety scale" based on the Cornell Medical Inventory, with such questions as:

- Do you bite your nails or chew your pencil?
- Can you feel your heart pounding in your chest?
- Have you had a lot of trouble with your teeth?
- Are your feelings easily hurt?
- Do you worry about many things?
- Do you cough a lot?
- Do you often feel unhappy and depressed?
  (Erickson & Schwartz, 1969, p. 7.4)

Students also were asked to respond to "acculturation pictures"—hand drawings of Navajo adult males in traditional and Euro-American attire (suit and tie)—intended to assess children's attachment to Navajo cultural values and lifestyle (Erickson & Schwartz, 1969, p. 7.11). Finally, they were asked "aspirational" questions such as, "Do most Navajo pupils sometimes wish they were Anglos?", "Who is smarter [Navajos or Anglos]?", and "What grade do you think you will go to before you stop going to school?" (Erickson & Schwartz, 1969, pp. 7.15, 7.16, 7.18).

The (in)validity and racist overtones of these measures speak for themselves. I mention them only to give readers a fuller picture of the evaluation procedures and the assumptions the evaluators made about what counted as appropriate and adequate evaluative evidence.

In fact, academic achievement was a minor focus of the evaluation, not even considered until the seventh chapter of the report. The report's major thrust concerned Rough Rock's community-based programs and the role of the school board—areas targeted by the Office of Economic Opportunity, and the centerpiece of Rough Rock's demonstration. Here, the evaluation team paints a picture of the school that we have heard repeatedly in the oral histories: "[E]ven casual observation at Rough Rock," Erickson and Schwartz (1969) say, "suggested that relationships between the school and its community were unusually, perhaps even phenomenally, rich and well developed"—

Local people were almost always present in the halls of the administration building, acting much as if they owned it—sitting, chatting, visiting the Arts and Crafts room, stopping at the dining hall for a meal, dropping into classrooms to see how their children are doing. They played basketball in the gymnasium, attended the school's movies, used the facilities for community affairs. They obviously

thought it a pleasant, accepting spot, a good location for meeting friends or passing the time of day (p. 3.30).

The report goes on to say that, "Almost all Rough Rock parents said their school
was following what most local Navajos wanted" (p. 3.32).

Given these observations, it is difficult to comprehend the intensity of criticism leveled at the school in this report, all of which is couched in condescend-
ing and emotionally loaded language. For example, the report is laced with
condemnations of school board "nepotism" and "patronage." "We think Rough
Rock's patronage system is badly out of control at present," the evaluators
write; " … for the sake of its own development, the Board needs to learn how to
function in terms of consistent policy" (Erickson & Schwartz, 1969, p. 3.54).

The evaluators' patronizing attitude is obvious in these remarks. But in light
of the school's mission and the fact that virtually everyone in the community is
related by kinship, clanship, or marriage, it is hard to see how the board could
do other than hire relatives for the jobs for which they were qualified. Hiring *no*
relatives, the evaluators acknowledge, "might make it difficult to run any program of significant size;" what they object to was the hiring of "close" relatives
"in the Anglo sense of those terms" (Erickson & Schwartz, 1969, p. 3.17).

The report also condemns the board's insistence on a policy of rotating employment for dormitory aides and participants in the school's various economic
development programs, on the grounds that the policy "made it virtually impossible to develop the skills … these people needed" within 6 or 8 weeks. There is
some truth to this, and indeed, it was a practice the school director also objected
to, but about which he was routinely overruled by the board. The evaluators'
criticism, however, ignores board members' and their constituents' expectations that school resources, particularly jobs, be distributed *throughout* the
community. Rotating employment among positions that required little or no
formal education maximized the number of individuals eligible for jobs and, as
we have seen in the oral histories, contributed greatly to the "rich and well developed" school–community relations the evaluators appear to have admired.

The evaluation also suggests that arts and crafts program participants who
continued beyond the length of their original 8-week contract (presumably developing "the skills they needed" to pursue a craft independently) were moti-
vated by self-serving financial interests. Certainly people were and are
concerned about their economic survival and that of their families. But personal
income from the arts and crafts program amounted to $10 per participant per
month (Erickson & Schwartz, 1969, p. 3.45). Using the Navajo-Cornell Pro-

ject's estimation of per capita incomes prior to the demonstration school (Sasaki, 1961), this would raise these participants' annual cash incomes from $85 to $205. Given this, the following statement can only be interpreted as naive, mean-spirited, or both: A "discouraging proportion of arts and crafts trainees," Erickson and Schwartz (1969) say, "carved out full-time jobs by moving from rug weaving to sash belts to silversmithing to moccasin making, to basket weaving to leatherwork" (p. 3.44).

The Erickson Report (1969) contains much similar commentary; the overall tone is of disdain for school programs and personnel. Board members received biweekly stipends of $118, which, according to the evaluation team, "made the board members very wealthy" by community standards and distorted their roles (p. 3.27). The evidence for the latter was that the board spent a large amount of time on personnel matters, specifically the hiring and firing of local people, while devoting relatively little time to classroom or dormitory affairs.

Underlying the inflammatory accusations of patronage and nepotism are fundamental misconceptions of community leadership norms. Board members achieved their positions as had traditional leaders or *naat'áani*: They were senior household heads and prominent livestock owners; they had extensive kin ties throughout the area; and they possessed cultural knowledge considered to be protective of their constituency. Their concerns pivoted around these understandings of their positions as community, not "academic," leaders. Historically leaders had left educational matters to the family in the context of daily life. Leaving classroom and dormitory affairs to the individuals hired for their knowledge of those areas, board members instead devoted their energies to providing income and resources to their constituency, and to ensuring the financial survival and growth of the institution they had been elected to govern. This is exactly the point made by social anthropologist Murray L. Wax in his contribution to *School Review's* (1970) "Skirmish at Rough Rock": "The board acted in the areas where it had expertise, and it refrained from acting in the areas where with good reason it felt that [Robert] Roessel and his professional advisors and staff had their expertise" (p. 67). This pattern, Wax (1970) adds, is "little different from the pattern of schools in many small towns and rural areas" (p. 67).

Finally, the Erickson Report dismisses the school's many economic development programs as "big, flashy, attention-getting projects ... launched impulsively, without proper thought and planning" (Erickson & Schwartz, 1969, p. 3.43). In a concluding summary, the evaluators dismiss the demonstration project altogether:

... if Rough Rock's purpose was to prove that a copious continuing flow of Federal grants would do much to develop a community, it probably succeeded, but the demonstration then was unrealistic and unnecessary. Few people would doubt, demonstration or not, that using federal funds to create rotating employment opportunities for at least 50 per cent of family breadwinners ... would contribute considerably to the well being of an impoverished community. Furthermore, funds of this magnitude are not likely to be available to the vast majority of disadvantaged communities in the United States, particularly as far as politically impotent American Indians are concerned .... (p. 9.8).

THE POLITICS OF PROGRAM EVALUATION

We should, perhaps, allow these words to stand as their own indictment. What is particularly troubling about them and the report in general is the tone of superiority and the authors' supremely non-reflexive evaluative stance. By Erickson and Schwartz's own account, the demonstration school was following the wishes of the community, achieving a "phenomenal" level of community participation. Meaningful employment and its availability to a significant number of community members, even on a temporary or rotating basis, spurred and reinforced that participation. What is problematic is the evaluators' interpretation of these facts and their claims of scientific objectivity.

The social and moral interpretive contrasts are glaring. "Consideration for one's family and kin, which is a value in communal societies, becomes for the bureaucrats nepotism and corruption," notes Murray Wax (personal communication, April 9, 1999). And if nepotism is muted by distributing resources through a system of rotating employment, "then one has violated the tenets of 'civil service,' where only the qualified and virtuous should receive benefits" (M. Wax, personal communication, April 9, 1999).

At one level, the evaluation seems to be a classic case of the problem of bias in social research. Applying Western concepts of what it means to "do" school, and what leadership and participation should "look like," the evaluators reduced the complex social-cultural processes the demonstration project represented to a caricature. The ultimate, well publicized portrayal not only was singularly unhelpful in enabling school personnel to make improvements, but caused them to reject the evaluation entirely.

At another level, the evaluation highlights the difficulties inherent in using schools to achieve Indigenous community-defined ends. Should we be surprised that, after 2 years, the school had failed to achieve its long-term community-transformational goals? Or that such a process was entangled with bureaucratic difficulties and fraught with contention? As Wax (1970) points out, instituting a system of local control through an elected school board does not eliminate the potential for conflict, it "merely establishes a new framework within which the struggles for control continue to occur" (p. 65).

Perhaps we should not be surprised, moreover, that a Federally funded evaluation of a Federally funded program used normative criteria and measures that legitimized the larger power structure within which both the evaluation and the Rough Rock Demonstration School coexisted. This effectively veiled the evaluative process in an aura of objectivity, screening from scrutiny any critical consideration of evaluative norms, and, more importantly, of how Indigenous self-determination might actually be achieved. Indeed, the Erickson Report implicitly suggests that genuine Indigenous self-determination was not an appropriate aim.

AFTERMATH

The Erickson Report raised more commotion outside Rough Rock than it did within; in our interviews, few community members even mentioned it. "I am not worried about the report," one board member said at the time, "since this is our school and we control it" (Kiyaani, 1969, p. 335).

Outside Rough Rock, the report generated a great deal of backlash and debate. In a "counter-evaluation" by Robert Bergman, a psychiatrist and head of the U.S. Public Health Service Mental Health program in Window Rock, attorney Joseph Muskrat, and anthropologists Sol Tax, Oswald Werner, and Gary Witherspoon—several of whom had served as consultants to Erickson and Schwartz—culture shock was cited as a cause of bias in the report (Bergman, Muskrat, Tax, Werner, & Witherspoon, 1969). In the first issue of the Council on Anthropology and Education's *Newsletter,* Donald Erickson (1970a) responded with this one-paragraph comment:

> I agree that there ought to be a study of Rough Rock done by a competent anthropologist. One problem as I see it is that most of the anthropologists who would try to acquire the assignment are unqualified by disposition to do the study. I have been astounded at the almost complete lack of objectivity of numerous anthropologists concerning Rough Rock .... One would think the place had been founded by God Almighty ... (p. 26).

Erickson's comment in the *Newsletter,* the counter-evaluation, and a series of articles in the November 1970 *School Review* (including a piece by Erickson entitled, "Custer *did* die for our sins!" [Erickson, 1970b]), all suggest a subtext of representation or who speaks for whom, even as they expose underlying racisms and the problems of assessing minoritized schooling by dominant society norms. Navajo educator Gloria Emerson's critique in *School Review* best illustrates these points. Dismissing culture shock as an "easy label," she relodges the debate within the arena of greatest concern to stakeholders: How can Indigenous communities achieve Indigenous education control? "Change must come," Emerson (1970) states, "but not by mimicking antiquated Anglo-American education. New forms must be created to represent the resiliency and the genius for adaptation for which the Navajo is famed" (p. 98).

In the same volume, Dillon Platero, then Rough Rock's executive director, makes a similar point while emphasizing the demonstration school's larger objectives. Countering Erickson and Schwartz's assertion that the demonstration project was "unnecessary," Platero (1970) responds that Rough Rock *does* matter:

> [I]t will not be shrugged off. Although little referred to, probably one of our most important accomplishments has been to infuse into Indian education in general, and Navajo education in particular, a refreshing spirit that has so long been missing. Rough Rock's very existence fosters the hope of inspiring other tribal groups to attempt to realize greater control of their own destinies … (p. 58).

In the aftermath of the Erickson Report, the school board sent a telegram to the Office of Economic Opportunity disavowing the report's "slanted interpretation" (Kiyaani, 1969, p. 319). The board then hired an all-Navajo evaluation team to reassess the demonstration project (Begaye, Billison, Blatchford, & Gatewood, 1969), and voted to forbid future external evaluations. This policy would remain in effect until 1975, when new Federal legislation made external evaluation a requirement of the BIA school contracting procedure.

FIG. 9.1. "We have a school board that decides what it wants for their children."
—Teddy McCurtain, 1969. (Photograph from RRCS archives of school board
members [*from left to right*] John Dick and Teddy McCurtain, courtesy of Rough
Rock Community School.)

The Two Faces
of Self-Determination

... I think in some ways, we ... had a window of opportunity of about 10 years where we were allowed to do our own thing, and communities were willing to try these things, and that also ... the government was set up in such a way that they weren't down on us so hard ...

> —*Wayne Holm, in oral history testimony, Window Rock, January, 1996*

The system we operate under would defeat the President of General Motors. The system is a monumental fake and hoax. It is a political game in which the community that refuses to lie down and die wins just enough to stand up for the next punch.

> —*Rough Rock School director Ethelou Yazzie, in Federal testimony, Washington, D.C., 1976*

This chapter tells two stories, both of which take place during the same time period, and both of which are true. One is the story of a revolution in Navajo and Indigenous education—an account of opportunity seized in the name of self-determination, and of how the "unimaginable became doable" (Pfeiffer, 1993). The other is a story of a school and a process held hostage to a Federal bureaucracy that, despite its rhetoric, stymied self-determination at every turn. The two stories intertwine. They are two faces of the struggle for Indigenous education control.

* * * * * * *

WHEN THE UNTHINKABLE BECAME DOABLE

People were shocked when we suggested using Navajo [language]. Nobody *ever* suggested using Navajo in the school to learn, so how can you do that? School is to learn English.

> —*Agnes Holm, Window Rock,* January 1996

113

During the 1970s and 1980s, a quiet revolution in Navajo education took root and began to grow. Whereas only a few years before, as Agnes Holm said, "None of us ever thought of teaching in Navajo," the demonstration at Rough Rock and the Holms' experimental work at Rock Point had opened up a host of new possibilities. "For a long time," Wayne Holm added, "people really couldn't believe that you were both a teacher *and* a Navajo, ... because being a Navajo or being a teacher ... were mutually exclusive terms." Rough Rock and other Indigenous schools changed that forever.[1]

Robert Roessel wrote prophetically of Rough Rock in 1966 that, "The challenges confronting the school, if successfully met, will literally reshape Indian education" (Roessel, 1966a, p. 1). We have already learned of some of those challenges: the need for more Navajo bilingual teachers and for more Native teaching materials. How Rough Rock and other Navajo schools addressed those needs fueled a revolution that would, literally, reshape Navajo and American Indian education and transform the community of Rough Rock as well. To better understand this, we must place Rough Rock and Navajo education in a larger social and political context.

Bilingual Education and Self-determination

The late 1960s and early 1970s were periods of incredible activity in bilingual and bicultural education. A spirit of innovation and a willingness to make leaps of faith characterized the field (Crawford, 1995, p. 12). Along with good faith came a good measure of political support. Presidents Kennedy and Johnson laid the foundation by directing national attention to public education (Thompson, 1975, p. 21). In 1968, Congress passed the Bilingual Education Act, calling for "new and imaginative" programs that used children's native language while they learned English. Authorized as Title VII of the Elementary and Secondary Education Act, Title VII provided for bilingual teaching assistants and other education personnel, and for bilingual teacher preparation, materials development, and parent involvement activities. At the same time, the BIA embraced bilingual education as one of "the most promising" approaches to educating Indian students, largely on the basis of the methods being tried at Rough Rock and Rock Point (Bauer, 1970, p. 223). In a 1970 article, Evelyn Bauer, an ESL specialist for the

---

[1]"In all fairness," Wayne Holm later reflected, "you have to admit that there had been some use of Navajo in some mission schools. And that Willie [William] Morgan was trying out Navajo readers ... when World War II disrupted all that" (personal communication, February 21, 2000). These are valid points. Still, they indicate that the use of Navajo in children's schooling had, to that point, been extremely limited.

Bureau, predicted optimistically that the "national and international attention given to bilingual programs ... make it likely that these programs will continue to expand" (Bauer, 1970, p. 227).

It is difficult to imagine any greater attention than that focused upon Rough Rock at the time. "From its birth," one school report says, "Rough Rock was almost as big a curiosity as the New York Mets or color television" (Nix, 1970, p. 5). School board members and administrators received frequent invitations to share their experiences at conferences, in Congressional testimony, and at meetings of civic and private organizations. Each month, an estimated 100 to 500 visitors—anthropologists, educators, psychiatrists, film crews, politicians and others—passed through Rough Rock's classrooms, the community, and board room, leading the school board to hire a full-time public relations officer. "We always had visitors," Lynda Teller remembers, and "every time we had a visitor, we would perform something or do a presentation for them." "There were so many people who came to visit," John Dick told us, "I don't recall their names. They were very appreciative of the school."

The roster of visitors included individuals with considerable political clout. Caroline Kennedy and her uncle, Senator Robert Kennedy, visited the school in 1967. When the first class of 8th graders graduated in 1968, Senator Edward (Ted) Kennedy gave the graduation address. "I remember when Ted Kennedy

FIG. 9.2. John Dick with then-Senator Walter Mondale (interpreter in center), 1969. (Photograph from RRCS archives, courtesy of Rough Rock Community School.)

was here," Benjamin Bennett reminisced when Galena Dick and I spoke with him nearly 30 years later. "People were coming from *all over* to hear Ted Kennedy. As far as celebrities," he continued, "what about [former U.S. Vice President] Walter Mondale? He was here when he was a senator. He was talking to Dillon [Platero] until 2 in the morning." This reminded Galena of her family's encounter with the senator:

> That Senator Mondale, he came just the day our oldest child, Ernest Jr.—just that day we were having a ceremony for him. There comes Senator Mondale! And he was introduced to us in a hogan. And he sat there for a whole afternoon to observe the ceremony. I think he was the one that wanted to take a goat skin back, so that's what my in-laws gave him ....

How are we to interpret these events? In one sense they can be viewed as a rare instance of the joining of Indigenous and state interests. In terms of the on-the-ground realities at Rough Rock, it seemed that the social and political climate was *right* for constructing a very different kind of Indigenous school. Rough Rock's founders and early leaders seized that opportunity.

The school board minutes are full of references to board members' and administrators' Congressional testimony on Navajo and Indigenous education. Following one set of hearings in Flagstaff, Arizona in 1968, before the Senate Special Subcommittee on Indian Education, Robert Kennedy, then Chairman of the subcommittee, addressed the annual Navajo Education Conference in Window Rock. "Why not Indian parents living in every dormitory?" he asked, referring to Rough Rock's community-based programs—

> Why not adult education activities in every school? Why not Indian parents enriching the curriculum with Navajo crafts and cultural activities? Why not community development dimensions and programs for every school? (U.S. Congress, 1969, p. 1057).

"Rough Rock has proven its point," Kennedy concluded, proclaiming that it should serve as a model for a comprehensive "new national Indian policy" (U.S. Congress, 1969, p. 1055).

Robert Kennedy did not live to see that policy come to fruition, although the seven-volume testimony before his subcommittee—headed, after his assassination, by his brother Edward Kennedy and summarized in what is commonly called the *Kennedy Report*—led to legislation that inaugurated the Federal policy of self-determination. In 1972, Congress passed the Indian Education Act, a Title

IV (now Title IX) amendment to the ESEA and the first Federal legislation to specifically support Indigenous bilingual/bicultural materials development, teacher preparation, and the involvement of Indian parents in the schools. In 1975, the Indian Self-Determination and Educational Assistance Act was passed (Public Law 93–638), formalizing the procedures for tribes and Indigenous communities to contract for the operation of social and educational services. By formally legitimating the experimental contracting procedure first tried at Rough Rock, P.L. 93–638 paved the way for other Indigenous communities to contract to operate their own schools.

"A Lot of People Were Experimenting"

Title VII (Bilingual Education), Title IV (Indian Education), and P.L. 93–638 created the legal and financial potential for placing Indigenous education under local community control. By 1978, just 12 years after the demonstration school's founding, 34 Indigenous schools were under contract, and these and other schools had begun bilingual/bicultural programs. Bernard Spolsky counted 84 American Indian bilingual programs in 1974 (Spolsky, 1974).

Ernest Dick remembers this as a time when "a lot of people were experimenting, all kinds of grants, and all kinds of training programs." Words on a page do faint justice to the excitement of the time, or to the distinct but mutually reinforcing local, tribal, and national initiatives that fanned the flame of local education control.

Rough Rock people were the driving force behind many of these initiatives. The first tribal college, Navajo Community College, was founded at Many Farms in 1968 by Guy Gorman, Ned Hatathli, Dillon Platero, Robert Roessel, and Allen Yazzie.[2] That year, Robert Roessel left Rough Rock to assume the college chancellorship. In 1970, the Navajo Division of Education (NDOE) was established as the coordinating office for Navajo education; 3 years later, Dillon Platero left Rough Rock to head up the Division. Under Platero's leadership and an advisory council that included former Rough Rock Educational Services Director Anita Pfeiffer and DINÉ, Inc. trustee Guy Gorman, NDOE established a site-based delivery system of university-accredited, bilingual teacher preparation courses coordinated with local Title VII and Title IV projects (Iverson, 1981; Roessel, 1979). Ernest Dick directed one such project at Rough Rock. He recalls:

---

[2]Navajo Community College (now called Diné College and located at Tsaile, Arizona, about 40 miles southeast of Rough Rock), was the harbinger of the 1978 Tribally Controlled Community College Act. As of this writing, there are 33 such colleges.

We did a lot of things. We developed the curriculum which is being used throughout the Navajo Nation now, and we were working with Navajo Community College also. And then we asked the school to run the Navajo Teacher Training
program in conjunction with the University of New Mexico. I did that for about 3
years. I learned a lot from there .... A lot of teachers have graduated from that.

The Diné Bi'ólta Association (DBA) was the brainchild of Platero, Pfeiffer,
and Samuel Billison, a member of Rough Rock's "post-Erickson" Navajo evaluation team and NDOE's Teacher Education Advisory Council. DBA, Wayne
Holm recalls, "grew out of Rough Rock"—

> ... it was basically Rough Rock teachers in effect, and Rough Rock administra-
> tors. But it was very effective in enabling other people to get training materials
> and all that. It came directly out of Rough Rock.

People still speak passionately of DBA and its summer and winter workshops on Diné language, culture, and linguistics. The workshops helped standardize the Navajo orthography and develop a corpus of Indigenous literacy
materials, even as they nurtured a cadre of Native linguists and teachers.[3]
Lorinda Gray, whose teacher education courses up to that point had equated bilingual education with special education ("We picked up some courses, but it
was geared to dealing with kids that are mentally retarded"), describes her very
different experience with DBA:

> After the DBA started holding workshops for teachers and assistants, that's when
> we learned to pick up some Navajo writing, Navajo reading, and instruction
> geared to teaching Navajo students. I think that's where all the bilingual inspira-
> tion came in ... that's when we got more involved with the bilingual program.

And, as Robert Roessel pointed out (personal communication, February 11,
2000), DBA had a major emphasis on Navajo culture teaching as well.

In her written reflections on these events, Irene Silentman (1995), a linguist
who taught Navajo literacy to Rough Rock staff members during the school's
early years, recalls how DBA provided "a better perspective on my culture and
language" and "stimulated my interest in Navajo linguistics"—

> Out of these workshops and seminars came many materials on Navajo language
> and culture and much refinement on Navajo-relevant curriculum. I recall feeling

---

[3]The Bureau of Indian Affairs and Center for Applied Linguistics in Washington, D.C. also
played critical roles in helping to standardize the Navajo orthography.

excited about all that was occurring as far as Navajo education was concerned. Meetings were occurring constantly on the refinement of Navajo language. Speakers and experts (both traditional and academic) were brought in to help us decide on bilingual education concerns and issues (p. 10).

Local initiatives linked effectively with regional and national resources, such as the BIA, Teacher Corps, and a special program to prepare Native linguists at the Massachusetts Institute of Technology (MIT). In the early 1970s, the BIA contracted with Northern Arizona University in Flagstaff to develop Indigenous literacy materials, and with the Center for Applied Linguistics in Washington, D.C. to develop a bilingual kindergarten program for Navajo schools (Bauer, 1970, p. 227). Teacher Corps projects proliferated at regional universities, including Diné Teacher Corps at Northern Arizona University just 40 miles west of the reservation. MIT offered graduate fellowships in linguistics for Navajo speakers, prompting several Rough Rock staff members to undertake studies there and one, Paul Platero, to complete a Ph.D.

There was also the Navajo Reading Study, a multi-year project begun in 1969 by sociolinguist Bernard Spolsky of the University of New Mexico, to explore "the feasibility and effect of teaching Navajo children to read in their own language first" (Spolsky, 1972, p. 11). Spolsky and his associates (including Agnes and Wayne Holm, Irene Silentman, and others who had worked or would go on to work at Rough Rock), surveyed the language use patterns of over 5,000 Navajo 6-year-olds, taking a lexical inventory as a basis for developing Navajo reading materials. It was essential, Spolsky believed, that "all books we develop should be written originally in Navajo," so teacher education in the context of materials development became a central part of the project (Spolsky, 1976, p. 350; 1972, p. 16). When the Navajo Reading Study ended 6 years later, it had produced 50 children's books, booklets, and readers, and two dozen technical reports on Navajo and American Indian bilingual education.

Finally, there was the Native American Materials Development Center (NAMDC), established in the mid-1970s through a consortium of Title VII-funded community-controlled schools, including Rough Rock and Rock Point, to develop Navajo language, social studies, and science curricula. Based in Albuquerque, NAMDC produced dozens of Navajo teaching materials and served as a training center and clearinghouse on American Indian bilingual education.[4]

---

[4]Borrego Pass and Ramah-Pine Hill, both Navajo community-controlled schools in New Mexico, also were NAMDC consortium members. When the U.S. Department of Education insisted on a single fiscal agent, Ramah-Pine Hill assumed responsibility for the grant, moving NAMDC to Albuquerque.

Irene Silentman (1995) recalls these years as a period when "Navajo bilingual programs were at their peak" a time that produced a growing Indigenous literature hand-in-hand with a cadre of bilingual teachers:

> Many more Navajo teachers were certified and trained for bilingual programs, the state's public schools were implementing some form of bilingual instruction with state bilingual funds, minimal though they were, and everyone was developing sequential curricula for their schools. Support was coming from the local communities and school administrators .... There was even support from the tribal headquarters, the Navajo Division of Education (pp. 12–13).

These were times, too, of a more general assertion of Indigenous rights, manifested most visibly in protests by members of the American Indian Movement (AIM) and the Alcatraz–Red Power Movement (ARPM).[5] AIM and ARPM raised national consciousness that "Indians have cultures, traditions, history, and communities that they want to preserve," and "that they also want equal justice, economic opportunity, access to education, and more accurate portrayal of Indians in the media and in history books" (Johnson, Champagne, & Nagel, 1999, p. 309). During the early 1970s, Indigenous educators also established the National Indian Education Association and the Coalition of Indian Controlled School Boards. Both organizations helped push an agenda of local, Indigenous control and influenced the findings of the American Indian Policy Review Commission, whose 381-page report called for overhauling Federal Indian education policy to emphasize bilingual/bicultural education, Indigenous language restoration, and "support and financing for Indian community control of all aspects of Indian education" (American Indian Policy Review Commission, 1976, pp. 11–13).

"I saw this as a time for the native people to renew their strengths, preserve their cultures and languages, and improve the education of their children," Irene Silentman (1995) writes—

---

[5]The American Indian Movement was founded in Minneapolis in 1968, and "quickly established chapters in several U.S. cities" (Johnson, Champagne, & Nagel, 1999, p. 305). Its membership came primarily from younger, schooled, urban Native people. The Alcatraz-Red Power Movement or ARPM grew out of three separate occupations of Alcatraz Island, a former Federal penitentiary in California's San Francisco Bay, during the 1960s. "The underlying goals of the Indians on Alcatraz were to awaken the American public to the reality of their situation and to assert the need for Indian self-determination," Johnson et al. write (1999, p. 303). The Alcatraz occupations became a springboard for Indigenous activism that continued well into the next decades, and included a takeover of BIA headquarters in 1972 and the historic siege at Wounded Knee, on the Pine Ridge Sioux reservation in South Dakota, in 1973 (Johnson et al., 1999).

The 1970s were also a time of pan-Indianism and reaffirming oneself as Indian. There was a bonding developing among the Indian nations of the country. The American Indian Movement was at its peak, and so were programs in bilingual education (p. 7).

"We Grew Up With The School"

In this social and political climate, Rough Rock and other Indigenous schools began to grow their bilingual/bicultural programs, with local educators at the programs' core. Ernest Dick's experience, recorded in a 1997 interview, typified that of many young adults at Rough Rock and elsewhere at the time:

> In 1967, I started working as a dormitory aide. I worked as a bus driver, and a teacher's aide, and at the same time, my wife and I were starting to go to school down there at Arizona State University on Teacher Corps. And from there we started going to Navajo Community College and taking classes. I remember an organization called Diné Bi'ólta' Association which ran trainings during the summer and at the same time you could get credit through the University of New Mexico. From there we just kept on going, kept on going until we got a degree, both of us at the same time.

Galena Dick describes her experience as "growing up with" the school. "As I worked on my degree and in my classroom," she writes, "I began to learn to read and write my language along with my students. I had to pick up where I stopped when I entered boarding school, because my language and culture had been taken away from me" (Dick, 1998, p. 25).

Clearly bilingual/bicultural education was much more than a credentialing process or a new kind of curriculum (see, e.g., Read, Spolsky, & Neundorf, 1975). Bilingual/bicultural education was cultural reclamation, the unseating of historical relations of authority and control. "We came to value our own language, particularly when we saw it in print," Irene Silentman (1995) says; "our language was just as valuable and was on equal status with, if not above, the English language" (pp. 16–17). Navajo educators, Silentman adds, came to see themselves as "equals with non-native teachers and administrators" (p. 16).

At Rough Rock, bilingual/bicultural education accomplished even more: It brought young adults back home, provided new career paths and employment, and enabled children to remain close to home while attending school. In effect, the school and its bilingual/bicultural program reunited the generations, knitting families and the community back together through an intergenerational education enterprise and a local opportunity structure in which young people,

FIG. 9.3. On-site teacher preparation class, c. 1975. *In foreground from left to right:* Sally Begay, Linda McCurtain Begay, Darlene Redhair, Mary Benally, and Rena Tsosie. (Photograph from RRCS archives, courtesy of Rough Rock Community School.)

especially, could build their lives. To rephrase Galena Dick's account, an entire community began growing up with—and around—the school.

"We Had a Window of Opportunity"

Viewed through this lens, what was the situation at Rough Rock nearly 15 years after the demonstration school began? Supported by Federal legislation and policies of self-determination—much of which Rough Rock and other Navajo community-controlled schools fought to bring about—the school had produced a core group of local teachers and a substantial number of Navajo literacy materials. Bilingual teachers were relearning Navajo even as they taught it to their students and worked toward teaching degrees. And Rough Rock had been joined in its efforts by the growing numbers of community-contract school boards, a comprehensive Navajo teacher education effort, the financial support of Title IV and Title VII grants, and an expanding national network of bilingual/bicultural programs and personnel.

"Before Rough Rock," Wayne Holm reflected in a 1996 interview, "the notion that you have to have community-responsive curriculum, or that you had to have some forms of empowerment in the community—it isn't that people were against it—it was just literally unthinkable. You didn't *think* about these things." Within a short time, he said,

> the thing that happened was that if you weren't doing something in this line, you had to justify why you weren't doing it .... I mean if you were not attempting to have community-based curriculum, to use [the Native] language, if you did not have something dealing with the culture, the question was, why not? .... There was just an enormous change of opinion.

Rough Rock threw open a window of opportunity that had been barred shut just a few years before. The 10 or 15 years following the founding of the demonstration school marked a watershed in Indigenous schooling. In the words of Anita Pfeiffer, a leader in the struggle for local control, a major shift in opinion and orientation was under way. What was unimaginable only a generation before, had, in her words, become "doable" (Pfeiffer, 1993).

A SECOND REALITY

Another view of this time reveals the reality of a Federal bureaucracy that constrained, even throttled, local opportunity. If we listen to other accounts of these times—the voices in school documents, peoples' memories, and the voluminous testimony before the American Indian Policy Review Commission—we see a different reality:

It is 1969. Rough Rock school enrollments have grown to over 400 pupils in preschool through grade 8, and school leaders are hopeful that a new high school can be built. In February, the school board and director Dillon Platero meet with William Benham and Graham Holmes of the BIA area office to request their support for school construction funds. The Bureau's position, according to Benham and Holmes, is that Congress will not allocate monies for additional classroom space at Rough Rock when school "seats" remain unfilled at other reservation boarding schools. They urge the board to "sacrifice" 7th and 8th graders to schools in Many Farms for a few years, thereby filling more BIA school seats and helping to justify a request for new facilities at Rough Rock.

In response to this proposal, school board president Teddy McCurtain (in Platero, 1969b) reminds his audience of the community's vision of the demonstration school—

It was ... decided to have a demonstration project set up where this new school would be separate and recognized as the Navajos' school and in this project Navajo culture would be taught ... and the school would be operated differently from ... other schools. From the suggestion given it seems that we're being asked to go back to Bureau operation and I feel what we have been teaching at Rough Rock the past years would be forgotten ....

We have a school board that ... decides what it wants for their children. We feel this makes our school quite different from other schools, ... and if we are to send some of our students to Bureau schools this would be working in a different direction from what we want. I feel we are not here to tell you that we will send our children to other schools but we are here merely asking you for additional facilities to take care of our needs ... (pp. 188–189).

The board votes unanimously to extend the demonstration school to the secondary level and requests that a feasibility study for a new high school be undertaken (Dunlap, 1972, p. 1).

It is 1971. After 5 years of operation, the board still has received only the most general guidelines on the contracting procedure from the Bureau's central office in Washington, D.C. Lacking specific Federal directives and timelines, policy is defined de facto by the area office, which imposes more stringent standards on contract schools than regular BIA schools and either fails to identify or ignores its own timelines (American Indian Policy Review Commission, 1976, p. 122). Annual negotiations are continuously held up and require frequent trips by board members and administrators to Window Rock, Gallup, and Washington, D.C. Thomas James, board secretary at the time, remembers having to "follow" school funds around:

Back then, the money did not come directly here. It came to Gallup. When the money arrived we would have to follow it up there. There were uncaring people there in the BIA. It would take a long time for it to be approved .... That's how difficult it was.

The school is by now on a perilous financial path. When BIA funds are not forthcoming, school officials are forced to suspend payroll and dip into employee withholding taxes and other accounts with funds on hand to meet expenses (Kiyaani, 1971). Expenditures begin to exceed the budget. By June, the school shows a deficit of nearly $200,000. Two years later, the debt has more than doubled. The Federal government, the major source of the problem, disowns it, refusing to negotiate a new contract until the debt is cleared up and effectively holding the school—and its students—hostage.

It is August 1973. DINÉ, Inc. declares bankruptcy and the board accepts a new corporation title, the Rough Rock School Board, Inc., required by the BIA for contract accreditation. The BIA further stipulates that the school "guarantee sound fiscal management" by hiring an external accounting firm. The school board complies and hires a firm in Phoenix, some 350 miles away. This lengthens the time between requests for and the receipt of funds, creating a chronic financial backlog in which invoices take nearly a month to process. Paychecks are more often late than on time. One school report cites this as a leading contributor to "teacher frustration and high turnover" (Tonigan, Emerson, & Platero, 1975, p. 28).

It is 1974. After the departure of Dillon Platero to head the Navajo Division of Education, the school board hires a new director, former Rough Rock elementary teacher Ethelou Yazzie. The school now has an enrollment of 451 students in preschool through grade 12; it also is helping Kitsillie, a small community on Black Mesa, secure a school contract by acting as their fiscal agent, receiving and dispensing funds, overseeing personnel, and assisting with a summer school there.

Lacking BIA support, the director and board members lobby Congress directly for funds to build a new high school. An impressive new facility opens near the Friends Mission and old day school (then in use as a middle school). But the Congressional appropriation has financed only a portion of the school plant. The board still is seeking funds to build a gymnasium and library. In the interim, high school students are bused each day to the elementary and middle schools for physical education and library classes. This upsets class schedules, leading to the cancellation of some secondary Navajo language and culture classes.

Meanwhile, Ethelou Yazzie and the board are waging an ongoing battle for the school's financial survival. This year, contract negotiations commence in June, 1 month before the new fiscal year, and are not completed until November, 4 months after the fiscal year begins. No employee contracts can be signed, no supplies can be ordered, and the school administration is in negotiations instead of at school when the school year begins (Tonigan et al., 1975). Rough Rock is only one of many schools experiencing such problems; according to the American Indian Policy Review Commission, budget and contracting runarounds are widespread, making a mockery of self-determination and jeopardizing the very future of community contract schools (AIPRC, 1976, p. 122). Ethelou Yazzie (AIPRC, 1976) submits this testimony to the Commission:

It is June:

The BIA contract is not signed. We have no idea what our budget for fall will be. No teacher is certain that his/her job will be funded. No money has yet arrived .... The curriculum center will stay open half-time because there is no money. There is no capital to produce its product, or to train apprentices in writing, editing, and printing ....

This is the way it is at Rough Rock. We expect a crisis a month, and we are never disappointed (p. 259).

To keep the school afloat, its leaders rely on a host of discretionary grants—Title I (remedial math and English reading), Title IV (Indian Education Act funds), Title VII (Bilingual Education Act funds), Follow-Through, the National Institute of Mental Health, and private foundation support—all of which must be renegotiated annually and some of which have competing or overlapping aims. This, too, requires frequent cross-country trips and regular meetings at Rough Rock between board members, administrators, and school sponsors. From the simple tripartite organizational structure with which the school began, Rough Rock's infrastructure has ballooned into 19 mostly independently funded and operated offices (see Fig. 9.4). According to one school report, all of this means that "Far too many persons report to the Director. Their inability to see her when they need supervisory assistance means they often go without it" (Tonigan et al., 1975, p. 21).

It is 1977. The BIA imposes an indirect cost rate to be negotiated as a percentage of each school's budget. Later, the Bureau discards the percentage system in favor of lump sum agreements. The question of how the school will receive indirect cost monies continues to disrupt and delay contract negotiations and the receipt of school funds for years.

It is 1978. Ethelou Yazzie has taken a position at another school, and the board appoints Rough Rock high school principal Jimmie C. Begay as the new director. High school students still lack a library and gymnasium, the floors of some middle school classrooms are rotting and some rooms are without electricity, there are 33 middle school students for each teacher, and there are not enough textbooks to go around. Assisted by Robert Roessel, who has rejoined the staff as a book writer and special assistant to the director, the school obtains $3.5 million in Congressional add-on funds for the high school. A year later, the BIA approves $4.3 million to build a new middle school. Funding and logistical problems will delay completion of the middle school plant nearly 5 more years. During that time, students will receive their instruction at the 40-year-old day school and in trailers set up near the high school.

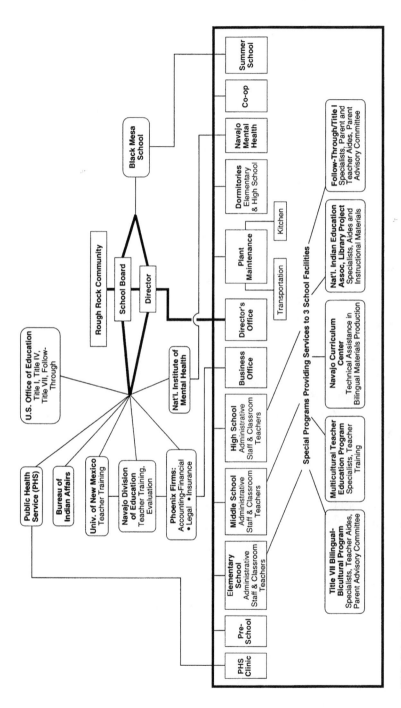

FIG. 9.4. School organizational structure, c. 1975.

It is 1979. Congress passes P.L. 95–561, introducing a BIA school funding formula based on numbers of enrolled students. All BIA-funded schools, including contract schools, are now required to establish "formal accountability systems" that regularly document student enrollment and instructional needs (Bliss, 1980; Foster & Boloz, 1980). A phenomenon called count week ensues—5 days during each school year when school officials scramble to get as many students in classrooms and dormitories as possible. Each student carries a funding quota.[6] The budget and contracting runarounds persist, hamstringing school operations and tying up school leaders in endless meetings. The Phoenix accounting firm continues to profit from the school in return for legitimizing its fiscal management. And the school is again $50,000 in debt.

* * * * *

Two Stories, One Reality

The two stories here reflect a single multilayered reality. That reality is much more complex than can be gleaned from the memories of those we interviewed or from the pages of a report, but perhaps these sources suggest the tightrope Indigenous schools and their leadership have had to negotiate in the name of self-determination. The rhetoric of self-determination was and is betrayed by a Federal bureaucracy tethered to a colonial system of patronage and control (see also Senese, 1986). Except for their body count, nowhere is it clear how this system addresses students or their needs. The fact that communities such as Rough Rock were able to gain a foothold in the system, seizing that moment of opportunity for self-empowerment, is a tribute to their ingenuity and resolve to realize the promise of local, Indigenous education control (see also Manuelito, 2001).

This, at least in part, was the situation at Rough Rock and many Indigenous schools by the early 1980s. The struggle would not abate, but only intensify.

---

[6]Sixteen years later, in anticipation of count week, one school administrator remarked, referring to students: "Anything that runs between two trees is fair game. We don't care if we have to shanghai them—bring them in!"

FIG. 10.1. "I want my children to get an education on both sides, Navajo and English."—Rough Rock parent (Photograph of Rough Rock school children, 1982, by Fred Bia, courtesy of Rough Rock Community School.)

10

Transitions and Turmoil

At the time the school started they were demonstrating .... The intentions then were good, but compared to what we have established here, and what has taken place when I was on the board about 15 or 16 years later—as I compare those things, they're different. The intentions there at the time the school began were more for economic development. And now it's different .... I guess time has changed.

—*Ernest W. Dick, Rough Rock,* May 1997

As we sat at the kitchen table in his home near the junction to Many Farms and Kayenta, Ernest Dick reflected on the transitions in the community and school before and during his 13-year tenure (1983–1996) on the Rough Rock School Board. Time and the presence of the school itself *had* changed Rough Rock by the early 1980s when Ernest Dick and four other new board members were voted into office. The Rough Rock Chapter, revived by the school board in 1968 after it had been informally dissolved during stock reduction, had a relatively new chapter house and again played a prominent community role. A U.S. Public Health Service clinic, another early school board initiative, operated on the elementary campus. In 1976, years of pressure on Federal officials exerted by the previous board had resulted in a paved road to Many Farms. Speaking of the road when we interviewed him in 1981, then-school board president Wade Hadley said, "That was like opening up the door to the community." Six years later, a paved road was built to Kayenta, about 35 miles to the northwest.

In addition to making it easier for outsiders to visit Rough Rock, these transportation improvements gave community members easier access to nearby border towns, with all their amenities, and to English. Thanks to school jobs and school-initiated opportunities for professional development, family incomes had risen five-fold, although they still were far below national poverty levels. Most families had pickup trucks or other vehicles, and at least in employee homes on the school compound, radio and television were common. Children thus had a much more extensive English-language environment than their counterparts just a few years earlier.[1]

The school had grown, too, into a pre-K–12 facility with over 500 students in separate elementary, middle, and high school complexes. Office of Economic Opportunity funding had long since ended, curtailing the school's early economic development projects and turning school programs more and more toward the explicitly classroom-based mandates of Title I, Title IV, and Title VII. In addition, the BIA had adopted policies emphasizing standards, reform, and "accountability." Although the board and the director continued to be active in community affairs (in fact, some board members also served simultaneously as chapter officers), Federal budget slashing and changing Federal mandates demanded school leaders' constant vigilance over the contracting procedure and school finances. As a result, board members and the school director spent a great deal of time lobbying Congress and working with a national network of Indian educators, and a great deal of time *away* from the community and school.

In terms of the 30-year retrospective that inspired this book, these were Rough Rock's "middle years." They were years of explosive internal turmoil—of continuing financial uncertainty, curricular instability, and incredibly high staff turnover—as the school struggled constantly with a conservative new Federal administration intent on downsizing bilingual and Indian education. And yet, they also were years of recognition and praise for the school; in 1986 the school marked 20 years of survival and began the process of seeking accreditation through a national school accrediting board. At the same time, during these "middle years" the seeds of promise planted during the previous 2 decades came to fruition in a cadre of bilingual teachers who would give new life to the school's bilingual/bicultural program. These also were years during which I participated directly in the school and community. The account that follows derives from personal experience as well as school documents and the accounts of others.

Many who witnessed or were active at Rough Rock during this time saw the school on a virtual collision course with its own administration and the Federal bureaucracy, navigating one financial, curricular, and personnel obstacle after

---

[1]Bernard Spolsky and Wayne Holm (1977) found a high correlation between ease of access to school and a general linguistic shift toward English on the Navajo reservation. The situation at Rough Rock was representative of Spolsky and Holm's findings; by the 1980s the school had become a place where, at least in classrooms and during staff meetings, English was as likely to be heard as Navajo. This was a major change from the linguistic ecology of the school during its early years.

another. Laced throughout these conflicts were the ever-present subtexts of fluctuating Federal funding, inadequate per pupil allocations within the school contract, and the seemingly divergent interests of Federal Indian education program agencies and the program participants themselves.

THE SETTING

> It was always like Rough Rock was in transition—almost like a classic state of turmoil—not a turmoil like they would have sensed, but it was just ... because they were so different .... I think the hard part was the Native language, culture, and history ...
>
> —*Abbie Willetto, 1979 Rough Rock graduate and teacher,*
> *Mesa, Arizona, April 1996*

Abbie Willetto attended Rough Rock during the heyday of the opportunities described in chapter 9. For all the positive changes of those years, they had been treacherous ones for Rough Rock's bilingual/bicultural program, as Abbie's remarks suggest. Although the board remained adamant that children receive instruction in Navajo language and culture throughout their school careers, the constant need to contend with shifting and inadequate funding took its toll in myriad ways. By 1975 the Navajo Curriculum Center was reduced to providing assistance to school sports programs and student publishing projects; there simply was no money for anything more. When the school's Title VII grant ended that year, the board had to cut several bilingual teaching positions. Only one teacher taught Navajo language and culture to the 119 students at the middle school. At the high school, although four units of Navajo language were required for graduation, these classes sometimes went for weeks or months without a regular teacher (Blie, 1978). Through a combination of Federal grants, the board established a Navajo Culture Center, and this supported classroom cultural demonstrations by parents and elders. But with board members and the director occupied almost solely with the school contract and the pursuit of funds, the responsibility for teaching Navajo language and culture fell to individual teachers and a handful of specialists. High turnover among the teaching staff, a product of funding inconsistencies and the need to import non-Navajo teachers from outside the community, conspired to create a highly volatile Navajo Studies program.

Teachers, students, evaluators, and parents all complained to the board about these problems, and in May 1977, the board hired a team of prominent educators from Navajo Community College, including Navajo Studies director Ruth

Roessel, to study and help rectify the situation. Noting the overlapping functions of the Culture and Curriculum Centers, the NCC team recommended a single coordinating office for Navajo Studies at the school (Ruth Roessel, 1977, p. 60). That fall, again combining several Federal grants, the board established the Navajo Resource Center as that coordinating office. Later, Ruth Roessel rejoined Rough Rock as the Resource Center director, and Robert Roessel returned to work as a book writer and special assistant to Executive Director Jimmie C. Begay.

In the midst of all of this, school enrollments dropped precipitously. Fearing that parents were transferring their children to other schools because of Rough Rock's lack of curriculum guidelines—and knowing that a lower student count meant a reduction in Federal funds—the board hired a curriculum supervisor, a White educator from the Midwest, to overhaul the K–12 curriculum. What followed is a story of several coterminous and philosophically distinct curriculums.

BASIC SKILLS

"Welcome to the Rough Rock Basic Skills Project Newsletter!" So begins a description of the programmed reading and mathematics curriculum adopted in 1980 for Rough Rock School. Readers may recall this as a time when, under President Ronald Reagan and Vice President George Bush, "back-to-basics" became code words for remedial education for the poor. Title II of the ESEA supported basic skills programs, and with the curriculum supervisor's assistance, Rough Rock secured a Title II grant. Two commercial curriculum packages were identified to implement it: the Conceptually Oriented Mathematics Program (COMP), "a comprehensive management system with a hierarchy of skills" (Harness, Keller, & Studyvin, 1981, p. 3), and the Exemplary Center for Reading Instruction (ECRI). In a slide presentation on ECRI at Rough Rock, the program's teaching strategies were outlined this way:

> First, the teacher demonstrates the skill to the students ... Second, the students are given a chance to practice the new skill in small steps with the teacher prompting them when necessary, [t]hird, the students are expected to practice the new skill independently, [f]inally, if the students begin to show too many errors during their independent practice, the teacher goes back through the previous three steps once again, making sure that students demonstrate high accuracy. The ECRI program ... must be comprehensive because a basic assumption of the program is that children can only be expected to master those skills they have been taught *(Script for Presentation on ECRI at Rough Rock Demonstration School,* n.d., p. 5).

I remember walking down the hallway of the elementary school, passing classrooms and hearing the chorus of student voices calling out English sounds and words. This was ECRI. Years later, I mentioned this to colleagues at Rough Rock. Yes, they agreed, students had acquired perfect English diction in those classrooms, but little oral comprehension or comprehension of text. Still, teachers accepted and even praised ECRI because, as Galena Dick explained to me, "at least it was something stable we could rely on."

By the end of the 1980 academic year, Basic Skills had become the core of the K–12 curriculum, particularly at the elementary school where the curriculum supervisor assumed the principalship. Consuming 4½ hours of classtime each day, Basic Skills took up most of teachers' and students' daily schedules. Except at the beginners level, in special cultural presentations, and in periodic 30-minute Navajo language lessons, all instruction took place in English.[2]

"WE'RE TRYING TO MOVE THIS BILINGUAL/ BICULTURAL CURRICULUM"

Just as Basic Skills got under way, and under the direction of the Roessels and the Navajo Resource Center, the school obtained a Title IV Indian Education Act grant for a K–12 Navajo Materials Development Project. Hired as one of the project's curriculum developers, I was drawn into the swirl of competing interests at the school. Separately funded and physically distanced from Basic Skills by our location in a government-issue metal quonset across campus, I and my Navajo colleagues in the project—language and culture specialist Gene Johnson, artist Fred Bia, and secretary and editorial assistant Regina Hadley Lynch—began contemplating our charge of developing and restructuring the school's Navajo Studies curriculum. We had 3 years and approximately $400,000 to complete the job.

In the project's first year, we interviewed 40 parents and elders, soliciting their ideas on what kind of curriculum should be developed. We also sent out

---

[2]A 1981–1982 evaluation of the Basic Skills program claims that "significant pre/post gains were made at every grade level (1–6) for nearly every sub-test area" of the Comprehensive Test of Basic Skills (CTBS). Furthermore, the report states, "more dramatic gains were made by students in grades 2 and 3 (Reading and Math) and grade 6 (Math) where teachers were high implementors of [Basic Skills] program strategies" (Educational Evaluation Systems, Inc., 1982, p. 13). The documentation for these gains is grade-equivalent scores, the limitations of which are discussed in chapter 8 (see footnote 1). Moreover, it is not clear that the gains are attributable to the Basic Skills program, since no data are available for the same students prior to its implementation, and no control group was used as a basis for comparison. In fact, the program evaluation reports some of the highest pre/post gains by students whose teachers were identified as "low implementors" of Basic Skills (Educational Evaluation Systems, Inc., 1982, p. 24).

questionnaires to students, teachers, and other school personnel. "What do students need to know to be successful both on and off the reservation?" we asked. "What kinds of Navajo knowledge should be taught?" "What shouldn't be taught [e.g., what shouldn't be left to the school]?" "Who should teach Navajo language and culture?"

Everyone agreed that the school should prepare students to participate in economic opportunities both on and off the reservation. They disagreed, however, on how this should be done. Many parents said they wanted children to learn "both sides"—Navajo and English—well. "I don't want my grandchildren to come out uneducated," a woman who reported having "two busloads of grandchildren" at Rough Rock said; "I want them to get an education on both sides." But a number of parents believed bilingual education would "confuse" their children. "I placed my children in school to learn the White man's way," an elderly man insisted. "When you teach both Navajo and English, you just confuse kids."

Trying to make sense of these responses, we consulted the staff of the Native American Materials Development Center (NAMDC) in Albuquerque, many of whom were former Rough Rock teachers, as well as a local advisory committee of parents, students, and teachers. In our many discussions it was pointed out that those who objected to bilingual education had themselves been the victims of English-only schooling. "From the 6th grade on," Fred Bia observed, "we started sampling Anglo culture"—

> That made a big impression on some people. They put a bar of soap down your throat when you speak your language—that puts a latch in your mind against your culture. You say, "I don't want to go back to that!" That's what we've got to deal with, when your own people are against this bilingual/bicultural philosophy.

Like the teachers in John Collier Jr.'s earlier film study, we struggled against the oppressive backdrop of colonial education. "It's taken so long for us to start developing materials," Fred Bia remarked one day, "but we haven't even gotten a foothold. We're trying to move this bilingual/bicultural curriculum. It's not the thing of the real traditional people, or really like the Anglo way."

Eventually, we established the "foothold" we had been searching for within local stories of people and place. Drawing on Paulo Freire's (1970) *Pedagogy of the Oppressed* and Hilda Taba and associates' (1971) inquiry-based curriculum, we envisioned Navajo students' curriculum explorations as participatory, dialogic, and inquiry-oriented. This basic orientation led us to develop a spiraling framework of concepts, topics, and themes that would engage students in researching their community, tribal nation, and world. The nub of that web, the anchoring knot, was *k'é*. Figure 10.2 illustrates this curriculum framework.

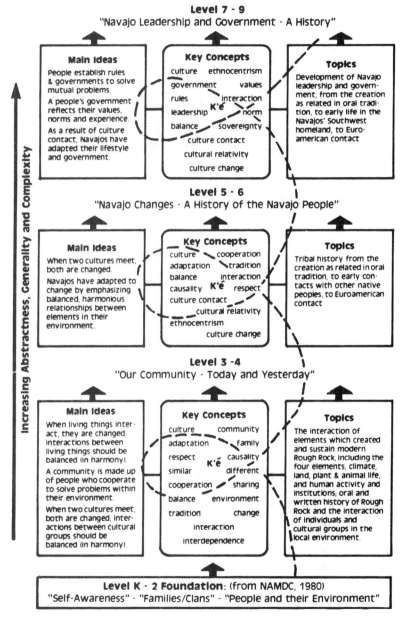

FIG. 10.2. Framework for an inquiry-based Navajo Studies curriculum (reprinted from McCarty et al., 1991, p. 47).

This framework became the foundation for a series of colorfully illustrated and professionally printed bilingual/bicultural texts, the result of nearly 30 oral history interviews. Having collaborated with parents, elders, teachers, and students all along, we felt certain these materials would be warmly and immediately received.

We quickly were proven wrong.

THE BARRICADES TO CHANGE

"But Navajo students won't *respond* to questioning!" That was the initial reaction of many staff members when we introduced the newly published bilingual texts. A significant body of research seemed to support that claim. Native American children were characterized as nonverbal, nonanalytical, and afraid "to disagree in public or to risk hurting someone's feelings by speaking up in class or stating an opinion" (Decker, 1983, p. 47; see also Kaulbach, 1984; Marashio, 1982; More, 1989; Rhodes, 1988; Ross, 1989). The problem, we believed, was not that Navajo children are intrinsically "nonverbal"—simple playground observations dispel this myth—but that the only available models for questioning and "speaking up" were the silencing practices of Federal boarding schools and, more recently, the scripted, right-wrong "dialogues" of the TESL program and Basic Skills.

Challenged by our colleagues at the school to show that Rough Rock students would respond well to an inquiry-based approach, we conducted a demonstration lesson in one 4th-grade class. As we have reported elsewhere (McCarty, Wallace, Lynch, & Benally, 1991), students responded eagerly and verbally to questioning; they also showed themselves to be quite capable of and keen to engage in inductive/analytical reasoning. We attributed these responses to the materials' clear cultural and linguistic relevance, and to the fact that inductive inquiry and participatory learning are very much the patterns of learning and teaching *outside* the classroom as well.

But the larger problem remained: How to insert these materials and a critical, inquiry-based pedagogy into a school schedule dominated by Basic Skills? Just at this time, and for reasons unknown to us, the school's director, Jimmie C. Begay, requested an accounting of the extent of students' participation in Navajo Studies. An investigation by the elementary principal revealed that at most, students participated in Navajo Studies for 1½ hours each week; many received no Navajo language and culture instruction at all. When this became public, the principal directed teachers to make use of the new bilingual/bicultural materials. Several teachers had already volunteered.

A top-down mandate was not what we envisioned or preferred. Still, this did get the materials into classrooms. By the end of the project's third year, they were adopted as a "Navajo Humanities" complement to Basic Skills.

INEQUALITY AND INDIGENOUS CURRICULUM REFORM

It is often assumed that curriculum reform is a rational process: If materials are developed, if they are pedagogically sound, and if teachers are properly "trained" in their use, everything will fall neatly into place. At the end of this line of reasoning are student gains on standardized tests.

The experience of the Materials Development Project demonstrates that curriculum reform is a social and political process full of contradictions, which in fact possesses little rationality at all. "Politics can engulf the curriculum," Levinson and Holland (1996) note; coalitions "form and reform trying to appropriate the schools to their own ends" (p. 1). But, unlike curriculum change in non-Indian schools, the process at Rough Rock was entangled in a particularly insidious web of circumstances that is best described as institutionalized racism.

By 1983, Rough Rock students were subjected to several curricula, each informed by distinct pedagogical philosophies and each representing a different interest group at the school. Those interest groups grew out of disparate funding sources and became rooted in the school's institutional structure as representatives of each group, myself included, secured influential positions within that structure. Each curriculum had school board approval, yet no mechanisms existed to ensure their compatibility or coordination. In fact, the school's infrastructure guaranteed just the opposite effect.

Rough Rock's base budget—its negotiated contract with the BIA—provided only for facilities maintenance and basic operational and instructional costs. Anything else had to be financed by supplemental grants. During my tenure at Rough Rock, Title I funded remedial English and mathematics instruction; Title II supported Basic Skills; Title IV supported the Materials Development Project; Title VII funded an early-exit, transitional bilingual program; Follow-Through funded an early childhood program; and the National Institute of Mental Health supported the Navajo Mental Health project. Each of these programs had distinct aims, each operated autonomously, and each was ultimately accountable not to teachers, parents, students, or the school leadership, but to Federal agencies in Washington, D.C.

As a participant in these arrangements, I came to question their destabilizing consequences and to research the history of discretionary funding at the school.

Figure 10.3 illustrates that history over 17 years. As can be seen, school leaders were navigating a financial roller coaster, a budgetary process that was not only wildly unpredictable, but that required vast amounts of time and energy just to sustain. Invisible in Figure 10.3, but part of the picture as well, were enormously high rates of staff turnover. During these same 17 years, 30% to 60% of the staff were new each year. And, hidden beneath all of these figures was movement among the students themselves. Accompanying parents trying to make a living in a reservation-wide soft-money economy, students continuously dropped in and out of school, an epiphenomenon represented in the fact that nearly 25% of Rough Rock students were new to the school each year (McCarty, 1984, pp. 113, 121–123). Many had never participated in a bilingual/bicultural program, making the provision of a consistent and cumulative language program at Rough Rock even more difficult.

Figure 10.3 is a portrait of inequality. It is a picture of structural arrangements shot through with natural cleavages and impossible conditions with which non-Indian schools do not have to contend.[3] As we scrutinize the picture more closely, we see a downward-trailing trend in funding after 1980—a trend that corresponds precisely with a national election. As it turns out, the curricular and personnel issues represented in Figure 10.3 were but the tip of the iceberg. Underneath lay what one school board member would describe in Congressional testimony as "the life and death issues" of American Indian community-controlled schools.

"SUDDEN DEATH … "

In March 1983, U.S. Secretary of Education Terrell Bell announced President Ronald Reagan's fiscal year 1984 education budget:

> In concert with the Administration's overall policy regarding separate funding for *Indians* (emphasis in original) … we are proposing to terminate assistance under the Indian Education Act. Indian students and adults will continue to be eligible for services under other programs …. Services to federally recognized tribes … will continue to be provided by the Bureau of Indian Affairs, in recognition of the special relationship between Indian tribes and the Federal Government.
> —*Statement by the Secretary of Education on the Fiscal Year 1984 Budget,*
> March 1983, pp. 1, 4.

---

[3]It may be, as Wayne Holm suggested to me, that schools serving economically disenfranchised communities in other settings have similar problems, "because money is available but comes in separate, sometimes contradictory packets" (personal communication, February 21, 2000).

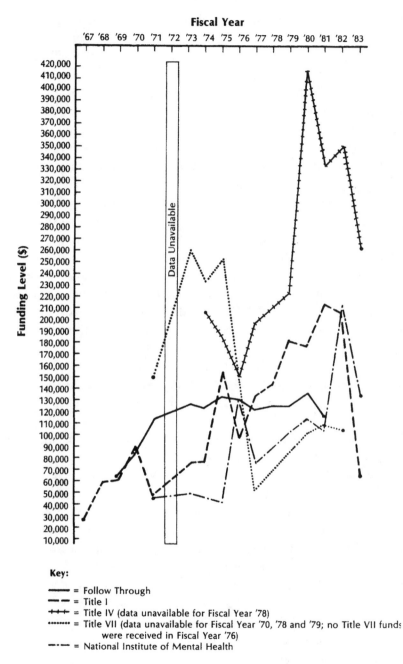

FIG. 10.3. School funding from sources other than the Bureau of Indian Affairs and U.S. Office of Economic Opportunity, 1966–1983 (reprinted from McCarty, 1989, p. 496).

By early 1983, the full impact was beginning to be felt of the Reagan Administration's euphemistically named budget consolidations. The future of Title IV, the Indian Education Act that had ushered in the Federal policy of self-determination a decade before, hung in the balance. Title IV, tribal educators were told, would be replaced with the Indian Student Equalization Program (ISEP), which allocated funds on the basis of annual student "counts."

In February of that year, school director Jimmie C. Begay traveled to Washington, D.C., hoping to influence the four Congressional subcommittees charged with overseeing Indian education programs and funds. ISEP funds, he pointed out to the representatives, were woefully inadequate, and securing indirect cost monies was elusive at best. "What about Title IV and contract schools using this source of funding?" Begay asked. Assistant secretary for Indian affairs Ken Smith responded that, "The Indian Student Equalization Program formulae will replace Title IV" (*Notes from Jimmie C. Begay's Trip to Washington,* February, 1983).

The funding frustrations experienced by school leaders and personnel did not subside. Less than a year later, Jimmie C. Begay was in Washington reiterating the same problems. Rough Rock's immediate concern was that it still had no contract, even though the fiscal year had begun some 6 months earlier. There also was the problem of indirect costs. "Presently there are no guidelines available by which [indirect costs are] negotiated," the *Rough Rock News* reported (February 1984, p. 4), and the school had experienced shortfalls since 1975. The Indian Student Equalization Program formula fell far short of covering the difference.

None of these issues had been resolved by late September, and the school still had no contract for the fiscal year begun the previous July. A tentative budget had been worked out with the BIA, but, Jimmie C. Begay cautioned, "I cannot say the budget has increased or decreased because the per capita [ISEP] figure has not been finalized." Further, he warned, "ISEP may get a 2% cut across the board from Washington .... if this happens, the tentative budget may be thrown off again" *(Rough Rock News,* November 1984, p. 2). The contract would not be finalized until February of the following year.

Undoubtedly this financial insecurity took its toll on staff morale, but students paid the dearest costs. One incident is particularly revealing and troubling. On January 19, 1984, the 55 students in the boys' dormitory drew up a petition and threatened to walk out of the dorm. The major problem at the dormitory, their petition read,

> ... is that we have little heat and at times have no heat at all .... When the boiler goes on the blink ... the hot water supply is affected ... we take cold showers in

the mornings and have to work in a cold dormitory every day.
—*Rough Rock News,* February 1984, p. 1

Further, the boys said, there were not enough blankets to go around—the "little boys get priority for blankets over big boys" (*Rough Rock News,* February 1984, p. 1). Their petition also protested the many broken windows, which they had used cardboard to mend.

These conditions scream of the most brutal inequalities. Yet the prospects for alleviating them grew dimmer as the school year proceeded. In late fall, the BIA proposed new school boundary restrictions on Bureau-funded schools. Although the boundary policy was not enforced for several years (the school board was still contesting it in 2001), the fear at Rough Rock was that this policy would effectively withdraw 133 out-of-district students—and the ISEP monies they generated.

Testifying before the Senate Select Committee on Indian Affairs at hearings in Phoenix that December, then-board president Emmitt Bia was given 3 minutes to address these and other "life and death issues" of contract schools. The first problem, he noted, was delayed school funding. The second was the issue of "sudden death"—termination of school contracts if schools failed to meet BIA standards. Third was the drawn-out process by which the Bureau funded facilities improvements such as those needed so desperately at Rough Rock's dormitories. Finally, there was the imposition of boundary restrictions, an "aberration of parental choice" *(Rough Rock News,* January 1985, p. 1).

In the spring of 1985, all of these crises came to a head when the BIA authorized an extensive evaluation and audit of the school. Whispers of school closure were rampant. Jimmie C. Begay left Rough Rock under pressure and the White director of education, Carl Levi, was named acting director of the school.

Levi and the board immediately launched a new marketing campaign to increase school enrollments and recruit teachers, including radio and television spots translated into Navajo. That fall, the quest for more enrollments came to fruition in an unexpected way, when the Bureau of Indian Affairs asked Rough Rock to absorb an additional 350 high school students from Many Farms whose classrooms and dormitory had been declared unsafe. To many observers, this looked like a BIA takeover of Rough Rock School. According to the *Navajo Times* (Oriole, 1985):

Rough Rock has had administrative and curriculum problems over the past two years and recently got an extremely poor evaluation report from the BIA, so some people were afraid the Bureau was trying to take over the Rough Rock contract school … [Carl] Levi said that is not the case, but the high school will use the BIA's curriculum next year. "This should bring some stability to the high school," Levi said. "It reduces the pressure to develop the high school curriculum" …. The merger also will help Rough Rock because the school's enrollment had dropped to just 360 students in kindergarten through 12th grade …. (pp. 1–2).

The agreement to accommodate hundreds of new students and the BIA curriculum may seem to have been an abdication of local choice. The fact is, Rough Rock was compelled to comply. At the end of the year, in an open letter to Rough Rock students and staff, Levi summed up the pressures the school faced:

> Most of you are pretty much aware of how the year started, the last minute call from the Chinle Agency … asking if we could handle an additional 350 or so students from Many Farms, the frantic plans which changed from minute to minute and day to day, the threatening cloud of the BIA's Spring '85 evaluation, the talk of the high school possibly closing, the hurried recruiting and hiring and the visitors from Washington. There had been no budget negotiated for FY '86, we were concerned over how many students would actually enroll, and later on, there was worry over the impending audit by the Office of the Inspector General ….
>
> —*Rough Rock News,* December 1985, p. 4

… AND SURVIVAL

As a new year dawned in 1986, Rough Rock prepared to mark its 20th year. Although the school was far from financially sound, it had outlived an amazing barrage of institutional assaults. In January, the school launched a self-study to become a candidate for accreditation by the North Central Association, a process school leaders hoped would return some sense of common purpose, but which, more urgently, was now required for contract eligibility. In October of that year, Rough Rock held a 2-day conference to celebrate its 20th anniversary. In his keynote address, former school director Dillon Platero reflected that while the Navajo Nation had not fully achieved its policy of providing Navajo language and culture instruction in every school,[4] it was "largely because of the pioneering efforts of Rough Rock that we are closer to it today than we were in 1966" (Platero, 1986).

Soon, school leaders would change their school's name to the Rough Rock Community School. When I asked Ernest Dick at the time why "dem-

---

[4]The reference here was to the recently passed *Navajo Tribal Education Policies*, which specified that Navajo language and culture instruction would be available for all grade levels in schools serving the Navajo Nation (Navajo Division of Education, 1984).

onstration" had been dropped, he explained, "We're not demonstrating any more." And, as he would remind me years later, the school and its goals *had* changed. By the late 1980s Rough Rock had ceased to demonstrate, but it had survived.

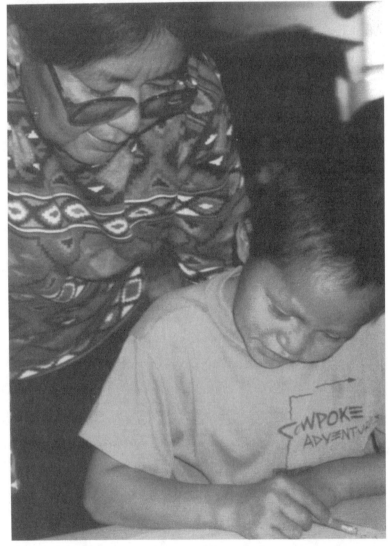

FIG. 11.1. "When students are full members of the classroom, they become lifelong learners with control over their learning."—Rough Rock Elementary School teachers (Photograph of bilingual teacher Rita Wagner with Raynard Bia, 1992, by T. L. McCarty.)

"If We Want To Be Powerful, We Have To Exercise Our Power": Indigenous Teachers as Change Agents

Teacher 1: You know, as a teacher, you sometimes feel hesitant to speak up … especially when you don't get any support.

Teacher 2 (nodding): Praise. And then when they [district administrators] come into the classroom, if they could just give you feedback.

Teacher 3: District administrators need to be here for Parent Night …. They need to be here right by our side, greeting parents …

Teacher 4: Teachers, parents, administrators—everyone needs to work together to make things happen.

T. McCarty: So what can we do? (… a moment of silence …)

Teacher 2: If we want to be powerful, we have to exercise our power.[1]

This conversation took place in the Rough Rock Elementary School teachers' lounge during one of my visits to the school in 1993. I was then a consultant to Rough Rock's K–3 bilingual/bicultural program. The conversation reflected growing unrest among the bilingual program faculty—seven women, all community members—about what they perceived to be top-down curricular mandates from White male administrators at the district office—individuals who rarely, if ever, stepped into teachers' classrooms. Referring to an outcome-based "mastery learning" curriculum recently introduced by an administrator relatively new to the district, one teacher observed, "It's forced upon us. It's another thing laid on us from the top."

---

[1] Although the bilingual faculty gave their permission to use real names, to preserve their privacy I have not used teachers' names in the dialogues presented in this chapter.

Previous chapters have examined issues of Indigenous self-determination as they are manifest within the macro structure of state and national interests. Those same relations of power penetrate the micro level of the classroom, and are manifest in teachers' interactions with students, each other, and the school's administrative hierarchy (Cummins, 1989; 2000; in press). This chapter analyzes power relations at this level, focusing on the ways in which Indigenous teachers struggle for voice and to (re)claim an Indigenous pedagogy.

A NEW BILINGUAL/BICULTURAL PROGRAM

During the difficult second decade of the Rough Rock School's existence, personnel changes were constant. Between 1983 and 1986, the elementary principalship was vacated four times, with one individual holding the position for less than 4 months. As the revolving door of non-Native administrators continued to spin, a group of bilingual teachers at the elementary school quietly began working to transform the curriculum. Serendipity and these teachers' agency united to create a social space within which they were able to carve out new pedagogical possibilities.

In the fall of 1983, at the invitation of the elementary principal at the time, personnel from the Hawaii-based Kamehameha Early Education Program (KEEP) arrived at Rough Rock "for the express purpose of doing our own research" (Lynn Vogt, personal communication, August 18, 1988). In Hawaii, KEEP had established a lab school featuring comprehension-based oral language and literacy development and cooperative-interactive participant structures keyed to Native Hawaiian cultural processes (Vogt et al., 1993). KEEP was then beginning to disseminate its approach. The work at Rough Rock was an extension of those dissemination efforts. The purpose, Vogt and Au (1995) say, was to determine "which [KEEP] features would transfer and which would require adaptations" (p. 113).

One of the most significant and lasting impacts of Rough Rock's many Federal grants was building a local, bilingual faculty. When KEEP personnel arrived, there were eight Native teachers at the elementary school. KEEP researchers report (Vogt et al., 1993):

During the fall semester of 1983, Cathie Jordan, KEEP anthropologist, and Lynn Vogt, KEEP research teacher, lived in the Rough Rock community and worked in a 3rd-grade class at the school. Vogt taught the KEEP reading program, and Jordan organized and ran the research effort. The project involved intensive collaboration with one 3rd-grade teacher, Afton Sells, and her aide, Juanita Estell, and some involvement with the rest of the faculty and staff. All of the faculty except the librarian were Navajo and members of the Rough Rock community (p. 59).

The work that fall launched a collaboration that would continue for 5 years and provide the foundation for re-establishing bilingual/bicultural education at Rough Rock. Afton Sells found that KEEP's approach reinforced what she was already doing despite Basic Skills. As she recalled years later, "I didn't want to give it [KEEP] up." Other bilingual teachers, also dissatisfied with Basic Skills, joined Afton Sells in trying out KEEP teaching strategies. KEEP research teacher Lynn Vogt made periodic visits to Rough Rock, providing workshops, observing, giving feedback to teachers, and generally working alongside them in their classrooms. In the context of fluctuating administrative leadership and a school board and executive director locked in the "life and death" bureaucratic and financial battles engulfing the school, KEEP emerged as the only consistent curricular force at the elementary school. "It gave us something to go by," one teacher said. "It was something stable," Galena Dick reflected. "It got us going."

The freedom to experiment and to change had been absent at Rough Rock for some time. At one point, Vogt and Au (1995) report, "teachers were required to submit lesson plans once a week to the [non-Indian] principal who monitored the allocated time for each subject written on the plan. The plan was to be on the teacher's desk at all times, and if he [the principal] walked into the room he expected the teacher to be teaching the lesson noted on the plan" (p. 118). "I felt like a parrot, repeating lines," one teacher recalled of her practice during those times. "We were used to that type of teaching: teachers as technicians," another teacher said.

Although the teachers never spoke to me of it in these terms, the gender and racial politics of White-male authority and Indigenous-female subordination are clear. These power relations had marginalized teachers within their own school and classroom, positioning them as the voiceless and devalued "Other" (Aronowitz & Giroux, 1991; Goffman, 1959, 1963). The inequality carried over to students; how can teachers construct empowering learning environments for children when teachers themselves are devalued within an environment of domination and control?

Under these difficult conditions the collaboration with KEEP took root. In addition to contextualized and culturally relevant instruction, KEEP introduced a crucial process that liberated teachers from their assigned role as readers of curriculum scripts: They were given the opportunity to work cooperatively and to engage in critical reflection on their practice. Numerous researchers have identified teacher reflection and collaboration as essential to positive change (see, e.g., Cochran-Smith & Lytle, 1993; Duckworth, 1986; Goswami & Stillman, 1987; Hollingsworth et al., 1994; Kincheloe, 1991; Lipka et al., 1998; Schön, 1983; Short, 1993; Strickland, 1988; Ulichny & Schoener, 1996). At Rough Rock, the opportunity to engage in reflective, collaborative practice enabled teachers to re-fashion KEEP—which focused on English language development—into a *bilingual/bicultural* program. "At first," one teacher explained, "we thought we should follow KEEP strategies strictly" ("cloning KEEP," as the elementary principal later described it). "Then we started sorting things out for ourselves," the teacher continued. "We thought of our own ideas and felt comfortable—we felt confident."

One additional development helped this process along. In January 1987, after the fourth elementary principal in 4 years resigned, the school board hired Dan Estell as principal. A non-Navajo who had married into the community, Estell held the position of principal for 8 years, actively and enthusiastically supporting teachers' efforts and lending administrative permanency to the bilingual/bicultural program as it took shape. The summer after his appointment to the principalship, Afton Sells and Lynn Vogt recalled, "RRENLAP [the Rough Rock English–Navajo Language Arts Program] was born."

I resumed my involvement with the school the following year, when Afton Sells, Dan Estell, and the school's education director invited me to return to Rough Rock to serve as a consultant to the new program. Our first task was to obtain funding. In 1989, just as KEEP ended its formal association with Rough Rock, the school received a 3-year Title VII bilingual education grant. The grant not only enhanced the credibility of teachers and the bilingual/bicultural program within the school bureaucracy, it opened a horizon of time and resources, freeing teachers to plan, experiment, and effect change.

"WE CAME A LONG WAY"

Over the next 8 years, RRENLAP grew from a K–3 transitional program that moved students out of bilingual instruction at grade 4, to a K–6 Navajo–English language maintenance program. None of this occurred as a linear, lock-step process. Rather, change occurred through a gradual, recursive, and sometimes painful engagement in which teachers observed and provided feedback to one another, critiqued and tried various approaches, and came to embrace—and own—a pedagogy grounded in local linguistic and cultural knowledge.

This section sketches a portrait of the process of teacher empowerment, using excerpts from my field notes to highlight activity within RRENLAP at different moments in time. I also discuss one particular experience, a teacher study group, that accelerated the transformation of literacy teaching and assessment, and that, in retrospect, seemed to be a defining moment in the transformation of teachers' professional identities and roles.

Thursday, December 5, 1991. RRENLAP coordinator Galena Dick and I begin what has become customary during my bi-monthly visits to the school: observing in RRENLAP classrooms, taking notes, talking with teachers and students about their work, and later meeting with teachers as a group, where they share their ideas, questions, and projects, and where Galena and I provide feedback on our observations. We also offer feedback in the form of individual memos to teachers, which Galena and I compose together, huddled in front of a computer or typewriter. In our observations and written responses to teachers, we are consciously attentive to strengths. We view this as an opportunity to nudge teacher reflection and critique from a point of strength, and within a safe and caring environment.

In the kindergarten class, the teacher tells us that most of her 12 students speak both Navajo and English. Students sit at one of two u-shaped learning center tables, one group with the teacher and another with the teacher assistant. Standing beside the teacher's center, we observe students working on a worksheet labeled with the English nursery rhyme, "Little Jack Horner." At the other center, students read this nursery rhyme aloud. Virtually all interaction is in English.

On the walls, a bulletin board features commercial pictures of the Mayflower, Pilgrims, and Native people; other walls show cut-outs of the four sacred mountains that delineate *Dinétah* or Navajoland. The teacher shows us students' writing contained in folders labeled "Halloween" and "Thanksgiving." The Halloween writings include stories about various "trick-or-treat" characters—goblins, ghosts, and so on. The Thanksgiving writings include student-made books on Euro-American holiday themes. The student writing folders are the beginning of the teacher's plans to implement a system of portfolio assessment.[2]

---

[2]A useful description of portfolio assessment comes from Robert Tierney and his associates in the opening pages of their (1991) book, *Portfolio Assessment in the Reading-Writing Classroom.* The concept of portfolios, they say, is "driven by an attempt to actually approach the issue of assessment in a manner which befits different classrooms and different students. Our goal ... was to have assessment which was responsive to what students were doing .... We were concerned that traditional assessment was both limited and subversive" (Tierney, Carter, & Desai, 1991, p. 4). Explaining the portfolio process and products, Tierney et al. (1991) go on to say that, "Over the course of the year, students accumulate in their folders stacks of their own writing .... Students sort through [their folders], select materials to go in and out of them, share them with their parents and classmates .... These portfolios represent the work students do across time and serve as the catalyst and basis for self- [and teacher-] assessment" (p. 45).

We move on to another kindergarten class, where again, 14 students are working at two learning centers. Galena remarks that, "Everything they do over there [at one center] is in English, and then at the other center, it's in Navajo." We are struck by the colorful, engaging environment. A *Késhmish* (Christmas) brainstorming web hangs from the ceiling, along with conventional Christmas decorations. Everything is at child height. The bulletin boards and walls are covered with students' art and writing projects on Navajo hogans, clowns, and Santa Claus. The teacher shows us student-made storybooks about *Shash,* a sheepdog, and tells us students are also making an English dictionary "big book."

In the 1st-grade class down the hall, 21 students sit at seven tables scattered throughout the room. Pumpkins and students' written work hang from the ceiling, next to scenes of the Mayflower and Pilgrims. A bulletin board features student-made pumpkin books along with worksheets on letter-shape formations. The teacher and teacher assistant work with students on a Christmas art project at separate tables.

Galena says that the teacher is emphasizing thematic units, which she plans and shares with the kindergarten teacher whose room we visited first. The teacher explains that her students have also been reading nursery rhymes. Working in small groups, "they start out reading a rhyme, then go on to make up their own rhyme or poem."

Our final visit is to a combination 1st/2nd-grade classroom of 30 students. Bulletin boards are covered with students' writing in Navajo and English, and with Diné figures, dolls, and a chart showing the sources of natural dyes used in weaving Navajo rugs. Students are busy writing in their journals; we notice that spelling and grammar have been corrected by the teacher in red or blue ink. One student, whose primary language is Navajo, leans over and asks an English-dominant peer how to spell "brother," then looks at her text. The teacher says, "He knows there's an 'r' in there." But he copies "bother" anyway. The teacher asks him to read from his journal. He reads the word "brother" perfectly.

Thursday, February 13, 1992. This is the first meeting of the RRENLAP teacher study group, and teachers have been given release time for the day to meet. Galena Dick, the seven RRENLAP teachers, and I constitute the group; elementary principal Dan Estell also joins us for this first meeting and for several others. Over the past few years, teachers have become increasingly concerned about the limitations of standardized tests and their damaging and demoralizing effects on students and teachers. Although far more authentic than standardized tests, the criterion-referenced assessment system adapted from KEEP does not seem to capture the rich, multilayered quality of the literacy processes and performances we observe in RRENLAP classrooms. Late in the fall of 1991, we decide to embark on a pilot project—a study group on alternative forms of literacy assessment. Like study groups reported elsewhere (e.g., González et al., 1995; Matlin & Short, 1991), our group is voluntary, organized by teachers for their own purposes, and designed to connect a body of professional literature on assessment to our own, action-oriented classroom research. The bilingual coordinator, 3rd-grade teacher, and I facilitate the group, but at this initial meeting Galena Dick makes it clear that, "This study group is not just a place where we have to listen to one person and have them give us all the answers. We know our kids better than anybody else .... Teachers intuitively know there is more going on than what is represented on standardized tests."

We begin by tapping prior knowledge with a discussion of student evaluation. For a few moments, the room is silent. One veteran teacher with 21 years of professional experience claims not to know anything about evaluation. Having collected a number of student writing samples, she says she is "waiting to be told what to do" with them. Later in the school year, this same teacher will write, "We started off so bare .... It was challenging to develop such a powerful [new] means of assessment."

Gradually, this discourse deepens with words that speak of the practices that have silenced teachers for so long: "We tend to accept what somebody else develops—standardized tests." "OBE" (Outcome-Based Education, the mastery learning program advocated by district administrators). "Not sure." And then, a breath of possibility: "Why not use our own teacher-developed tests?"

We list questions we want to have answered through the study group: "How do Navajo children become biliterate?" "How do we manage portfolio assessment and have time for other instructional activities?" "How many forms of assessment do we want?"

Later in the day, we break into pairs and read excerpts from Robert J. Tierney et al.'s (1991) *Portfolio Assessment in the Reading–Writing Classroom.* When we come together as a group to discuss our reactions to the text, we resonate with Tierney's et al.'s dual messages that "teachers know their craft," and that conventional, "teacher-proof" assessments subvert children's *and* teacher's creative potentials.

We agree on a plan for the remainder of the spring: We will read the book by Tierney et al., along with Sarah Hudelson's (1989) *Write On.* We will keep and exchange journals with our reflections on the readings, our observations of students' literacy and biliteracy processes, teachers' experiences in trying new forms of assessment, and our questions and concerns. Once a month, the group will be released from classroom teaching to meet for a full day; once a week, teachers will meet for a few hours after school to discuss what they are reading and their research on students' literacy and biliteracy development. I am able to attend only the monthly meetings, but am in contact with the group by telephone or through journaling throughout the month.

March–May, 1992. Over the next several months, the work of the group continues. During each monthly meeting we literally lay students' writing on the table, examining writing styles, problems, and questions. We critique the professional texts we are reading and share the literacy assessment strategies teachers are piloting. (For more on this, see Begay et al., 1995; McCarty, 1993). We see, as a teacher points out in our March meeting, that regardless of whether students are acquiring English as a second language or have English as their primary language, "They can do it"—they are writers and readers. It also becomes evident that understanding students' English literacy processes and demonstrations requires serious attention to those same processes and demonstrations in Navajo. Teachers articulate that the best judges of this are not outsiders, but teachers and students: "Students' writing has taught me a lot," one teacher says. "I need to work at giving my students their responsibilities and control over their learning."

And we talk about teachers' experiences in English-only boarding schools, the suppression of their literacies, and their desire to "reverse the type of schooling we went through" (Dick, 1998, p. 25). This relates to difficult practical questions, such as how to involve parents in assessment, and how to respond to conditioned beliefs that literacy is a unidimensional skill that can be captured in a single-moment-in-time examination and distilled into a number or letter grade. The kindergarten teacher asserts, "I would tell parents that this [portfolio] is a rich description of a letter grade."

By the end of the school year, teachers have developed sophisticated bilingual writing checklists geared toward their own classrooms and students. One teacher shares a graphic model of portfolio assessment based on the Diné ceremonial basket and cornstalk. Several teachers are experimenting with some form of portfolio assessment. They write of their accomplishments:

> We as a group have learned what a portfolio is all about .... We feel confident enough to use a portfolio for parent conference, open house and parent visitation .... We feel we know enough to establish a portfolio involving parents, administrators and our principal.

And they speak of the changes in their images of themselves and their students:

The role change involves taking a new stance towards the profession. [When students are] invited to be full members of the classroom … they become lifelong learners with … control over things that they're learning.

Finally, teachers speak directly of the value of reflection and collaboration in generating these changes. A teacher who had written simply, "disenfranchised," in one of her first journal entries, talks at the end of the year about her sense of ownership in effecting positive change, her excitement at the possibilities in the year ahead, and the pride she feels toward her students and herself. "In talking and working with the group," she says, "I found out that I actually do some of these things we read and talked about in the classroom." "You know," another teacher states, "when you involve yourself in discussion, little things come up that you never thought to be important and it turns out they are …. I feel empowered … "

Friday, March 4, 1994. Two years later, Galena and I continue our research in RRENLAP classrooms. Throughout this time, teachers have participated in ongoing collaborative and reflective work with each other; they have attended university institutes and workshops on Indigenous language education, and they have given a number of formal presentations on RRENLAP at national and international conferences. Several have obtained master's degrees. These experiences have increased their pride and ownership over their practice and widened their network of collegial support.

Walking down the hall, we see bulletin boards featuring students' Navajo writing on traditional Diné topics. All the classroom doors are decorated with student- and teacher-made banners featuring various trade books. A new Title VII grant has enabled the purchase of a sizable collection of multicultural children's literature. Galena explains that the banners are part of the school's "Love a Book" initiative. Each class will be able to order copies of its favorite book, featured on the banners, for each child.

Our first stop is the 3rd-grade class taught by the teacher whose kindergarten class we documented in our December 1991 observations. Fourteen students work at desks grouped into tables that make three long double rows. Several students are drawing pictures to illustrate number concepts. A few are engaged in a lively discussion, code-switching from Navajo to English, about Olympic ice skaters Tonya Harding and Nancy Kerrigan. The teacher tells us students have been fascinated by the controversy surrounding charges that Harding's bodyguard intentionally injured Kerrigan, Harding's chief rival. Every morning, the teacher says, "we discuss what's in the news."

Students also are engaged in a thematic unit on Navajo creation stories. As part of their inquiry, they read Ethelou Yazzie's (1971) *Navajo History,* and Marilyn Maberry's (1991) *Right After Sundown—Teaching Stories of the Navajo,* both published by local presses. A bulletin board displays students' English texts on their Diné forebears. Insects and insect people are central to these stories, and the teacher uses this as an opportunity to connect literature study to science investigations. Another link is to social and political studies: The class is researching and writing stories about the creation of the Navajo Nation. Evaluation of this work includes student portfolios.

In the 3rd/4th-grade class down the hall, the teacher is reading a biography of Martin Luther King to seven students grouped around a u-shaped table. When she finishes, she asks in English, "So, what's a biography?" One student responds, "You write about someone."

"What did you learn from this book?" the teacher continues.

"He won a medal."

"He won a medal—for what?"

The discussion continues, in Navajo and English, about how, during the 1960s, people of all ethnicities and backgrounds came together for "the poor people's march." While this discussion is under way, two other students work on math at a cluster of desks; two work on an art project, and the school's reading specialist reads a book to a student in the corner of the room.

As we leave, we notice student-made dioramas on a wall, from a study of whales. On the other side of the room are student constructions of hogans. The teacher explains that the latter are part of a literature and social studies unit on Navajo kinship.

The last room we visit today is a 1st-grade class where the Navajo language specialist is reading *Na'ahóółaiłchí'í,* "The Little Red Hen," a favorite of Rough Rock students and teachers.[3] Five boys sit at the front of the class with cut-outs of each of the story's animal characters. Ten other students are seated around them on the floor; they read the text aloud in Navajo, as the boys in the front hold up their props and act their parts. When they finish reading, the language teacher

---

[3]During a meeting with RRENLAP teachers, I questioned the authenticity of this text, since it is a translation of a traditional Anglo-European story. Teachers seemed puzzled by my question; they clearly considered *Na'ahóółaiłchí'í* to be a Navajo story. In our discussions, I came to understand that the story's familiar animal characters and message of the value of cooperation and sharing are, in fact, quintessential Diné storytelling themes.

leads students in a Navajo song about animals. Other Navajo songs follow. Students participate excitedly and seem genuinely to enjoy this activity.

As Galena and I walk back down the hallway to her office, we talk about the changes we have observed in Rough Rock classrooms. Virtually all teachers are using authentic Navajo or multicultural children's literature, around which they and their students organize thematically-based research and writing projects. "You don't see any basal readers on the desk," Galena notes, "and the teachers are making up their own questions to accompany their literature studies." And teachers are using some form of qualitative assessment, although the use of portfolios is spotty. Activity in RRENLAP classrooms resembles real-world work environments: Not everyone is doing the same thing at once. Instead, students and teachers come together for activities that require everyone's involvement—storytelling, songs, games, and drama, for example—but they also work independently and in small groups, depending on what needs to be accomplished at a given time. Peer assistance is the norm. There is much greater consciousness and use of Navajo. Finally, where there had been an emphasis on other peoples' histories and stereotypical representations of Native peoples ("Pilgrims and Indians"), Galena points out that teachers and students are now "studying our own history."

FIG. 11.2.   RRENLAP Coordinator Galena Sells Dick assisting students with creative writing projects, 1992. (Photograph by T. L. McCarty.)

FIG. 11.3. Teachers Emma Lewis and Lynda Teller, with 1st-grade student, showing her bilingual book, *Coyote Stories*, 1992. (Photograph by T. L. McCarty.)

FIG. 11.4. Evelyn Sells reading *Na'ahóółaiłchí'í, The Little Red Hen,* to her kindergarten class in 1992. (Photograph by T. L. McCarty.)

FIG. 11.5. Kindergarten teacher Lorene Tohe van Pelt with RRENLAP students in an oral language and cultural activity of Navajo string games, 1992. (Photograph by T. L. McCarty.)

Later in the day, we meet with teachers to reflect on 5 years of RRENLAP and the 10 years that have passed since the initial collaboration with KEEP. "We came a long way," the 3rd-grade teacher begins. "Instead of seeing students as a whole group, each child is working at the student's own rate," the 1st-grade teacher adds. "Students are more confident of themselves," she continues. Speaking of alternative assessment, the 3rd-grade teacher reiterates, "You know where your students are. This helps you a lot with your teaching."

Teachers also articulate the political dimensions of their work: their increasing confidence and willingness to take risks and implement approaches that access local knowledge; reclaiming control of their classrooms; and adapting district-level mandates to their own ideas of sound pedagogy. The process, Galena Dick says, "gave us ways of *how* to develop appropriate materials and assessment .... It gave us that confidence and empowerment."

CHILDREN'S BILITERACY, SELF-EFFICACY,
AND ACADEMIC ACHIEVEMENT

I cannot leave this discussion of RRENLAP without commenting on its influence on students' biliteracy development, self-efficacy, and school achievement. In addition to portfolio assessment and the ethnographic observations
just noted, we were required by the terms of the school's Title VII grant to document students' performance on locally developed and standardized tests. We
used a cohort design, following students from kindergarten to 6th grade and
comparing their performance on these multiple assessments with Rough Rock
students who had not participated in RRENLAP. We also examined RRENLAP
students' performance on the Comprehensive Test of Basic Skills.

On locally developed assessments of English listening comprehension,
RRENLAP kindergartners at the end of the 1989–1990 school year posted
mean scores of 58%. After 4 years in the program, students' mean scores rose to
91% (McCarty, 1993; 1995). On standardized reading subtests, discriminatory
as they are, the same students' scores initially declined, then rose steadily. By
the end of third grade, their scores had stabilized, although they were still below
national norms. Similar patterns were observed in mathematics (McCarty,
1993; 1995). While these findings were less dramatic than some school personnel might have hoped, RRENLAP students consistently outperformed a local
comparison group who had not participated in RRENLAP or any other form of
consistent bilingual/bicultural schooling. RRENLAP students also were assessed by their teachers as having stronger oral Navajo and Navajo literacy abilities than their non-bilingual education peers. Overall, our data showed that
bilingual students who had the benefit of cumulative, uninterrupted initial literacy experiences in Navajo made the greatest gains on both local and national
measures of achievement.

ZONES OF SAFETY AND RISK

The changes effected by RRENLAP teachers occurred within a site of possibility and hope. Elsewhere we have described this as a zone of safety—a socially
constructed space within which teachers moved from a deficit view of their
teaching and learners, to a stance focused on their and students' agency and
strengths (Begay et al., 1995; Lipka & McCarty, 1994). Analyzing a similar
process among Yup'ik teachers and elders, Jerry Lipka et al. (1998) write, "We
believe that a slow, deliberate process of teachers becoming empowered by
forming their own groups and by considering questions of teaching, learning,

methodology, and school-community relationships becomes an excellent forum for ... school change and reform" (p. 199).

At Rough Rock, those changes arose through a fortuitous encounter with KEEP. They were helped by an infusion of long-term financial assistance and administrative support by the building principal, and by a fundamental democratization of the teacher-principal relationship. Although it was not a relation of symmetry, teachers' relationship with their building principal *was* one of mutual concern and support. Within this context, and over a period of nearly 10 years, teachers worked as both apprentices and peer mentors (Lave & Wenger, 1991). In Vygotskian terms, they created and worked within a zone of proximal development—an interactional space in which each individual was able to achieve more through collaboration than alone (Cole, John-Steiner, Scribner, & Souberman, 1978). Importantly, these were the very conditions teachers strove to create with and for their students.

Risk also resided within this safety zone. It explicitly was *not* a "comfort zone"; indeed, this was often a site of pain and discomfort as teachers revisited their own educational histories and challenged the pedagogical assumptions internalized in the course of their schooling (Lipka & McCarty, 1994). The process was equally one of contention and fear, as teachers spoke out against the silencing practices within their community school. The remainder of the dialogue with which this chapter began reveals the tension between institutional constraints and teacher empowerment: "We're just teachers," a teacher noted, describing shared perceptions of a lack of district-level support for teachers' work. "Peons," another said. "We're just teachers of the kids ... "

How is it that, in a single dialogue, teachers can imagine themselves as both powerful and "just teachers"—"peons"? This discourse, I believe, must be situated within a conception of schools as contested, contradictory spaces. Rough Rock teachers and students *did* empower themselves through the creative co-construction of new pedagogies based on their language and culture strengths.[4] But sustaining that power required continuous negotiation carried out within a context of historical oppression and bureaucratic coercion. To clarify how Indigenous teachers operated within a context marked by both hope and constraint, I return to the macro level of Federal Indian policy.

---

[4]Ruiz (1991) notes problems with use of the term "empowerment" in the lexicon of critical pedagogy. "Empowerment," he states, "may not be desirable ... because of our tendency to use it as a transitive verb [passing from subject to object] ; this denies both voice and agency to students and communities" (p. 227). Ruiz's (1991) point "is that voice and agency are central to critical pedagogy;" without them, he states, "there is no such thing as 'empowerment'" (p. 227; see also Cummins, 1989; 2000).

THE QUEST FOR ACCREDITATION

On April 28, 1988, just as RRENLAP was taking shape, Congress authorized the Hawkins–Stafford Elementary and Secondary School Improvement Amend-ments, known as Public Law 100–297. In introducing the Indian education bill that would become part of P.L. 100–297, Senator Dennis DeConcini, Democrat from Arizona, reaffirmed the Federal government's "special duty to the Indian tribes to assure the availability of the best educational opportunities," a duty he insisted "must be fulfilled … in a manner consistent with … Indian self-determi-nation" (White House Conference on Indian Education, 1992, p. 6).

Among other things, P.L. 100–297 provided a forward-funding system for Indigenous community-controlled schools, allowing school boards to opt out of the contracting procedure that had frustrated budgetary planning for nearly 2 decades. Instead, these schools could seek "grant status," an arrangement that would assure a lump sum base budget each year, although the final budget would await the outcome of student count week and any discretionary funding the school might obtain. Grant status seemed to offer a pathway out of chronic financial insecurity in two ways: first, it would add predictability to the budget process, and second, schools could generate income by investing the lump sum. Rough Rock's leadership eagerly anticipated these changes.

But achieving grant status was not as straightforward as it might appear. Congress and the BIA required grant schools to meet certain standards deter-mined by national or regional accrediting boards. Thus, Rough Rock began the process of seeking accreditation through the North Central Association (NCA).

North Central accreditation at the time was a 3-stage process involving a self-study by school staff, an external assessment by a visiting team of educators, and development and implementation of a "planned program of school improve-ment" (Commission on Schools, 1983, p. 4). NCA school improvement guide-lines directed schools to a set of 12 "quality education principles" addressing such things as school–community relations, staff competencies, curriculum, school climate, and physical facilities (Commission on Schools, 1983, p. 7).

In 1990, the Navajo North Central Association asked that I chair Rough Rock's NCA evaluation team. Despite deep misgivings about the process, I agreed, knowing the high stakes for the school. From 1990 to 1991, I met reg-ularly with teachers, school officials, and community members to discuss the accreditation procedure. In these meetings, I attempted to demystify NCA's expectations and the accreditation process. At the same time, I emphasized the school's strengths; this seemed a perfect opportunity to direct greater attention to the work within RRENLAP and to encourage similar community-directed change.

As part of the self-evaluation, the Rough Rock staff organized into 12 sub-committees reflecting NCA's 12 school improvement principles. It was under these circumstances that Rough Rock's central administration introduced a program called Outcome-Based Education (OBE). Outcome-Based Education was intended as a "master plan" for school improvement. OBE's philosophy is stated in positive terms ("All students can learn and succeed;" "success breeds success"). If we read the program's documents more closely and critically, however, the underlying message is clear: *Some* students are guaranteed to achieve school-defined "success," while *others* [those constructed as Others] must be drilled and coaxed, and even then, are likely to fall short. Objectified, neutralized, and screened from scrutiny are the efficacy and appropriateness of the program itself.

The OBE *Practitioner's Implementation Handbook,* for example, identifies "corrective activities" to ameliorate student "deficiencies," including reteaching and instructing students to re-read their textbooks. Juxtaposed to these are "enrichment" activities for "fast learners to broaden their horizons" (Danielson, 1989, pp. 82–86). In mandated workshops described by one staff member as "brainwashing" sessions, Rough Rock teachers were presented with flow charts from the *Handbook* outlining student "role performances" and instructing teachers to fill in boxes with student objectives that would, allegedly, enable students to perform those roles and "succeed."

Not surprisingly, RRENLAP teachers viewed OBE as a rejection of their work with alternative assessment and curriculum reform. Tensions mounted when the district administration tied teacher evaluation to students' performance on standardized tests. The ironic and troublesome fact was that, at the end of the NCA process, the external evaluation explicitly recommended RRENLAP as a model for district-wide improvement. Further, the evaluation called for "meaningful dialogue" about curriculum decisions among teachers, district administrators, building principals, the school board, and community members (Navajo North Central Visitation Team, 1990, p. 14). With the exception of the RRENLAP staff and the elementary principal, these recommendations went unaddressed.

Rough Rock succeeded in its dual bids for North Central Accreditation and grant status—a fact that still inspires pride by those involved (see Fig. 11.6). The NCA process also succeeded in ensuring the school's survival. But the process did little to change district-level curriculum and assessment policies.

FIG. 11.6. Rough Rock officials accept a plaque recognizing the school's accreditation by the North Central Association, Chicago, 1992. *From left to right:* high school principal Steve Strong, school board member Ben Deswood, school board president Ernest W. Dick, unidentified NCA official, and Rough Rock education director Ronald White. (Photograph from RRCS archives, courtesy of Rough Rock Community School.)

It certainly did not direct greater administrative attention to RRENLAP teachers' attempts to restructure curriculum and pedagogy. Hence, despite Senator DeConcini's call for a policy "consistent with Indian self-determination," the conditions for Indigenous schools authorized by P.L. 100–297 continued to lock these schools in a system of Federal constraint and control. Filtered throughout that system, and the daily reality teachers faced, was a web of power relations that buried their voices and privileged instead the authority of non-Indian school administrators.

Within this institutional context, RRENLAP teachers continued to carve out possibilities for positive change. Their relationship with the elementary principal buffered these attempts, protecting and supporting their efforts to develop the elementary school's bilingual/bicultural program. Eventually, teachers modified OBE to include Navajo language and literacy, and to accommodate the teaching innovations they had developed and made their own. To use Lois

Weis's (1996) words, teachers exercised agency and imagination even as they grappled with the "structures wrapped around their … lives" (p. xii).

ELUSIVE TEACHER EMPOWERMENT

In an analysis of their researcher–teacher collaboration, university educator Polly Ulichny and ESL teacher Wendy Schoener (1996) say that teacher empowerment "was the precondition, as well as the outcome, of the transformation process" (p. 520). In reading their account, especially Schoener's words, one is impressed with the way Ulichny and Schoener's collaboration at once affirmed Shoener's pedagogy and encouraged greater scrutiny and risk-taking on her part. Their story is not unlike the experience reported here for bilingual teachers at Rough Rock.

The research and professional literature is liberally sprinkled with similar accounts of teacher empowerment. But the words researchers choose to describe this process often fail to do justice to the complicated and treacherous terrain through which the collaborative "we" must walk. The work within RRENLAP suggests that teacher empowerment is neither a precondition nor an outcome, neither a starting point nor a destination. Instead—and especially in the context of minoritized schooling—it is a complex and entangled negotiation at every turn, mediated by coercive relations of power.

The processes glossed by the words "teacher empowerment" are as ephemeral as they are significant. Their importance, Lipka and Yup'ik teacher-researchers point out, "may only be in the 'now'"—the moments of opportunity constructed within a zone of safety that evolve into productive work (Lipka et al., 1998, p. 203). The transferrable lessons within RRENLAP, then, lie in the ways in which such moments of possibility can be created and effectively employed. Those lessons also lie in the recognition that, within Indigenous and minoritized schooling, individual and collective empowerment is neither a given nor a final state, but rather an ongoing struggle for identity, agency, and voice.

FIG. 12.1. "It was widely known, 'At a place called Tsé Ch'ízhí is a great school.' Now they have changed it." —Thomas James (Photograph from RRCS archives, courtesy of Rough Rock Community School.)

Protest

In the fall of 1995, not long after the school became accredited, the Rough Rock faculty, staff, and school board prepared to celebrate the school's 30th anniversary. Committees were formed to coordinate various aspects of the event. The atmosphere was one of optimism and pride. But as we conducted the interviews for the book that would mark this anniversary, a current of conflict surfaced. Within a few months, that conflict would erupt in a protest and boycott of the school. This chapter is an account of the protest and its aftermath.

In trying to make sense of this incident, I have come to view it as both an unexpected rupture in the community and the school, and, paradoxically, the almost predictable culmination of all that preceded it. The protest was, un-questionably, one of the most debilitating and difficult episodes in the recent history of Rough Rock—an event that shattered long-term relationships of kinship and trust, and caused school enrollments to plummet. At the same time, the protest was an occasion for people at Rough Rock to assess the school's future course and to summon the personal and communal resources to move on.

As traumatizing as it was for those at Rough Rock, the protest raises broader questions as well. Are schools inherently divisive institutions in communities such as Rough Rock? Can local communalism overcome or accommodate new and conflicting interests and values—or are local values inevitably undermined by the larger, diverse social forces schools reflect and reproduce? How does the role of the school as the community's primary economic resource influence community cohesiveness and values? Within Indigenous and other minoritized communities, can schools—institutions structured to serve dominant class interests—ever be truly reformed?

These questions have no simple answers. But if some larger benefit can be realized from this account of the protest at Rough Rock, it is this event's instructiveness for Indigenous schooling. The protest lays bare the historically rooted and systemic challenges to Indigenous and minoritized community empowerment.

This event also illustrates the extraordinary resiliency that has enabled communities such as Rough Rock to persevere in the face of those challenges.

I begin this account with the first months of 1996, and the oral testimony of elders.

"THIS IS WHAT THIS SCHOOL WILL BE KNOWN FOR: IT WILL BE RUN BY THE COMMUNITY"

When we interviewed him early in 1996, former school board secretary Thomas James recalled the first school board's mission: "What the school is best known for is [that], 'It will be run by the community.'" He elaborated: "It was widely known, 'At a place called Tsé Ch'ízhí is a great school. Navajo is taught there as well as everything else,' it was said about us for a time. Now they have changed it. Now there is nothing."

The "they" to which Thomas James and others whom we interviewed referred, were non-Indian, mostly male school administrators. "There are too many White people running the school," Thomas James said. In addition to allowing the bilingual/bicultural program to decline, the White central administration was seen as diverting school jobs and income to non-Navajos. Readers will recall that when the school began, one of the key factors promoting a sense of openness and community ownership over the school was the presence of jobs for local people. "Let the local people work," Thomas James insisted.

Others shared Thomas James's disillusionment, pointing to the fact that Navajo language and culture had been dropped as requirements at the high school. "When this school opened," Dorothy Begay reminisced, "there was learning of Navajo traditions. The school is emitting a kind of force .... We are forgetting and losing our traditions."

Bilingual teachers, too, worried that the school was "turning to more the English way." When the school began, a bilingual teacher said, "there was a lot of community involvement, whereas today, you don't see that anymore. It seems like the community is just drifting further and further away from the school."

"Do you think Rough Rock is going in the direction that was originally envisioned for it?" I asked.

"Yes and no," she replied—

Because we as a school are limiting the involvement of the community people. If the school would just listen to the community people, I think we would see that vision. And if our administrators are supportive of the bilingual program, and just do things—put more bilingual programs into the classroom, into the school—we could see that vision. But it seems like the community people have a very limited say-so.

These opinions were widely shared among those we interviewed and with whom I worked at the school. From its beginnings as a school "known for being run by the community," Rough Rock had become, in many people's view, a school controlled by outsiders.

"THIS SCHOOL TENDS TO OPERATE SEPARATELY FROM THE COMMUNITY, ALMOST LIKE AN EMBASSY"

The growing alienation of the community from the school was not lost on some central office administrators. In December 1995, I attended a meeting of department directors to present the ideas my Rough Rock colleagues and I had developed for this book. Following my presentation, a non-Navajo administrator presented a proposal for a cultural center at Rough Rock as a tourism and money-making enterprise. A White administrator with a relatively long history at the school asked, "Has anyone gone to the community to see if they would like it? Because this would be a radical change for this community. It would be an invasion of the community. This school tends to operate separately from the community, almost like an embassy."

It is impossible for me to disassociate this embassy-like quality from the structure of school finances. Much of the December 1995 meeting, for example, was taken up with finding ways to pay support staff for time worked over the Christmas holidays. Despite the forward-funding arrangements conferred by accreditation and grant school status, there remained uncertainty about exactly what the school's budget would be. "We're waiting for the word to come down on how much money there is," the director of administration observed. "OK," he said, referring to the hoped-for receipt of "the word." "You can start stealing from next year's budget now." Another administrator asked, "Do we go ahead and borrow from the future?"

With more Federal cutbacks on the horizon, the future looked bleak. "It's amazing how much energy goes into obtaining that waning support," Executive Director Carl Levi remarked after the meeting.

Like past school administrations, Levi and the board were absorbed with doing whatever needed to be done to secure school funding, a situation Levi likened to "dueling the devil at the door." It is unclear whether or how well the administration communicated this situation to school staff and community members. I observed staff meetings at which school finances were discussed, but none was attended by community members who were not school employees. What is clear is that the director and board members were frequently called away from the school for out-of-town budget and legislative sessions, and to participate in numerous organizations involved in the movement for Indigenous education control. Over the long-term, school leaders' absence and their focus on finances nurtured the growth of intolerable local conditions, particularly at the high school.

"WE CAN'T EVEN TALK ABOUT SCHOOL THINGS"

To increase flagging high school enrollments, the administration had for some time recruited out-of-district students who had been expelled or otherwise forced to leave other schools. This raised Rough Rock's student count, and hence, the school's base budget. Because out-of-district students resided in the school dormitories, their enrollment generated additional funding under the Indian Student Equalization Program (ISEP). These funds were essential to keeping the school financially afloat.

The problem was that little support was provided to faculty or staff to address the out-of-district students' special needs. Reports of student drug use and vandalism were widespread. The local news media alleged that high school teachers were openly selling and using illegal drugs (*Navajo Times,* April 25, 1996; May 2, 1996). These reports caused grave concern among parents and grandparents, who held the board and school administrators responsible. Dorothy Begay's comments were typical of many individuals we interviewed: "When the children get out of school, they get into trouble," she sighed. "The school should look after the students and counsel them to help develop their minds, because children who have good minds don't get into trouble."

In addition, high school teachers and students lacked basic texts and supplies. According to the *Navajo Times,* the high school lacked "textbooks, dictionaries in the English classes, has no tissue in the bathrooms, no science labs and no water stations in the science class" (Shebala, 1996, p. A2). Inadequate school funding was partly to blame. Per pupil expenditures at Rough Rock were approximately $3,000, a third less than the amount expended per pupil in Arizona public schools, which themselves rank at the bottom of the nation on per pupil expenditures.[1] Moreover, charges of fiscal mismanagement encircled the central administration. In the spring of 1996, this situation was inflamed by accusations of child sexual abuse at the dormitory.

---

[1]Per pupil expenditures in Arizona are abysmally low—among the bottom tenth in the nation. In 1998, the $4,481 expended per pupil in Arizona public schools earned the state a "D–" in a January 1 *Education Week* report.

The crisis was brought to a head by disputes between Executive Director Carl Levi and the director of administration, Justin Jones, a Navajo from outside the community. The dispute is part of the public record, which is why I name both individuals here (see, e.g., *Navajo Times,* April 25, 1996; June 6, 1996). When Levi recommended that the board not renew Jones' contract, Jones and his supporters mobilized a recall initiative. On Sunday, April 21, 1996, the Rough Rock Chapter passed a resolution calling for a tribal investigation of Levi and the school board. Although some chapter officials, including the president, refused to sign the resolution, the resolution passed and a school boycott went forward the next day. As the *Navajo Times* reported it:

> About a hundred parents, community members, students and staff stopped school buses and other vehicles from entering the elementary school, junior high and high school about 5 a.m. .... About 12 uniformed police officers in nine Navajo Nation police cars and one sheriff's Jeep reopened traffic about 8:30 a.m. The protesters remained at the entrance to the elementary school throughout the day … demanding the immediate removal of [the executive director], student services director …, secondary school principal … and procurement specialist.

> They also urged the community to recall six of the seven school board members .... [The] Parent Advisory Committee president … said the community is fed-up with the lack of administrative and school board support for Navajo language and culture studies (Shebala, 1996, p. A2).

As protesters picketed outside the elementary school, some teachers and staff tried to enter the school building. They were forced to leave their vehicles and walk from the perimeter of the school compound where protesters blocked the road, carrying signs that read, "RRCS, Diné Bi'ólta'" (The People's School). As it was described later by those who managed to enter the school: "We had to cross a strike line to get into the office … parents were just yelling at us." Tribal police cars engulfed the campus. High school students and teachers picketed the administration building, saying their books were worn out and they had no books, and called on central office administrators to resign.

The protest continued through much of the week, with some protesters camping outside the school. At the end of the week, on letterhead with the title, "Celebrating 30 Years of Navajo Education," the school director called for "business as usual" and ordered all employees back to their work stations. Meanwhile, the school board met almost daily, listening to parents', teachers', and students' concerns.

People on both sides of the incident spoke of it with shock: "I still cannot believe this is happening," one person said to me in the midst of the controversy.

By June, according to a community member, the "battle was still going on." Tribal officials had just spent 3 days at the school, interviewing school staff and board members and investigating school finances. A separate FBI investigation of the allegations of child sexual abuse also had been launched; those charges were later determined to be unfounded.

The protest exacted a terrible cost, pitting mother against daughter and sister against brother, as people aligned on one side with the embattled central office administration and board, or on the other with Jones and the protesters. At the elementary school, where the work of RRENLAP teachers had proceeded despite the district's escalating troubles, tensions ran high. "We can't even talk about school things" one staff member told me shortly after the protest.

Later in the year, community members elected a new school board, and the executive director and most central office administrators were forced to resign. Dozens of other school employees resigned or lost their jobs. In July, the *Navajo Times* carried an advertisement for 11 secondary teachers and a librarian, principal, and special education coordinator at the high school; an elementary physical education teacher, 3 residential student services specialists, and the entire central administration—25 positions in all. By the middle of the following school year, so many parents had removed their children from school at Rough Rock that the board was forced to impose a 4-day school week to cut operational costs, and to institute further layoffs and pay cuts.

This was the situation at the end of Rough Rock's 30th anniversary year.

"THE ADMINISTRATORS WILL GO THEIR WAY, BUT WE HAVE TO LIVE HERE"

In May, 1997, more than a year after the protest, I traveled to Rough Rock at the invitation of the elementary bilingual program staff. I had not been to Rough Rock in more than a year. On that late spring day, I wrote in my field journal:

> A storm hovers over the mesa above Rough Rock when I arrive .... The parking lot is barely half full. I realize later that these were the first signs of the deserted feel of the school. After being away for more than a year, I am surprised to find the hallways so empty of life. I walk into the Title VII office and it is empty .... I go back out into the hall to see if anyone is around. I find several staff members in the elementary school office. We greet each other, hugging .... Elementary school enrollments are down to 119 students [from 199 the previous year]. The staff members say they almost hope the school will close so that they can all "start over." I am to hear this from several other staff members before I leave the next day.

The wounds inflicted by the protest remained open and raw. The original group of RRENLAP teachers, several of whom had participated in the protest, had been split by the incident. "It's enough to shed tears over," a bilingual teacher told me. "We're all torn apart."

The administrators involved in the controversy had left the community; none was from Rough Rock. What remained were community members—kin and clan relatives—to pick up the pieces and move on. "The administrators will go their way," a bilingual teacher said ruefully. "But we have to live here. The people in the community will live with this bitterness for the rest of their lives, and pass it on to their children."

Remarkably, bilingual teachers at the elementary school were able to come together for a group meeting during the second day of my visit. For several hours, we discussed the recent accomplishments of the elementary bilingual/ bicultural program. Funding for the program was due to expire, and the teachers wanted to begin planning for another grant proposal to be submitted in the coming year. As we talked, much of the interpersonal tension I had noted earlier seemed to be suspended, at least for the moment. Teachers spoke with cautious optimism about the work ahead. "If we get together, a lot of the cultural activities we developed this year could be put into our language assessment," one teacher said. "We should work on this in our curriculum workshop this summer," another teacher urged.

"LET'S WORK TOGETHER"

By the start of the new school year—nearly 1½ years after the April 1996 protest—the chaos of the incident seemed to have subsided. Over the summer, a new executive director had been appointed. In September, I was invited to the school to assist with a staff inservice. I was eager to hear what the new director would have to say. As the inservice began in the elementary school gym, the director stood before an assembly of about 40 staff members. Raising a copy of a May 1968 *Journal of American Indian Education* in which the original Rough Rock demonstration project was featured, he said:

Let's pretend this is the year 1966.

Let's pretend this is the start of the Rough Rock Demonstration School.

Let's pretend we're here to bring Navajo language and culture into the curriculum.

Let's pretend we're here to involve the community.

Let's pretend we want to have a school anyone and everyone can be proud of.

With passion in his voice, the new director went on to describe the vision underlying the founding of the demonstration school: "We were trying to build a school that had no walls .... We had a revolutionary Navajo arts and crafts program .... We tried to make the dormitory a warmer place for students."

"Now we're in 1997. We have an opportunity to equal or exceed what's in that book," he continued, pointing to the *Journal of American Indian Education* in his hand. He went on:

I'm 71 years old. I've got gray hair. But I can still fight. I want to help make this school the best school possible ....

We have division. But we're trying to correct that. The only way we're going to do this is to work together ....

There are not many schools that are trying to do what we are doing. So I ask you, I plead with you, I pray with you, let's work together.

The speaker was Robert A. Roessel, Jr., who had returned after 31 years to once again head the Rough Rock School. His commitment was to remain in his position for a maximum of 2 years to help stabilize the school and reinvigorate its Navajo Studies program and community-based emphasis. Roessel vowed that his replacement would be a Navajo educator, as it had been when he left the director's position and Dillon Platero was named director in 1968.

The board's decision to appoint Robert Roessel as director, and the fact that the school once again was under the leadership of a non-Indian, took many observers, including me, by surprise. But at Rough Rock, the school staff, and certainly Roessel himself, seemed not surprised but determined. While the pain of the protest still lingered, people no longer seemed paralyzed by it. They seemed to have found the resources and the desire to move forward.

This became evident later in the inservice, during a group discussion of schoolwide goals for bilingual/bicultural education. The staff entitled their ideas, *"Díí éí ólta' bá laanaa niidzin,"* "This is what we wish to happen at the school." Their vision was of student empowerment: Children should become literate in English and Navajo. Children should be able to use both languages "with enjoyment and without difficulty;" they should "understand and feel confident in both Navajo and Anglo cultures." Finally, children should "have positive self-esteem, self-discipline, and self-awareness" to prepare them for their lives in the future. The staff articulated this as the Diné philosophy of *Sa'ąah*

Naagháí Bik'eh Hózhóón, the "path of long-life happiness" (House, 1996/97; Matlock, 1995).[2]

About a week after the inservice, Rough Rock held a Blessing Way ceremony to rededicate the school and community to the principles upon which the demonstration at Rough Rock had been founded. According to the *Navajo Times* (September 25, 1997), "Those principles included having Navajo history, language, and culture form the heart and foundation of the school's curriculum" (p. A7). Guy Gorman, one of the original DINÉ trustees, spoke to the more than 160 community members, students, and school staff assembled for the event. Urging them to again work together, he called for "unity as there was when the school began" *(Navajo Times,* September 25, 1997, p. A7).

Shortly after the ceremony, I spoke by telephone with staff members from the bilingual/bicultural program. "If you're here every day, you wonder if you're going in the right direction," a teacher remarked. "You listen to a person from outside the community, and it helps," she added, referring to the speakers at the ceremony and the inservice. "Things are getting better here," she said softly.

REFLECTIONS ON THE PROTEST

In reflecting on what I have labeled "the protest," I recognize that it had different meanings for different individuals, depending on their positions within the community and school. In the same way that we would not expect the interests of school employees to be fixed and unitary, community interests at Rough Rock are not monolithic but multiple and often contradictory. Family loyalties, political alliances, career ambitions, and philosophical stances all align and collide within a complex network of local and larger power relations. A text such as this provides but one situated glimpse into these dynamics.

It seems to me that the immediate precipitators of the protest had been seeded more than a decade before. The school was on the precipice of receivership, an outcome the new board and director wanted to avoid at all costs. NCA accreditation, grant status, and the importation of out-of-district students were means toward that end. As former school board president Ernest Dick explained, "There

---

[2]According to House (1996/97), who uses Navajo language instructor Frank Morgan's translation, "*sạ*' means 'old age'; *ah* means 'up to; a long ways to and beyond.' *Naa* means 'around; cyclical; repetitive'; *ghái,* 'it walks there.' *Bi* means 'its' (3rd person, singular, possessive); *k'eh* 'according to; in line with; in sync with.' *Hó* means 'there is; the whole place'; *zhóón* means 'beauty; balance; harmony; the way; the path of balance or harmony or beauty' " (p. 50). Morgan's free translation of *Sa'ạh Naghái Bik'eh Hózhóón* is 'past old age, the one that walks there in ultimate balance and harmony or on the balanced path.' This is sometimes shortened and referred to as 'long-life happiness' " (House, 1996/1997, p. 50).

are still a lot of people who believe the BIA should run our schools. That's what we're trying to get away from. We need to move forward."

This was the "devil at the door." But as the duel proceeded, the concerns of the central administration drifted further and further away from those of the community and many among the school staff. Communications from the administration were unidirectional and declarative rather than dialogical—informing the staff of the Outcome-Based Education curriculum being adopted, or of an inservice they were required to attend, or of the troubles in obtaining school funds. As chapter 11 indicates, these top-down mandates sidelined local teachers' attempts at curriculum reform. Worse, teachers feared retribution—loss of their jobs—for challenging White administrative authority. Teachers were effectively silenced from exposing the conditions that oppressed and disabled them. Meanwhile, the situation at the high school and dormitories was rapidly deteriorating. Parents and grandparents worried about the safety and well-being of their children and grandchildren. The high school Navajo Studies program was in disarray.

These conditions, and a bitter public dispute between two school administrators, were the observable circumstances underlying the protest. But I believe there are deeper, structural roots of this incident. Cameron McCarthy (1993) writes that, "School knowledge is socially produced, deeply imbued with human interests, and deeply implicated in the unequal social relations outside the school door" (p. 295). At Rough Rock, school knowledge had become vested in the authority of non-Indian outsiders. Race, gender, and social class privilege were undeniably complicit in this. Saying this, however, skirts the deep structure of the protest, for race, gender, and social class privilege are mapped onto the very institutional arrangements that enable Indigenous schools to establish themselves and survive. This is the heart of the struggle for Indigenous self-determination: It was must be exercised within a framework of historically constituted power relations that work to suppress, co-opt, and distort local, Indigenous authority.

One manifestation of these power relationships is a system of school funding that is both volatile and inadequate. The ISEP formula that drove many Rough Rock school policies, for example, does little more than distribute poverty equally. It does not change the fact that Indigenous schools are the most poorly funded in the nation, that they must rely almost solely on Congressional appropriations, or that Congress has little incentive, given small Indigenous constituencies, to substantially improve the material conditions of Indigenous communities and schools. These are fundamental inequities, historically constituted and institutionally legitimated. And *they* are what the protest was about.

* * * * * * *

Dii éi ólta' bá laanaa niidzin. "This is what we wish to happen at the school." In the aftermath of the protest, educators at Rough Rock came together to articulate a transformative and liberating vision of the future. They spoke of communal values, children's futures, and of their own roles in charting Rough Rock's future. Theirs was a discourse of resiliency, but even more, of reclamation and action to reposition local knowledge within the school curriculum. This discourse worked past the either/or dichotomies of Navajo versus English, local knowledge versus academic knowledge. Children should be able to use both languages "with enjoyment and without difficulty," teachers said; children should "understand and feel confident" in multiple social worlds.

These ideas would become the foundation for a new bilingual/bicultural program to extend from preschool through grade 12. That the mechanisms to support the program would be two new Federal grants speaks to the constancy of the institutional constraints under which Rough Rock and other Indigenous educators operate. That the program was conceived and implemented at all speaks to the creative working and reworking by people around, through, and beyond those constraints. Within the deep structure of the protest, it seems, also lay possibility and hope.

FIG. 13.1. "If a child learns only English, you have lost your child."—Dorothy Secody (Photograph of Rough Rock school children, 1982, by Fred Bia, courtesy of Rough Rock Community School.)

"What If the Children Forget the Navajo Language?"

What then, if the children forget the Navajo language? What will be our shield as we move into the future? This is what I say and think, my daughter. For this reason, both Navajo and English should be learned, without emphasizing one over the other .... So in the future, our language will not be forgotten.

—*Dorothy Begay, Rough Rock, 1996*

My language, to me, ... that's what makes me unique, that's what makes me Navajo, that's what makes me who I am. That's what going to Fort Sumner and coming back, and all that—it was *worth* it. The language, my language.

—*Fred Bia, Rough Rock, 1997*

When Fred Bia and I began working together on the Materials Development Project in 1980, we could safely assume that virtually all Rough Rock students spoke Navajo as their primary language. The recent data Rough Rock teachers and I have compiled indicate that between 50% to 60% of Navajo kindergartners speak Navajo reasonably well, and moreover, that their numbers and native language proficiencies are declining each year (McCarty, 1995; 1998). These data are slightly more optimistic than those of Navajo linguist and former Rough Rock teacher Paul Platero, who, in a 1991 survey of 682 Navajo preschoolers, found that over half were considered by their teachers to be English monolinguals (Platero, 1992). And, in 1993, Wayne Holm conducted a study of over 3,300 kindergartners in 110 Navajo schools, and found, similarly, that only half spoke any Navajo and less than a third were considered reasonably fluent 5-year-old speakers of Navajo (Holm & Holm, 1995; Wayne Holm, personal communication, February 14, 2000).

Like other Indigenous groups, the Navajo Nation is caught up in a tidal wave of language shift, a situation in which there are fewer and fewer heritage language speakers every generation (Fishman, 1991, p. 1). Of the 210 remaining languages indigenous to what is now the United States and Canada, only 34 are

179

still spoken by members of all generations (Krauss, 1998).[1] Put another way, fully 84% of all Indigenous languages in the United States and Canada are in danger of falling silent within the next 20 to 40 years. Further, it is by no means assured that even those languages with child speakers, including Navajo, will survive the 21st century.

What then, if the children "forget" the heritage language? This chapter considers that question, and the role of Indigenous schools in reversing language shift, in light of experiences at Rough Rock.

LANGUAGE IDEOLOGY AND ENDANGERMENT: "WHY ISN'T OUR LANGUAGE WANTED?"

Although I have highlighted them here, numbers merely gloss the crisis of language loss. Joshua Fishman (1991) reminds us that numbers mirror the concrete "destruction of intimacy, family, and community" by more powerful, homogenizing forces (p. 4). Songs, prayers, greetings, blessings, stories, science, philosophy, geography, history—the cultural worlds exemplified by the oral narratives presented here—all are constructed and reconstructed, in everyday practice, through the language. "That's what going to Fort Sumner and coming back ... it was *worth* it," Fred Bia says. We have only to revisit Bit'ahnii Yéę Be'esdzáán's account in chapter 3, of her mother's birth in captivity, to appreciate the significance of Fred Bia's words. The terror and genocide were worth it, he says, because the survivors returned as Diné—an identity mediated, personalized, and symbolized by "the language, my language."

And so we come to one of the most recent "life and death struggles" at Rough Rock—the paradox of this linguistic ideology as it confronts the dominant discourses and practices that threaten to annihilate it (see also Hornberger, 2000). In my 1997 interview with him, I asked Fred Bia what he thought about the future of his language. Sighing deeply, he replied:

> It will be an honor if you just *knew* your language in another 20 years .... You know, you *wish* there is some way that you can do something about it .... It's happening [language loss is happening] now. There's people that don't value our lan-

---

[1]The fact that 210 Indigenous languages still are spoken is testimony to the remarkable resilience of their speakers. The losses are nevertheless enormous. Michael Krauss, director of the Native Alaska Language Center at the University of Alaska Fairbanks, estimates that 300 languages once were spoken by peoples Indigenous to what is now the U.S. and Canada (Krauss, 1996, 1998). Other authors place that number much higher (see, e.g., McCarty, Watahomigie, & Yamamoto, 1999). For more on the causes and parameters of Indigenous language loss in the U.S., see Crawford, 2000 (in particular, pp. 52–83), and Reyhner, 1996.

guage. "Why should we learn our language?" [they say]. "My kids are having a hard enough time trying to learn English."

To this can be added the testimony of Rough Rock elder Dorothy Secody: "If a child learns only *bilagáana* [English/the Anglo-American way of life]," she said, "you have lost your child."

If we take language ideology to mean, as made explicit by Dorothy Secody, Dorothy Begay, and Fred Bia, not language *per se* but "the very notion of the person and social group" (Woolard, 1998, p. 3), then these narratives reveal a crisis of identity. It is a crisis of values, morality, and ways of knowing—of the most basic question of what it means to be Navajo—and whether children will, indeed, be "lost," disconnected from the words and worlds of their forebears.

This crisis cannot be divorced from its historical antecedents or the structures of power that engulf it (Tollefson, 1991). While language loss is, at one level, the result of individual language choices, those choices are influenced in myriad ways by a host of social, political, and economic forces. "There's people that don't value our language," Fred Bia points out. Hasbah Charley asks: "Why *isn't* our language wanted? Why aren't our prayers that we speak, that we use to say, 'This is how it will be'—why are they not wanted?"

A study of language shift in two reservation-interior communities by Evangeline Parsons-Yazzie (1996/97) sheds some light on these questions. Parsons-Yazzie found that even in Navajo-speaking homes, young children tended to respond to their parents' and grandparents' Navajo *in English.* At the tender age of 4 and 5—in some cases *before they had entered school*—children had internalized the covert and overt silencing messages of an English-dominant society. Wayne Holm (in press) elaborates:

> We see situations in which the adult initiates in Navajo and the child responds in English .... We see situations where the adult initiates in Navajo and the child responds—but non-verbally .... We see situations where the adult initiates in Navajo and the child fails to respond—the child hears the adult as so much "static."

In these and other ways, Holm (in press) asserts, "young children set the language policy of the home; they 'train' the adults around them to talk only English."

Parsons-Yazzie (1996/97) attributes the propensity for children to favor English to the prevalence of English among family and friends, English media, and feelings of shame. "[T]hey are afraid their friends will laugh at them for speaking Navajo," she says (p. 62). Some parents, Parsons-Yazzie (1996/97) states, "claimed television was taking the place of grandfather stories" (p. 63).

An elderly man said that "television was stealing the thoughts of the children" (Parsons-Yazzie, 1996/97, p. 63).

These are proximate causes, and although illuminating, they raise several key questions: *Why* the prevalence of English among family and friends? *Why* the shame and ambivalence about Navajo?

Certainly colonial education has played a crucial role in changing language attitudes and patterns of use. In American Indian, Alaska Native, and Native Hawaiian communities, schools have been the *only* social institution to both demand exclusive use of English, and prohibit use of the Native tongue (Kari & Spolsky, 1973). According to sociolinguist Tove Skutnabb-Kangas (1999a), this constitutes linguistic genocide, defined by international convention as "prohibiting the use of the [mother tongue] ... in daily intercourse or in schools" (p. 47). In the case of Navajo, the hardships of boarding school life left a firm resolve in many parents' minds that their children would not face a similar fate (Benally & McCarty, 1990). This is exemplified by this observation by a Rough Rock teacher: "What the boarding schools taught us," she remarked, "was that our language is second-best."

Parsons-Yazzie (1996/97) and Holm (in press) suggest other colluding forces. "The students see the Navajo employees in subservient positions [e.g., as teacher aides and low-paid service workers], and begin to see a glass ceiling ... over their own aspirations if they are Navajo speakers," Parsons-Yazzie says (1996/97, p. 63).[2] "[T]hey just preferred to speak English," she concludes, "and the adults were not persistent in responding in Navajo" (Parsons-Yazzie, 1996/97, p. 64). Holm (in press) adds: "In Navajo, ... one is expected to respect the integrity of the individual—even if they are children ... it is difficult if not unthinkable to 'force' a child to talk Navajo."

And yet the adults in Parsons-Yazzie's study, like those at Rough Rock, said they *want* their children and grandchildren to acquire Navajo, "[s]o we and our kids can talk the same language, and so we won't be mainstreamed with people of other races .... So they [the children] won't lose their native language and culture" (Parsons-Yazzie, 1996/97, p. 64). These desires, and their situatedness within a post-colonial present, make clear that language loss and reclamation are about *cultural* survival; they are fundamental issues of human rights and self-determination. The decline of Navajo among the young is not a "natural" process, but rather one that has been *naturalized* through historical experience and coercive relations of power.

---

[2]This is reminiscent of John Ogbu's (1978; 1993) theory of the "job ceiling" and its withering effects on the aspirations and school achievement of African-American and other "involuntary minority" youth.

"THE PARENTS NEED HELP"

For many at Rough Rock and others concerned with the crisis of language loss, the question now becomes, "What can be done to turn the present situation around?" Some, including the parents and grandparents we interviewed, believe the school must play a strong role in reversing language shift. "The school seems to be where parents place much of the responsibility for language learning," Parsons-Yazzie writes (1996/97, p. 64). And yet, no less distinguished a scholar than Joshua Fishman argues that schools are secondary to the struggle (Fishman, 1991). Schools "should be on tap and not on top of a language," Fishman (1996, p. 194) says, insisting that the bastion of mother tongue maintenance is the family and the home. Nothing "can substitute for the rebuilding of society at the level of … basic, everyday, informal life," Fishman maintains (1991, p. 112; see also Fishman, 2001).

The problem, as Parsons-Yazzie's study reveals, is that the pressures on families to abandon the mother tongue are so intense—the social injustices and dislocations so extreme—that if left to individuals and families alone, the crisis of language loss will go unabated. "When more children gain access to formal education, much of the … language learning, which earlier took place in the community, must now take place in the schools," Skutnabb-Kangas says (1999b, p. 10). "Parents need all the help they can get," Holm (in press) states. "Navajo schools must become the allies … of Navajo-speaking parents who want their children to acquire Navajo."

Can schools interrupt the crisis of language loss? I believe their role is essential (see Dick & McCarty, 1996; McCarty, 1998, 2001). It also is highly problematic. The school serving minority students is a "dual-edged sword," Fishman (1984) states; even when it is under minority-community control, it "leads away, out of and … partially undermines the very community it ostensibly serves" (p. 55; see also Wax, Diamond, & Gearing, 1971).

Rough Rock's biography seems to make Fishman's point. When the school was established in 1966, its mission was two-fold: to establish and demonstrate the effectiveness of local, Indigenous education control, and to make Navajo culture, history, and language central to the curriculum. Despite enormous challenges, the school has persevered in this mission. Yet the school's very presence has facilitated many of the social changes that lead to Native language loss. Can the school and its participants now position themselves as agents *against* those social changes? This is asking a great deal. But given the school's overwhelmingly important economic, social, and political role in the community, and the absence of similar community-wide institutions, the school in many ways is a natural, if imperfect, instrument for mobilizing language revitalization efforts. "[W]e have to depend heavily upon the school," Holm (in press) says. "We cannot know whether the schools are capable of helping. But we cannot give up on them without trying."

Rough Rock educators have not given up on their language or their school as a resource for reclaiming the Native language and the cultural knowledge it represents. The remainder of this chapter examines Rough Rock's attempts to construct a 21st century school in which children can be Navajo *in* Navajo. The story complicates issues of language and identity. It also shows how educational, linguistic, and cultural self-determination are inextricably linked. I begin by rejoining the narrative of the Rough Rock English-Navajo Language Arts Program.

"WE ARE REVERSING THE TYPE OF SCHOOLING WE EXPERIENCED"

A major finding of long-term evaluations of the Rough Rock English–Navajo Language Arts Project (RRENLAP) was that students who came to school speaking Navajo, and who had the benefit of cumulative early literacy experiences in Navajo, made the greatest gains on local and national measures of achievement (McCarty, 1993). This was true for students judged by their teachers to be fluent Navajo speakers as well as those whose proficiency in Navajo was limited. These findings reinforce those of other long-term evaluations of bilingual education, including the Navajo programs at Rock Point and Fort Defiance, Arizona (Holm & Holm, 1990; 1995; Rosier & Farella, 1976). In particular, the RRENLAP data show the effectiveness of gradual- versus early-exit (transitional) bilingual education (see, e.g., Cummins, 1989, 2000; Krashen, 1996; Krashen & Biber, 1988; Ramírez, 1992; Thomas & Collier, 1995). The RRENLAP data also demonstrate that literacy in a second language is mediated by first-language literacy—a finding supported by numerous earlier studies (see, for example, Holm & Holm 1990, 1995; Krashen, 1996; Moll & Díaz, 1993; Rosier & Farella, 1976). Children who learned to read first in Navajo learned how to read (period). That ability aided rather than hindered their English literacy development.

RRENLAP's effect was to reinforce teachers' confidence in the bilingual/bicultural approaches they had been developing, and to enhance the currency of Navajo as a language of instruction, at least at the elementary school. In 1994, Rough Rock received a Title VII bilingual education grant to expand

RRENLAP through grade 6, and to focus specifically on initial literacy in Navajo and the development of Navajo teaching materials. While the program stalled in the heat of the protest, in 1998, the school received two additional Federal grants for a pre-K–12 Navajo immersion/language maintenance program—also called a "language shelter" program (see, e.g., Skutnabb-Kangas, 1999b). This was the program envisioned at the post-protest inservice described in chapter 12. The metaphor of a language "shelter" seems most appropriate; it is reminiscent of Dorothy Begay's image of the Native language as a shield.[3]

Figure 13.2 outlines the language immersion/shelter program at Rough Rock as it was conceived and implemented in its first year. From preschool through grade 2, children participated in Navajo immersion classes, in which the majority of their instruction was in Navajo. Based on research showing that children need at least 4 to 7 years of heritage language development to acquire cognitive-academic proficiency in a second language, standardized testing was to be suspended until grade 3 (see, e.g., Crawford, 1995, 1997; Cummins, 1989, 1992; Cummins & Swain, 1986). Beginning in grade 3, approximately half the day was devoted to instruction in Navajo and half in English, with the language of instruction determined by teachers according to academic content.

At the middle and high schools, students, teachers, and community resource people worked together on in-class and field-based studies intended to integrate academic content with oral language and literacy experiences in Navajo. In her account of critical pedagogy in a community-based education program in New York, Klaudia Rivera (1999) calls such investigations "popular research projects—inquiries into the issues that affected [students'] lives and their positioning in society" (p. 486). An example at Rough Rock was a study of architecture and petroglyphs in Dinétah, the Navajo homelands in northwestern New Mexico. This was complemented by a study of local landforms and sacred sites that combined oral history, geography, geology, and mathematics. Research projects such as these not only brought interdisciplinary perspectives to bear on the construction of knowledge, they created natural contexts for hearing, speaking, reading, and writing Navajo, and for involving community members as teach-

---

[3]Ruiz (1995) notes that in order for schools to be effective agents of Indigenous language maintenance, they must consciously exercise endoglossic (community-oriented) policies that "give primacy to and promote an Indigenous language of the community" (p. 75). He contrasts such policies with those traditionally supported by Federal bilingual education grants (e.g., transitional bilingual education, a manifestation of what Ruiz calls "exoglossic" or English-oriented policies). Given the rapid rate of language loss within Indigenous communities and the ubiquity of English, explicitly endoglossic policies such as heritage language immersion may be the only programs capable of reversing Indigenous language shift. Anything else is likely to be too little, too late. For more on this, see McCarty (in press).

Pre-K–Grade 2:
Navajo Immersion
Structured ESL
(standardized testing suspended until grade 3)

Grades 3–6:
Half-day Navajo, Half-day English
(organized around learning centers and theme studies)

Grades 7–12:
Applied Research Projects in Navajo
Apprenticeships in Navajo
Navajo Language, Literacy, and Culture Courses

School- and Community-wide:
Summer Literature Camp

FIG. 13.2. Organization of a pre-K–12 "language shelter" Navajo immersion program at Rough Rock Community School, 1998.

ers. In these learning enterprises, the Native language and local cultural knowledge bridged students' past and future. Language was thus "at the center of the concept of community and … a domain of inclusion, strength, and potential" (Rivera, 1999, pp. 488–489).

The bilingual/bicultural program also sponsored a community-wide summer literature camp in which children of all ages worked with elders to study livestock management, ethnobotany, drama, storytelling, and Native arts.[4] The resulting demonstrations and interactions were recorded and placed on CD-ROM for future classroom use.

In these types of learning-teaching experiences, Rough Rock educators sought to blend the old with the new—to construct discourses and practices that, in Galena Dick's words, "prepare students to function in two languages and two worlds" (Dick, 1998, p. 25). This work can be seen as a form of resistance to the legacy of teachers' own educational pasts. Galena Dick (1998) re-

---

[4]These studies are very much like the "funds of knowledge" projects González et al. (1995) describe for Latino students in South Tucson.

members: "When we went to school, all we learned about was Western culture"—

> We were never told the stories that Rough Rock children are now told, and write themselves. We're telling those stories now. In the process we are reversing the type of schooling we experienced. We see both sides of it, and we're helping children, through schooling, make connections to their own language and lives (p. 25).

LANGUAGE AND SHIFTING IDENTITIES

Leaving Rough Rock after a recent visit, I was impressed by a conglomerate of signs posted on a fence surrounding the Chinle High School, 30 miles away. Positioned next to one another, the signs announced:

Navajo Traditional Song and Dance

Community Health Service

Parent–Teacher Social—Mexican Dinner

Halloween Party Friday Night

Across the street, an area once reserved for family fields and pasture, a strip mall featured a Taco Bell, Burger King, and Bashas' Supermarket. On the opposite corner, known in the early 1980s as Begay's Corner for the family-run cafe and gas station there, a Thriftmart ran a brisk business from dawn until late at night. Next door, A&W Rootbeer boasted "All American Food."

This social context complicates the "two-world" metaphor to which Galena Dick refers (see also Henze & Vanett, 1993). For those individuals now middle-aged and older, the image of two distinct, identifiable social worlds does seem to have been experienced as a dualized reality. "Back then we easily distinguished between the home and school cultures," Galena Dick has said; "when we returned to school, we identified ourselves as a different person with a different language" (Dick & McCarty, 1996, p. 75). And the testimony of elders speaks powerfully of the distinct social identities they constructed—as pupils in Anglo-American schools, railroad and domestic workers, and service men and women during World War II—and, simultaneously, as kin, apprentices, mentors, and keepers of livestock and the land.

In some respects, these dualized social–psychological worlds still exist. Abbie Willetto is a graduate of Rough Rock, and an accomplished bilingual educator with children of her own. The daughter of a Danish-American mother and Navajo father, Abbie Willetto began learning Navajo formally in 1974, when, at the age of 12, her parents came to work at Rough Rock School. "There was a lot of peer pressure," she said when I interviewed her in the spring of 1996, "because the [Rough Rock] kids only spoke Navajo, unless they were talking to a White teacher"—

> And I knew there were a lot of things being said about me because I was half-White and, you know, that was a big thing. I might as well have been a bleached blond .... So I wanted to know what they were saying, [and] I learned very quickly to understand what was being said.

Abbie Willetto refers proudly to her ability to read, write, and understand her language. "I knew there was a difference in me and I wanted to know more about what that difference was." She has made a conscious effort to teach her children Navajo. "I ... read things to my kids [in Navajo], and while they are not getting the amount of Navajo language in their life that I would want for them to get, they're proud and they know about their culture and history."

And yet, her son's experiences in school defy an easy reading of this account. Unlike the pressures that confronted his mother in 1974, Abbie Willetto's son describes the pressures to speak English and "be White." A native speaker of Navajo, he moved off-reservation with his mother at age 6. His mother recalls how he cried and cried one day, and said, "It's better if you are all White."

"'Why are you saying this?' I asked. Because he is three-quarters Navajo, and he said he knew English better."

Abbie Willetto's testimony speaks to the inter-connectedness of language, culture, and identity, and, at the same time, to their racialization within bureaucracies of power. Even for children whose parents endeavor to transmit the heritage language, the forces of a racially compartmentalized world persuade many young people that it is better—and easier—to speak English and "be White."

Like many younger people today, Abbie Willetto and her children are improvising new ways to be Navajo. "It can't just be that we've all got to raise livestock to get those values," Wayne Holm pointed out when we interviewed him in 1996. He described a group of parents who had enrolled their children in Navajo immersion classes at Fort Defiance. Every quarter they met to discuss what they were doing to support their children's acquisition of Navajo:

> And some people couldn't talk Navajo well enough—they'd have to talk in English. Or other people would talk Navajo and say, "Don't laugh at me" .... This was

about a sixth of the school population. But these parents really want their kids to be Navajo, and are really looking for ways to be Navajo.

These experiences suggest the multiple meanings informing young people's identities today. What it means to "be Navajo" and an "educated person" (Levinson, Foley, & Holland, 1996) have always been multilayered, manifold, and shifting (Ochs, 1993). These meanings are being renegotiated in a complex social terrain of increasing diversity, and yet, paradoxically, against the spread of a "McDonaldized, globalized, subtractive, and uncritically anglophile" world (Skutnabb-Kangas, 1999a, p. 10).

In a recent Rough Rock periodical, *Navajo Culture Today*, a headline reads: "Miss Navajo Nation says it's never too late to learn." The story is about Victoria Yazzie, the reigning Miss Navajo Nation at the time. Two years earlier, she "could hardly speak Navajo, although Navajo was her mother tongue" (Becenti, 1999, p. 2). Subtractive, English-only schooling had stripped her of her native language fluency. The Miss Navajo contest, however, stipulates that contestants be able to communicate in Navajo. "I had always wanted to be Miss Navajo," Victoria Yazzie reports. "So I spent about two years completely focused on the language" (Becenti, 1999, p. 2). Interviewed wearing a Navajo-style velveteen blouse, long satin skirt, and a silver and turquoise crown, Victoria Yazzie said she now prefers to speak Navajo. "I'm proud of our language," she told the reporter (Becenti, 1999, p. 2).

The Miss Navajo pageant is not a "traditional" Navajo activity in the sense that elders would attach meaning to that word. Yet it is a meaningful part of a contemporary cultural world that encompasses elders, their children, and their children's children. "[T]hings which don't shift and grow are dead things," Leslie Marmon Silko writes in her book, *Ceremony* (1977, p. 126). Miss Navajo represents a new kind of ceremony, one that valorizes the Native language and culture while recognizing, in Silko's words, "the different voices from generation to generation" (p. 126). And, as Victoria Yazzie's account demonstrates, this activity also acknowledges that, for many young people, the "educated person" is still one who is able to communicate effectively in Navajo.

SCHOOLS AND LANGUAGE RECLAMATION

There is no question that Indigenous peoples can survive and are surviving without their heritage languages (see, e.g., Warner, 1999, p. 77). But, being Navajo in Navajo is qualitatively different from constructing and enacting a Diné identity in English. And, language educator and activist Clay Slate

(1993) observes, "a society that allows people to be Navajo in Navajo is worth maintaining" (p. 10).

Schools such as Rough Rock are critical, if contentious, resources in this struggle. Because community schools are such dominating economic and therefore political institutions, the politics, language, and culture of the school *can* be assets for heightening collective consciousness and mobilizing community action. By their positions and their presence, bilingual educators demonstrate the instrumental value of the Native language. As we have seen at Rough Rock, bilingual educators can be opinion leaders; they can act politically on behalf of the language and the community of users it represents. Indigenous educators and their allies can assert the primacy of the Native language not only in the public domain of the school, they also can enlist the support of and assist community stakeholders in reinforcing the Native language at home.

In her 1996 book, *Indigenous Literacies in the Americas,* sociolinguist Nancy Hornberger refers to these processes as "language planning from the bottom up." The focus, she says, is on "the individual and the local community as active agents in dialogue and interaction within their social environment" (Hornberger, 1996, p. 11). It is undeniable that Indigenous schools and educators engage in such dialogue and interaction against a backdrop of oppression, and within school and community contexts that are contradictory and full of tension. For better or worse, schools are a prime arena in which these tensions are being confronted and negotiated. They are not the only place for language reclamation and the social transformations that must accompany it, but schools are a necessary place for this work. If school-based resources for linguistic and educational self-determination are not used, the remaining, largely negative forces at work will only speed the rate of language loss. Further, schools and their participants will be complicit in the loss.

* * * * * * *

I conclude this discussion on a note of possibility and hope. "I still have the feeling it's going to be possible to be Navajo in the 21st century," Wayne Holm told us in 1996. "I have a fire and here lies my fire stoker," Dorothy Begay ruminated in the winter of that year. "They are our maternal grandfathers and grandmothers .... With them we progress and gain strength. These things will not be forgotten. These things I teach my children," she said. And Abbie Willetto described the positive values her young daughter attaches to the Navajo language and culture: "She is so proud .... It sort of reminds me of me."

The testimony of Dorothy Begay, Fred Bia, Galena Dick, Dorothy Secody, Abbie Willetto, Victoria Yazzie, Agnes and Wayne Holm, and the many others whose words are included here shows that language and identity are "ever in process" (González, 1999, p. 433; see also González, 2001). This testimony also shows that schools have the potential to silence or give voice to identities rooted and mediated in the local language and culture. The linguistic and cultural choices children and their families make need not be either–or ones; no child should be forced to accept another language—or identity—at the expense of her or his own. In communities such as Rough Rock, "Indigenous" and "modern" need not be oppositional terms. School, especially, *can* be constructed as a place where children are free to be Navajo in Navajo—in all of its multiple and ever-changing meanings and forms.

FIG. 14.1. "We were trying to establish a place where our students can live in this so-called White man's world."—Ernest W. Dick (Photograph of Racey Sells, 1983, by Fred Bia, courtesy of Rough Rock Community School.)

Epilogue—"The Hopes and Dreams of Rough Rock"

When the planning for this book began in 1995, a bilingual teacher remarked that this "would be an opportunity to say what are the hopes and dreams of Rough Rock." In these final pages, I share my personal reflections on this unique demonstration in Indigenous schooling—its hopes and dreams, the knowledge and people it produced, and the larger issues and challenges it represents. I return first to voices we already have heard.

"And they said, 'Can you come home? We have a job for you here.'" When the demonstration school opened, it represented a kind of homecoming. The school's very presence, and especially its bilingual/bicultural program, brought the graduates of distant boarding schools back home, supporting them in building careers and raising families in the community of their birth. Parents and grandparents staffed the dormitories and classrooms. School jobs and economic development projects provided financial relief and new life opportunities. Physical facilities grew up around the school and with them, new social and political institutions. In countless intentional and unanticipated ways, the school *created* a community at Rough Rock. The school became and remains the community nexus.

"We said we wanted the Navajo language to be learned .... We wanted books in Navajo." One of Rough Rock's greatest achievements and most difficult challenges has been finding ways to incorporate Navajo language and culture into the school curriculum. "We paved the way for bilingual/bicultural education," Fred Bia pointed out when I interviewed him in December 1997. "We were trying to establish a place ... where our Native American students can live in this so-called White man's world," former school board president Ernest W. Dick told me earlier that year.

In addition to launching the first Indigenous publishing center, Rough Rock mobilized a far-reaching grassroots language planning movement. The Diné Bi'ólta' Association, Native American Materials Development Center, and numerous teacher preparation and materials development projects were inspired, directly or indirectly, by the demonstration at Rough Rock. "I saw this as a time for the native people to renew their strengths," Navajo linguist Irene Silentman (1995) writes (p. 7). Galena Dick (1998) recalls learning "to read and write my language along with my students" (p. 25). "We came to value our language," Silentman (1995) concludes, "particularly when we saw it in print" (pp. 16–17).

These words speak of a genuinely transformative pedagogy that defies reductionist paradigms of literacy as a technical skill. "Teaching literacy is, above all, a social and political commitment," Paulo Freire (1993) emphasizes (p. 115). Rough Rock educators have demonstrated the fulfillment of this commitment in a profoundly self-determinant and liberatory way.

"This type of education opened doors for many Navajo people." In her historical overview of Navajo bilingual/bicultural education, Silentman (1995) notes that the opportunities it provided helped "Navajo people to advance themselves career-wise, to become equals with non-native teachers and administrators" (p. 16). Galena Dick describes "growing up with the school." And Fred Bia observes that Rough Rock nurtured a class of Indigenous educators, giving "people the stepping stone to make a career in the bilingual/bicultural field. You see them in Washington D.C., you see them at other schools," he reflected during our 1997 interview. "They owe a debt to this school. I feel the same way."

The 30-year roster of Rough Rock employees reads like a *Who's Who* of American Indian education. Many who founded and worked at the school during its early years went on to assume leadership positions in tribal, state, and national organizations that drove the movement for Indigenous education control. Like Fred Bia, I consider myself fortunate to have learned from these educators, and to have witnessed and joined their activism. They "opened doors for many," Navajo and non-Navajo alike.

"There's a lot of things that we have done ... for our Indian children." During my interview with him, Ernest Dick remarked that Rough Rock educators had done "a lot of things ... to try to meet the needs of our people, our Indian children." Although volatile school funding constantly threatened those efforts, data from the longest-lived bilingual/bicultural program at the school, RRENLAP, show that students who experienced consistent, early Native language instruction significantly outperformed those who did not on academically challenging tasks. In Ernest Dick's words, constructing school as a place where children are helped to succeed because of, not despite, who they are, was "one of the most important things that we have done."

FIG. 14.2.   Writing in Navajo, 1992. (Photograph by T. L. McCarty.)

"This school ... will be run by the community." When we asked community members what the school's greatest accomplishment had been, all cited Rough Rock's demonstration in local control. "The people made the school for themselves," former school board member Simon Secody said; "they took ownership of the school." "We planted the seeds ... of Indian self-determination, Indian control," Ernest Dick maintained.

Before Rough Rock, Wayne Holm reminded us, the idea of Indigenous community empowerment was "unimaginable." "I think that it is important for ... people to understand what a profound influence that experiment has had," he added. "That's the *real* contribution of Rough Rock."

"It's how Indian education actually survived." The oral histories and other documentation reported here trace the struggle for self-determination at Rough Rock from the concentration camp at Hwéeldi and people's return home; to the coming of Anglo traders and school police; to Federal stock reduction and its devastating impacts on family economies and individual lives; to community

members' decision to "stand up" for the demonstration project in 1966, and their ongoing fight to sustain it. These events punctuate Rough Rock's biography, even as they illustrate the uneasy birth and growth of the movement for Indigenous education control. At the heart of the struggle are fundamental contradictions in the Federal–tribal relationship which, on the one hand, recognizes and protects tribal sovereignty, and, on the other, breeds bureaucratic arrangements that stifle and suppress sovereignty in myriad ways.

Rough Rock exemplifies the creative working through and around those contradictions—what Lomawaima (1993) characterizes as an insistence by Indigenous people to make decisions "according to their own values" (pp. 236–237). That insistence propelled major policy changes that began in the 1970s with the Indian Education and Self-Determination Acts, and continued to the end of the century with the Indian Nations at Risk Task Force and the White House Conference on Indian Education, two high-profile Indigenous initiatives that outlined plans for systemic education reform (U.S. Department of Education 1991; White House Conference on Indian Education, 1992). In 1990, Congress passed the Native American Languages Act, legislation drafted by Native people to protect and promote Indigenous languages and the cultural knowledge they encode. And in August 1998, President William Jefferson Clinton extended these initiatives with Executive Order 13096, reaffirming the Federal government's "special, historical responsibility for the education of American Indian and Alaska Native students," and calling for "a comprehensive federal response to address the fragmentation of government services available to American Indian and Alaska Native students" *(Federal Register,* August 11, 1998, p. 42681). These recent policies support Native language and culture instruction while attempting to ameliorate the problems of disparate Federal services and inadequate funding that have impeded consistency in academic programs and seriously compromised the quality of education available to Indigenous students.

Former U.S. Director of Indian Education, John Tippeconnic III (1999), notes that these policy developments "did not happen because of the goodwill of Congress or presidential administrations" (p. 37). Rather, he says, "it was because of the political wisdom and persistence of Indian educators, Indian institutions, Indian organizations, tribes, and other driving forces behind legislative and executive branch decisions" (Tippeconnic, 1999, p. 37). This is the terrain of opposition within which Rough Rock and other Indigenous communities are compelled to work. It is a social and political landscape in which the guideposts are ambiguous and shifting, the potential for change often only a mirage. Finding ways to negotiate this contested terrain and to broaden its horizons to advance Indigenous self-determination may be Rough Rock's greatest legacy. As Ernest Dick predicted when this book project began, that legacy is the testimony of "how Indian education actually survived."

* * * * * * *

From the start, the purpose of this book was to reclaim and privilege local narratives of experience—acts of remembering that tell of struggle and pain, but also of freedom and hope. It is their local character that gives these narratives their power, and within them lies the imprint of Rough Rock's hopes and dreams. But hope cannot go unrequited; it must be joined by efforts to create a socially just world. I conclude with a recent experience that suggests the urgency of this charge.

In September 2000, I visited Rough Rock again. Robert Roessel had recently retired as school director, and, as he had vowed, the school board had appointed a Navajo as his successor. The new director was Monty Roessel, the second youngest of the Roessel's five children. A published author of multicultural children's literature, Monty Roessel came to his position with a professional background in community development and photojournalism, and several years of experience as Rough Rock School's public relations specialist. Rough Rock teachers, some of whom had taught Monty as a child, remembered him fondly and seemed quite pleased that he had returned to the school. They expressed confidence in his leadership.

I met with Monty in his office in what had once been the old BIA day school. I had known him for nearly 20 years. Now a father of four with his oldest child in high school, he still wore the open, easy smile I remembered from his youth. I asked him about his greatest challenges as Rough Rock's new director. "Following in my father's footsteps," he replied, only partly in jest. Then he spoke of his desire to improve local access to technology and to build a 21st century learning center. His plans were visionary yet realistic, grounded in his experience growing up in a family that adhered closely to traditional Navajo values and beliefs.

Our discussion turned to the issue that had prompted my visit. As a consultant to the school, I had just completed two reports on Rough Rock's recently funded pre-K–12 bilingual/bicultural education projects. The reports noted that while the projects had made substantial progress in developing a Navajo language and culture curriculum, including a local assessment of Navajo language and literacy, the bilingual/bicultural program was seriously compromised by the growing influence of externally imposed standards for "accountability." The most disturbing evidence of this was in the ostensibly all-Navajo immersion preschool classroom, where, during a site visit, I had observed more English than Navajo spoken by both children and adults. When I asked the preschool teacher about this, she looked at me in dismay and asked, "Should I be teaching Navajo or teaching the standards?" Another elementary teacher put it more bluntly: "We don't have time for Navajo. We've been told to teach to the standards."

Standards and accountability are national obsessions that strike at the heart of Indigenous self-determination and minoritized community control. The very existence of Indigenous community schools depends on their compliance with standards that not only devalue Indigenous knowledge, but jeopardize children's life chances by threatening to deny them a high school degree. That children are subjected to these pressures in preschool is among the more perverse manifestations of a national education system that, while masquerading as an equalizing force, in fact begins to stratify and segregate the moment children enter school.

Like most parents and grandparents, those at Rough Rock and other minoritized communities want their children to grow up to lead fulfilling, productive lives. Like most parents and grandparents, they count on the school to provide their children with the resources to achieve this. And like most people, parents and grandparents at Rough Rock are not immune to the public and media rhetoric surrounding standards and high-stakes testing, which promise that their aspirations for their children will be fulfilled if only teachers, students, and schools become more "accountable."

Buried in the rhetoric is the fact that standardized testing is not accompanied by a parallel commitment to standardize the economic and social investment in children subjected to the tests. Clearly the tests are discriminatory in their English-only content and devaluation of the social and cultural capital Indigenous and other minoritized students bring to school. A more fundamental injustice is a system that bestows educational resources on the privileged, rewards their cultural capital (Bourdieu & Passeron, 1990), and then sanctifies their consequent advantage with standardized tests. There is nothing neutral or impartial about this process. It reifies existing racialized and class-based social structures, and ensures that the gap between those with and without access to opportunities, resources, and power will continue to grow.

This biography of Rough Rock is a call to confront and dismantle these pervasive, systemic inequities. Our lives are not separate from Rough Rock's history, nor can we, as Megan Boler (1997) warns, hear that history without considering its meaning for our work. The hopes and dreams that have materialized at Rough Rock are now imperiled by forces that would rob Indigenous people of their languages, cultures, and identities while threatening to drive Indigenous children into the lowest educational and economic stratum of the national society. These threats are not unique to Rough Rock, but are evident in a multitude of recent public policies that outlaw bilingual education, criminalize teachers who fail to speak only English in the classroom, and deny basic health and human services to the poor.

I close by returning to the metaphor of place and the questions with which I began. Can school be a place to be Indigenous, a place to be non-homogenized, a place in which *all* children learn, question, and grow from a position that values and builds upon who they are? Can we create schools, as Paulo Freire (1993) envisioned, that are sites of social justice as well as creativity, competence, and joy? Rough Rock has shown that school *can* be such a place, but with great difficulty and human cost. The larger question then remains: Can such places of difference be sustained without denying equality of economic, social, and educational opportunity to their inhabitants?

We are all implicated in these questions, and we are all called to act.

References

Allman, S. (1978). *Camps and family histories in the Rough Rock-Black Mesa area.* Map on file at Chinle Agency, Bureau of Indian Affairs, Chinle, AZ.

American Indian Policy Review Commission. (1976). *Report on Indian education.* Washington, DC: U.S. Government Printing Office.

Aronowitz, S., & Giroux, H. A. (1991). *Education under siege: The conservative, liberal and radical debate over schooling.* South Hadley, MA: Bergin & Garvey.

Atkins, J. D. C. (1887/1992). "Barbarous dialects should be blotted out … " In J. Crawford (Ed.), *Language loyalties* (pp. 47–51). Chicago: University of Chicago Press.

Babich, B. (1994). *Nietzsche's philosophy of science: Reflecting science on the ground of art and life.* Albany: State University of New York Press.

Baca, R. R. (1984). *Bilingual education evaluation: An overview.* Los Angeles: Evaluation, Dissemination and Assessment Center, California State University.

Baker, K., & de Kanter, A. A. (1983). Federal policy and the effectiveness of bilingual education. In K. Baker & A. A. de Kanter (Eds.), *Bilingual education: A reappraisal of federal policy* (pp. 33–86). Lexington, MA: Lexington Books.

Bailey, L. R. (1978). *The Long Walk: A history of the Navajo wars, 1846–68.* Pasadena, CA: Westernlore Publications.

Bauer, E. (1970). Bilingual education in BIA schools. *TESOL Quarterly, 4,* 223–229.

Becenti, D. (1999). Miss Navajo Nation says it's never to [sic] late to learn. *Navajo Culture Today, 2,* 2.

Begay, S., Dick, G. S., Estell, D. W., Estell, J., McCarty, T. L., & Sells, A. (1995). Change from the inside out: A story of transformation in a Navajo community school. *The Bilingual Research Journal, 19,* 121–139.

Begay, S. M., Clinton-Tullie, V., & Yellowhair, M. (1983). *Kinaaldá: A Navajo puberty ceremony.* Rough Rock, AZ: Navajo Curriculum Center Press.

Begaye, J. R., Billison, S., Blatchford, H., & Gatewood, H. D., III. (1969). *Navajo evaluators look at Rough Rock Demonstration School.* Rough Rock, AZ: Rough Rock Demonstration School.

Begishe, K. (1981). *Nitsáhákees bee haho'dilyaa, One's development through thoughts.* Mimeo on file at the Navajo Curriculum Center, Rough Rock Demonstration School, Rough Rock, AZ.

Benally, A., & McCarty, T. L. (1990). The Navajo language today. In K. L. Adams & D. T. Brink (Eds.), *Perspectives on Official English: The campaign for English as the official language of the USA* (pp. 237–245). Berlin & New York: Mouton de Gruyter.

Bennett, B. A., Pearson, K., & Plummer, A. (1967). Community development training on the Navajo reservation. In R. A. Roessel (Ed.), *Indian communities in action* (pp. 180–203). Tempe: Arizona State University.

Bennett, K. (1964). *Kaibah—Recollection of a Navajo girlhood.* Los Angeles: Westernlore Press.

Bergman, R., Muskrat, J., Tax, S., Werner, O., & Witherspoon, G. (1969). *Problems of cross-cultural educational research and evaluation: The Rough Rock Demonstration School.* Minneapolis, MN: University of Minnesota Training Center for Community Programs and Office of Community Programs Center for Urban and Regional Affairs.

Bia, F., Lynch, R., & McCarty, T. L., with Yellowhair, M. (1982a). *Nihił hahoodzodóó—Dííjįįdi dóó adą́ą́dą́ą́', Naaltsoos t'áálá'i góné yits'iłígíí. Our community—Today and yesterday, Book one.* Rough Rock, AZ: Navajo Curriculum Center Press.

Bia, F., Lynch, R., & McCarty, T. L., with Yellowhair, M. (1982b). *Nihił hahoodzodóó—Dííjįįdi dóó adą́ą́dą́ą́', Naaltsoos naaki góné yits'iłígíí. Our community—Today and yesterday, Book two.* Rough Rock, AZ: Navajo Curriculum Center Press.

Bia, F., McCarty, T. L., & Lynch, R. (1983). *Of Mother Earth and Father Sky.* Rough Rock and Flagstaff, AZ: Navajo Curriculum Center and Northland Press.

Bingham, S., & Bingham, J. (1976). *Navajo chapters.* Rock Point, AZ: Rock Point Community School.

Bingham, S., & Bingham, J. (1982). *Between sacred mountains: Stories and lessons from the land.* Chinle, AZ: Rock Point Community School.

Blie, M. (Recorder). (1978). *Minutes of school board meetings held in 1977–78 Rough Rock Demonstration School.* Chinle, AZ: Rough Rock Demonstration School.

Bliss, S. W. (1980). Financial planning under P.L. 95–561. In C. G. Foster, S. Boloz, & D. Salas (Eds.), *Reservation schools and P.L. 95–561: The administrator and the curriculum.* Flagstaff: Northern Arizona University.

Boler, M. (1997). The risks of empathy: Interrogating multiculturalism's gaze. *Cultural Studies, 1,* 253–273.

Bourdieu, P., & Passeron, J. (1990). *Reproduction in education, society and culture.* London & Newbury Park: Sage Publications.

Boyce, G. A. (1974). *When Navajos had too many sheep: The 1940s.* San Francisco, CA: The Indian Historian Press.

Cajete, G. (1994). *Look to the mountain: An ecology of Indigenous education.* Durango, CO: Kavakí Press.

Cochran-Smith, M., & Lytle, S. (1993). *Inside/outside: Teacher research and knowledge.* New York & London: Teachers College Press.

Cole, M., John-Steiner, V., Scribner, S., & Souberman, S. (1978). *L. S. Vygotsky, Mind in society: The development of higher psychological processes.* Cambridge, MA: Harvard University Press.

Collier, J., Jr., Laatsch, M., & Ferrero, P. (1972). *Film analysis of the Rough Rock Community School, phase one.* Unpublished manuscript on file at Rough Rock Community School.

Commission on Schools (1983). *The NCA K–12 guide: An instrument designed to help structure the self-study and team visit of a unit school evaluation.* Boulder,

CO: Commission on Schools, North Central Association of Colleges and Schools.

Conklin, P. (1967). Good day at Rough Rock. *American Education,* February, 4–9.

Crawford, J. (1995). *Bilingual education: History, politics, theory and practice* (3rd ed.). Los Angeles, CA: Bilingual Educational Services, Inc.

Crawford, J. (1997). *Best evidence: Research foundations of the Bilingual Education Act.* Washington, DC: National Clearinghouse for Bilingual Education.

Crawford, J. (2000). *At war with diversity: U.S. language policy in an age of anxiety.* Clevedon & Buffalo: Multilingual Matters, Ltd.

Cummins, J. (1984). *Bilingualism and special education: Issues in assessment and pedagogy.* San Diego, CA: College-Hill Press.

Cummins, J. (1989). *Empowering minority students.* Sacramento: California Association for Bilingual Education.

Cummins, J. (1992). Bilingual education and English immersion: The Ramírez Report in theoretical perspective. *The Bilingual Research Journal, 16,* 91–104.

Cummins, J. (2000). *Negotiating identities: Education for empowerment in a diverse society* (2nd ed.). Los Angeles: California Association for Bilingual Education.

Cummins, J. (in press). Commentary on Part III: Can schools effectively challenge coercive power relations in the wilder society? In T. L. McCarty (Ed.), *Language, literacy, and power in schooling.* Albany: State University of New York Press.

Cummins, J., & Swain, M. (1986). Bilingualism in education: Aspects of theory, research, and practice. London & New York: Longman.

Danielson, C. (1989). *Teaching for mastery* (2nd ed.). Princeton, NJ: Outcomes Associates.

Decker, B. C. (1983). Cultural diversity, another element to recognize in learning styles. *NASSP Bulletin, 67,* 43–48.

Deyhle, D. (1986). Success and failure: A micro-ethnographic comparison of Navajo and Anglo students' perceptions of testing. *Curriculum Inquiry, 16,* 365–389.

Dick, G. (1998). I maintained a strong belief in my language and culture: A Navajo language autobiography. *International Journal of the Sociology of Language, 132,* 23–25.

Dick, G., & McCarty, T. L. (1996). Reclaiming Navajo: Language renewal in an American Indian community school. In N. H. Hornberger (Ed.), *Indigenous literacies in the Americas: Language planning from the bottom up* (pp. 69–94). Berlin & New York: Mouton de Gruyter.

Duckworth, E. (1986). Teaching as research. *Harvard Educational Review, 56,* 481–495.

Dunlap, D. A. (1972). *The educational process of Rough Rock Community High School: A program for community and school.* Chinle, AZ: Rough Rock Community High School.

Dyk, W. (1938). *Son of Old Man Hat: A Navajo autobiography.* Lincoln: University of Nebraska Press.

Edelsky, C. (1991). *With literacy and justice for all: Rethinking the social in language and education.* London & New York: The Falmer Press.

Educational Evaluation Systems, Inc. (1982). *1981–82 evaluation of the Rough Rock Basic Skills program.* Report on file at Rough Rock Community School, Rough Rock, AZ.

Eisenhart, M. (1998). On the subject of interpretive reviews. *Review of Educational Research, 68,* 391–399.

Emerson, G. (1970). The Laughing Boy syndrome. *School Review, 79,* 94–98.

Emerson, G. (1983). Navajo education. In A. Ortiz (Vol. Ed.) & W. C. Sturtevant (Gen. Ed.), *Handbook of North American Indians,* Vol. 10, *Southwest* (pp. 659–671). Washington, DC: Smithsonian Institution.

Erickson, D. (1970a). Comment on Rough Rock. *Council on Anthropology and Education Newsletter, 1,* 26.

Erickson, D. (1970b). Custer *did* die for our sins! *School Review, 79,* 76–93.

Erickson, D., & Schwartz, N. (1969). *Community school at Rough Rock.* Washington, DC: Office of Economic Opportunity.

Espín, O. M. (1995). Foreword. In V. I. Muñoz, *"Where something catches": Work, love, and identity in youth* (pp. ix–xi). Albany: State University of New York Press.

Feld, S., & Basso, K. H. (Eds.). (1996). *Senses of place.* Santa Fe, NM: School of American Research Press.

Fine, M. (1996). Working the hyphens: Reinventing self and other in qualitative research. In N. K. Denzin & Y. S. Lincoln (Eds.), *Handbook of qualitative research* (pp. 70–82). Thousand Oaks & London: Sage.

Fishman, J. A. (1984). Minority mother tongues in education. *Prospects, 14,* 51–56.

Fishman, J. A. (1991). *Reversing language shift.* Clevedon, Avon: Multilingual Matters.

Fishman, J. A. (1996). Maintaining languages: What works and what doesn't. In J. Reyhner (Ed.), *Stabilizing indigenous languages* (pp. 186–198). Flagstaff: Northern Arizona University Center for Excellence in Education.

Fishman, J. A. (2001). *Can threatened languages be saved? Reversing language shift revisited: A 21st century perspective.* Clevedon, UK: Multilingual Matters Ltd.

Foster, C. G., & Boloz, S. A. (1980). The curriculum and 95–561: The administrator's salvation. In C. G. Foster, S. Boloz, & D. Salas (Eds.), *Reservation schools and 95–561: The administrator and the curriculum* (pp. 11–18). Flagstaff: Northern Arizona University.

Foucault, M. (1984). Nietzsche, genealogy, history. In P. Rabinow (Ed.), *The Foucault reader* (pp. 76–100). New York: Pantheon Books.

Freire, P. (1970). *Pedagogy of the oppressed.* New York: Continuum.

Freire, P. (1993). *Pedagogy of the city.* New York: Continuum.

Gipps, C. (1999). Socio-cultural aspects of assessment. In A. Iran-Nejad & P. D. Pearson (Eds.), *Review of Research in Education, 24* (pp. 355–392). Washington, DC: American Educational Research Association.

Goffman, E. (1959). *The presentation of the self in everyday life.* Garden City, NY: Doubleday.

Goffman, E. (1963). *Stigma: Notes on the management of spoiled identity.* Englewood Cliffs, NJ: Prentice-Hall.

Goodman, J. M. (1982). *The Navajo atlas: Environments, resources, people, and history of the Diné Bikeyah.* Norman: University of Oklahoma Press.

González, N. (Issue Ed.). (1995). *Educational innovation: Learning from households.* Special Issue, *Practicing Anthropology, 17.*

González, N. (1999). What will we do when culture does not exist anymore? *Anthropology & Education Quarterly, 30,* 431–435.

González, N. (2001). *I am my language.* Tucson: University of Arizona Press.n

González, N., Moll, L. C., Floyd-Tenery, M., Rivera, A., Rendón, P., González, R., & Amanti, C. (1995). Funds of knowledge for teaching in Latino households. *Urban Education, 29,* 443–470.

Goswami, D., & Stillman, P. (Eds.). (1987). *Reclaiming the classroom: Teacher research as an agency for change.* Upper Montclair, NJ: Boynton/Cook.

Grant, A. (1996). *No end of grief: Indian residential schools in Canada.* Winnipeg, Manitoba: Pemmican Publications.

Harness, A. M., Keller, M. C., & Studyvin, D. (1981). *Conceptually oriented mathematics program training manual.* Columbia, MO: COMP Consultants.

Henze, R. C., & Vanett, L. (1993). To walk in two worlds—or more? Challenging a common metaphor of Native education. *Anthropology & Education Quarterly, 24,* 116–134.

Hernstein, R. J., & Murray, C. (1994). *The bell curve: Intelligence and class structure in American life.* New York: Free Press.

Hoffman, V. (1966). TESL report for September, 1966. In R. A. Roessel (Compiler), *The third monthly report of Rough Rock Demonstration School month of September, 1966* (pp. 8–19). Rough Rock, AZ: Rough Rock Demonstration School.

Hoffman, V. (1968). *Oral English at Rough Rock: A new program for Navaho children.* Rough Rock, AZ: Navajo Curriculum Center Press.

Holland, D., Lachicotte, W., Jr., Skinner, D., & Cain, C. (1998). *Identity and agency in cultural worlds.* Cambridge, MA & London: Harvard University Press.

Hollingsworth, S., with Cody, A., Davis-Smallwood, J., Dybdahl, M., Gallagher, P., Gallego, M., Maestre, T., Minarik, L.T., Raffel, L., Standerford, N. S., & Teel, K. M. (1994). *Teacher research and urban literacy education: Lessons and conversations in a feminist key.* New York & London: Teachers College Press.

Holm, A., & Holm, W. (1990). Rock Point, a Navajo way to go to school: A valediction. *Annals, AASSP, 508,* 170–184.

Holm, A., & Holm, W. (1995). Navajo language education: Retrospect and prospects. *The Bilingual Research Journal, 19,* 141–167.

Holm, W. (1996). On the role of "YounganMorgan" in the development of Navajo literacy. *Journal of Navajo Education, 13,* 4–11.

Holm, W. (in press). The goodness of bilingual education for Native American students. In T. L. McCarty & O. Zepeda (Eds.), *One voice, many voices: Recreating Indigenous language communities.* Tucson: American Indian Language Development Institute, University of Arizona.

hooks, b. (1994). *Teaching to transgress: Education as the practice of freedom.* New York & London: Routledge.

Hornberger, N. H. (Ed.). (1996). *Indigenous literacies in the Americas: Language planning from the bottom up.* New York & Berlin: Mouton de Gruyter.

Hornberger, N. H. (2000). Bilingual education policy and practice in the Andes: Ideological paradox and intercultural possibility. *Anthropology & Education Quarterly, 31,* 173–201.

Horne, E., & McBeth, S. (1998). *Essie's story: The life and legacy of a Shoshone teacher.* Lincoln & London: University of Nebraska Press.

House, D. (1996/97). A Navajo paradigm for long life happiness—and for reversing Navajo language shift. *Journal of Navajo Education, 14,* 45–58.

Hudelson, S. (1989). *Write on: Children writing in ESL.* Englewood Cliffs, NJ: Center for Applied Linguistics and Prentice-Hall Regents.

Ilutsik, E. (1994). The founding of Ciulistet: One teacher's journey. *Journal of American Indian Education, 33,* 6–13.

Iverson, P. (1981). *The Navajo Nation.* Westport, CT: Greenwood Press.

Iverson, P. (1990). *The Navajos.* New York & Philadelphia: Chelsea House Publishers.

Johnson, B. H. (1968). *Navaho education at Rough Rock.* Rough Rock, AZ: Rough Rock Demonstration School.

Johnson, B. H., & Roessel, R. (Eds.) (1973). *Navajo stories of the Long Walk period.* Tsaile, Navajo Nation, AZ: Navajo Community College Press.

Johnson, T. R., Champagne, D., & Nagel, J. (1999). American Indian activism and transformation: Lessons from Alcatraz. In T. R. Johnson (Ed.), *Contemporary Native American political issues* (pp. 283–314). Walnut Creek & London: AltaMira Press.

Kari, J., & Spolsky, B. (1973). *Trends in the study of Athapaskan language maintenance and bilingualism. Navajo Reading Study progress report no. 21.* Albuquerque, NM: University of New Mexico.

Kaulbach, B. (1984). Styles of learning among Native children: A review of the research. *Canadian Journal of Native Education, 11,* 27–37.

Kawagley, A. O. (1995). *A Yupiaq worldview: A pathway to ecology and spirit.* Prospect Heights, IL: Waveland Press.

Kincheloe, J. (1991). *Teachers as researchers: Qualitative inquiry as a path to empowerment.* London: Falmer Press.

Kiyaani, D. (Recorder) (1969). *Minutes of school board meetings held in 1968–69 Rough Rock Demonstration School.* Chinle, AZ: Rough Rock Demonstration School.

Kiyaani, D. (Recorder) (1971). *Minutes of school board meetings held in 1970–71 Rough Rock Demonstration School.* Chinle, AZ: Rough Rock Demonstration School.

Kluckhohn, C., & Leighton, D. (1962). *The Navaho.* Garden City, NY: Doubleday & Co., Inc.

Krashen, S. D. (1996). *Under attack: The case against bilingual education.* Culver City, CA: Language Education Associates.

Krashen, S. D., & Biber, D. (1988). *On course: Bilingual education's success in California.* Sacramento: California Association for Bilingual Education.

Krauss, M. (1996). Status of Native American language endangerment. In J. Reyhner (Ed.), *Stabilizing indigenous languages* (pp. 16–21). Flagstaff: Northern Arizona University Center for Excellence in Education.

Krauss, M. (1998). The condition of Native North American languages: The need for realistic assessment and action. *International Journal of the Sociology of Language, 132,* 9–21.

Lather, P. (1999). To be of use: The work of reviewing. *Review of Educational Research, 69,* 2–7.

Lave, J., & Wenger, E. (1991). *Situated learning: Legitimate peripheral participation.* Cambridge, UK: Cambridge University Press.

LeCompte, M. D. (1993). A framework for hearing silence: What does telling stories mean when we are supposed to be doing science? In D. McLaughlin & W. G. Tierney (Eds.), *Naming silenced lives: Personal narratives and processes of educational change* (pp. 9–27). New York & London: Routledge.

Leighton, D., & Kluckhohn, C. (1974). *Children of The People: The Navaho individual and his development.* New York: Octagon Books.

Lessow-Hurley, J. (2000) *The foundations of dual language instruction* (3rd ed.). New York & London: Longman.

Levinson, B. A., Foley, D. E., & Holland, D. C. (Eds.). (1996). *The cultural production of the educated person: Critical ethnographies of schooling and local practice.* Albany: State University of New York Press.

Levinson, B. A., & Holland, D. (1996). The cultural production of the educated person: An introduction. In B. A. Levinson, D. E. Foley, & D. C. Holland (Eds.), *The cultural production of the educated person: Critical ethnographies of schooling and local practice* (pp. 1–54). Albany: State University of New York Press.

Link, M. (1968). *Navajo—A century of progress, 1868–1968.* Window Rock, AZ: The Navajo Tribe.

Lipka, J., & McCarty, T. L. (1994). Changing the culture of schooling: Navajo and Yup'ik cases. *Anthropology & Education Quarterly, 25,* 266–284.

Lipka, J., with Mohatt, G., & The Ciulistet Group (1998). *Transforming the culture of schools: Yup'ik Eskimo examples.* Mahwah, NJ: Lawrence Erlbaum Associates.

Lipsitz, G. (1990). *Time passages.* Minneapolis: University of Minnesota Press.

Lockard, L. (1996). New paper words: Historical images of Navajo literacy. *Journal of Navajo Education, 13,* 40–48.

Lomawaima, K. T. (1993). Domesticity in the federal Indian schools: The power of authority over mind and body. *American Ethnologist, 20,* 1–14.

Lomawaima, K. T. (1994) *They called it Prairie Light—The story of Chilocco Indian School.* Lincoln & London: University of Nebraska Press.

Lomawaima, K. T. (1995). Educating Native Americans. In J. A. Banks & C. A. M. Banks (Eds.), *Handbook of research on multicultural education* (pp. 331–347). New York: Macmillan Publishing.

Lomawaima, K. T., & McCarty, T. L. (2002, in press). When tribal sovereignty challenges democracy: American Indian education and the democratic ideal. *American Educational Research Journal, 39.*

Loughlin, B. W., & Dennison, K. (1961). A report of the demographical studies during the past five years. In R.W. Young (Ed.), *The Navajo yearbook* (pp. 113–120). Window Rock, AZ: Navajo Agency.

Maberry, M. V. (1991). *Right after sundown—Teaching stories of the Navajos.* Tsaile, AZ: Navajo Community College Press.

Manuelito, K. (2001). Self-determination in an American Indian community school. Unpublished Ph.D. dissertation, Department of Curriculum and Instruction, Arizona State University, Tempe.

Marashio, P. (1982). "Enlighten my mind ... " Examining the learning process through Native Americans' ways. *Journal of American Indian Education, 21,* 2–9.

Matlin, M. L., & Short, K. G. (1991). How our teacher study group sparks change. *Educational Leadership, 49,* 68.

Matlock, M. (1995). Sa'ąh naagháí bik'eh hózhóón: Tapping into the power of words. *Journal of Navajo Education, 12,* 19–24.

McCarty, T. L. (1984). *Bilingual/bicultural education in a Navajo community.* Unpublished Ph.D. dissertation, Department of Anthropology, Arizona State University, Tempe.

McCarty, T. L. (1987). The Rough Rock Demonstration School: A case history with implications for educational evaluation. *Human Organization, 46,* 103–112.

McCarty, T. L. (1989). School as community: The Rough Rock demonstration. *Harvard Educational Review, 59,* 484–503.

McCarty, T. L. (1993). Language, literacy, and the image of the child in American Indian classrooms. *Language Arts, 70,* 182–192.

McCarty, T. L. (1995). *The Rough Rock English-Navajo Language Arts Program (RRENLAP) Title VII Project, 1993–94 Year 5 summative evaluation report.* Manuscript on file at Rough Rock Community School, Rough Rock, AZ, and the U.S. Department of Education, Office of Bilingual Education and Minority Languages Affairs, Washington, DC.

McCarty, T. L. (1998). Schooling, resistance, and American Indian languages. *International Journal of the Sociology of Language, 132,* 27–41.

McCarty, T. L. (2001). Between possibility and constraint: Indigenous language education, planning, and policy in the United States. In J. W. Tollefson (Ed.), *Language policies in education: Critical issues* (pp. 285–307). Mahwah, NJ: Lawrence Erlbaum Associates.

McCarty, T. L. (in press). Bilingual/bicultural schooling and Indigenous students: A response to García. *International Journal of the Sociology of Language.*

McCarty, T. L., Wallace, S., Lynch, R. H., & Benally, A. (1991). Classroom inquiry and Navajo learning styles: A call for reassessment. *Anthropology & Education Quarterly, 22,* 42–59.

McCarty, T. L., Watahomigie, L. J., & Yamamoto, A. Y. (Guest Eds.). (1999). *Reversing language shift in Indigenous America: Collaborations and views from the field.* Special Issue, *Practicing Anthropology, 21.*

McCarthy, C. (1993). After the canon: Knowledge and ideological representation in the multicultural discourse on curriculum reform. In C. McCarthy & W. Crichlow (Eds.), *Race, identity and representation in education* (pp. 289–305). New York & London: Routledge.

McLaren, P., & Tadeu da Silva, T. (1993). Decentering pedagogy: Critical literacy, resistance and the politics of memory. In P. McLaren & P. Leonard (Eds.), *Paulo Freire: A critical encounter* (pp. 47–89). London & New York: Routledge.

McLaughlin, D. (1992). *When literacy empowers: Navajo language in print.* Albuquerque: University of New Mexico Press.

Meriam, L., Brown, R. A., Cloud, H. R., Dale, E. E., Duke, E., Edwards, H. R., McKenzie, F. A., Mark, M. L., Ryan, W. C., Jr., & Spillman, W. J. (1928). *The problem of Indian administration.* Baltimore, MD: The Johns Hopkins Press.

Moll, L. C., & Díaz, S. (1993). Change as the goal of educational research. In E. Jacob & C. Jordan (Eds.), *Minority education: Anthropological perspectives* (pp. 67–79). Norwood, NJ: Ablex Publishing Corp.

More, A. J. (1989). Native Indian learning styles: A review for researchers and teachers. *Journal of American Indian Education,* Special Issue, *August,* 15–28.

Muñoz, V. I. (1995). *"Where something catches": Work, love, and identity in youth.* Albany: State University of New York Press.

Navajo Division of Education (1984). *Navajo Nation education policies.* Window Rock, AZ: Navajo Nation, Navajo Division of Education.

Navajo North Central Visiting Team (1990). *Report on Rough Rock Community School self-study.* Window Rock, Navajo Nation, AZ: The Navajo North Central Association.

Nietzsche, F. W. (1887/1968). *On the genealogy of morals.* In W. Kaufmann (Ed. and Trans.), *Basic writings of Nietzsche.* New York: Modern Library.

Nix, E. (1970). *A feasibility study for a proposed Rough Rock High School.* Yuma, AZ: Arizona Western College.

Norris, R. (1968). Phase II—Navajo social living. In R.A. Roessel, Jr. (Compiler), *The twenty-third monthly report of Rough Rock Demonstration School month of May, 1968* (pp. 85–88). Rough Rock, AZ: Rough Rock Demonstration School.

Ochs, E. (1993). Constructing social identity: A language socialization perspective. *Research on Language and Social Interaction, 26,* 287–306.

Ogbu, J. U. (1978). *Minority education and caste.* New York: Academic Press.

Ogbu, J. U. (1993). Variability in minority school performance: A problem in search of an explanation. In E. Jacob & C. Jordan (Eds.), *Minority education: Anthropological perspectives.* Norwood, NJ: Ablex Publishing Corp.

Oriole, K. (1985, August). Rough Rock, Many Farms join schools. *Navajo Times,* 1–2.

Parsons-Yazzie, E. (1996/97). Niha'áłchíní dayistł'ǫ́ nahalin. *Journal of Navajo Education, 14,* 60–67.

Peshkin, A. (1997). *Places of memory: Whiteman's schools and Native American communities.* Hillside, NJ: Lawrence Erlbaum Associates.

Pfeiffer, A. (1967). Report from Educational Services for August, 1967. In R. A. Roessel, Jr. (Compiler), *The fourteenth monthly report of Rough Rock Demonstration School month of August, 1967* (pp. 11–31). Rough Rock, AZ: Rough Rock Demonstration School.

Pfeiffer, A. (1968). Educational Services. In D. Platero (Compiler), *The twenty-seventh monthly report of Rough Rock Demonstration School month of September, 1968* (pp. 7–11). Rough Rock, AZ: Rough Rock Demonstration School.

Pfeiffer, A. (1993, August). American Indian educational issues. Panel presentation at the Quarterly Regional Meeting of the Bilingual/Multicultural Personnel Training Alliance, BUENO Center for Multicultural Education, University of Colorado, Boulder.

Philips, S. U. (1983/1993). *The invisible culture: Communication in classroom and community on the Warm Springs Indian Reservation.* Prospect Heights, IL: Waveland Press.

Platero, D. (1969a). *Annual report of Rough Rock Demonstration School for 1968–79, July 1, 1968 through June 30, 1969.* Rough Rock, AZ: Rough Rock Demonstration School.

Platero, D. (1969b). *The thirty-first monthly report of Rough Rock Demonstration School month of February, 1969.* Rough Rock, AZ: Rough Rock Demonstration School.

Platero, D. (1970). Let's do it ourselves! *School Review, 79,* 57–58.

Platero, D. (1986). Keynote address presented at the 20th Anniversary Conference, Rough Rock Demonstration School, "What We Have Done in Bilingual Education over the Past 20 Years, 1966 to 1986." October 16, 1986, Rough Rock, AZ.

Platero, P. (1968). Phase II—Navaho language. In R. A. Roessel, Jr. (Compiler), *The twenty-third monthly report of Rough Rock Demonstration School month of May, 1968,* p. 81. Rough Rock, AZ: Rough Rock Demonstration School.

Platero, P. (1992). Navajo Headstart language study. Manuscript on file, Navajo Division of Education, Navajo Nation, Window Rock, AZ.

Popkewitz, T. S. (1998). Dewey, Vygotsky, and the social administration of the individual-constructivist pedagogy as systems of ideas in historical spaces. *American Educational Research Journal, 35,* 535–570.

Ramírez, J. D. (1992). Executive summary. *Bilingual Research Journal, 16,* 1–62.

Read, J., Spolsky, B., & Neundorf, A. (1975). Socioeconomic implications of bilingual education on the Navajo reservation. Paper presented at the Annual Meeting of the American Educational Research Association, Washington, DC.

Reno, P. (1981). *Navajo resources and economic development.* Albuquerque: University of New Mexico Press.

Reyhner, J. (Ed.). (1996). *Stabilizing indigenous languages.* Flagstaff: Northern Arizona University Center for Excellence in Education.

Rhodes, R.W. (1988). Native American learning styles: Implications for teaching and testing. In Arizona Department of Education (Ed.), *Proceedings of the eighth annual Native American Language Issues Institute* (pp. 11–21). Choctaw, OK: Native American Language Issues Institute.

Rivera, K. (1999). Popular research and social transformation: A community-based approach to critical pedagogy. *TESOL Quarterly, 33,* 485–500.

Roessel, R. A., Jr. (1966a). *The first monthly report of Rough Rock Demonstration School month of July, 1966.* Rough Rock, AZ: Rough Rock Demonstration School.

Roessel, R. A., Jr. (1966b). *The second monthly report of Rough Rock Demonstration School month of August, 1966.* Rough Rock, AZ: Rough Rock Demonstration School.

Roessel, R. A., Jr. (Ed.). (1967). *Indian communities in action.* Tempe: Arizona State University.

Roessel, R. A., Jr. (1977). *Navajo education in action: The Rough Rock Demonstration School.* Chinle, AZ: Navajo Curriculum Center Press.

Roessel, R. A., Jr. (1979). *Navajo education, 1948–1978: Its progress and its problems.* Rough Rock, AZ: Navajo Curriculum Center Press.

Roessel, R. A., Jr. (1983). Navajo history, 1850–1923. In A. Ortiz (Vol. Ed.) & W. C. Sturtevant (Gen. Ed.), *Handbook of North American Indians,* Vol. 10, *Southwest* (pp. 506–523). Washington, DC: Smithsonian Institution.

Roessel, R. A., Jr., & Platero, D. (1968). *Coyote stories.* Rough Rock, AZ: Navajo Curriculum Center Press.

Roessel, Ruth (1977). Evaluation of Navajo culture. In R. F. Tonigan et al., *1977 evaluation—Rough Rock Demonstration School* (pp. 54–62). Albuquerque, NM: Richard F. Tonigan & Associates, Ltd.

Roessel, Ruth, & Johnson, B. (Eds.). (1974). *Navajo livestock reduction: A national disgrace.* Chinle, AZ: Navajo Community College Press.

Rosier, P., & Farella, M. (1976). Bilingual education at Rock Point: Some early results. *TESOL Quarterly, 10,* 379–388.

Ross, A. C. (1989). Brain hemispheric functions and the Native American. *Journal of American Indian Education,* Special Issue, *August,* 72–76.

Ruiz, R. (1991). The empowerment of language-minority students. In C. Sleeter (Ed.), *Empowerment through multicultural education* (pp. 217–227). Albany: State University of New York Press.

Ruiz, R. (1995). Language planning considerations in indigenous communities. *The Bilingual Research Journal, 19,* 71–81.

Rushton, J. P. (1999). *Race, evolution and behavior* (special abridged edition). New Brunswick, NJ: Transaction Publishers.

Sasaki, T. T. (1961). Socioeconomic survey of the Many Farms and Rough Rock Navajos. In R.W. Young (Ed.), *The Navajo yearbook* (pp. 103–113). Window Rock, AZ: Navajo Agency.

Schön, D. A. (1983). *The reflective practitioner.* New York: Basic Books.

Sekaquaptewa, H. (1969). *Me and mine—The life history of Helen Sekaquaptewa as told to Louise Udall.* Tucson: University of Arizona Press.

Senese, G. (1986). Self-determination and American Indian education: An illusion of control. *Educational Theory, 36,* 153–164.

Shebala, M. (1996). School traffic flow stopped. *Navajo Times,* April 25, pp. A–2, A–8.

Short, K.G. (1993). Teacher research for teacher educators. In L. Patterson et al. (Eds.), *Teachers as researchers: Reflection and action* (pp. 155–159). Newark, DE: International Reading Association.

Silentman, I. (1995). *Navajo bilingual education in the 1970s: A personal perspective.* Unpublished manuscript.

Silko, L. M. (1977). *Ceremony.* New York: Penguin Books.

Skutnabb-Kangas, T. (1999a). Education of minorities. In J. A. Fishman (Ed.), *Handbook of language and ethnic identity* (pp. 42–59). New York & Oxford: Oxford University Press.

Skutnabb-Kangas, T. (1999b). Linguistic human rights—Are you naive, or what? *TESOL Journal, 8,* 6–12.

Slate, C. (1993). Finding a place for Navajo. *Tribal College, 4,* 10–14.

Soil Conservation Service (1939). *Statistical summary, human dependency survey, Navajo and Hopi reservations.* Washington, DC: Bureau of Indian Affairs.

Spicer, E. (1962). *Cycles of conquest: The impact of Spain, Mexico, and the United States on the Indians of the Southwest, 1533–1960.* Tucson: University of Arizona Press.

Spolsky, B. (1972). *The situation of Navajo literacy projects. Navajo Reading Study progress report no. 19.* Albuquerque: University of New Mexico.

Spolsky, B. (1974). *American Indian bilingual education. Navajo Reading Study progress report no. 24.* Albuquerque: University of New Mexico.

Spolsky, B. (1976). Linguistics in practice: The Navajo Reading Study. *Theory into Practice, 24,* 347–352.

Spolsky, B., Green, J. B., & Read, J. (1974). *A model for the description, analysis, and perhaps evaluation of bilingual education. Navajo Reading Study progress report no. 23.* Albuquerque: University of New Mexico.

Spolsky, B., Holm, A., & Murphy, P. (1970). *Analytical bibliography of Navajo reading materials. Navajo Reading Study progress report no. 7.* Albuquerque: University of New Mexico.

Spolsky, B., & Holm, W. (1977). Bilingualism in the six-year-old child. In W. F. Mackey & T. Andersson (Eds.), *Bilingualism in early childhood* (pp. 167–173). Rowley, MA: Newbury House Publishers, Inc.

Spring, J. (1996). *The cultural transformation of a Native American family and its tribe 1763–1995: A basket of apples.* Mahwah, NJ: Lawrence Erlbaum Associates.

Stefanakis, E. H. (1998). *Whose judgment counts? Assessing bilingual children, K–3.* Portsmouth, NH: Heinemann.

Strickland, D. S. (1988). The teacher as researcher: Toward the extended professional. *Language Arts, 65,* 754–764.

Szasz, M. (1974). *Education and the American Indian: The road to self-determination.* Albuquerque: University of New Mexico Press.

Taba, H., Durkin, M. C., Fraenkel, J. R., & McNaughton, A. H. (1971). *A teacher's handbook to elementary social studies: An inductive approach.* Reading, MA: Addison-Wesley Publishing.

Tate, W. (1997). Critical race theory and education: History, theory, and implications. In M. Apple (Ed.), *Review of Research in Education, 22* (pp. 195–247). Washington, DC: American Educational Research Association.

Thomas, W. P., & Collier, V. P. (1995). *A longitudinal analysis of programs serving language minority students.* Washington, DC: National Clearinghouse on Bilingual Education.

Tompkins, J. (1998). *Teaching in a cold and windy place: Change in an Inuit school.* Toronto, Buffalo, & London: University of Toronto Press.

Thompson, H. (1975). *The Navajos' Long Walk for education: A history of Navajo education.* Tsaile, AZ: Navajo Community College Press.

Tierney, R. J., Carter, M. A., & Desai, L. E. (1991). *Portfolio assessment in the reading–writing classroom.* Norwood, MA: Christopher-Gordon Publishers.

Tippeconnic, J. W., III (1999). Tribal control of American Indian education: Observations since the 1960s with implications for the future. In K. G. Swisher & J. W. Tippeconnic, III. (Eds.), *Next steps: Research and practice to advance Indian education* (pp. 33–52). Charleston, WV: Clearinghouse on Rural Education and Small Schools.

Tollefson, J. W. (1991). *Planning language, planning inequality: Language policy in the community.* London & New York: Longman.

Tonigan, R. F., Emerson, G., & Platero, P. (1975). *Annual review and evaluation of the Rough Rock Contract School—Second interim report.* Report on file at Rough Rock Community School, Rough Rock, AZ.

Troike, R. (1984). SCALP: Social and cultural aspects of language proficiency. In C. Rivera (Ed.), *Language proficiency and academic achievement* (pp. 44–54). Clevedon, Avon, England: Multilingual Matters.

Ulichny, P., & Schoener, W. (1996). Teacher–researcher collaboration from two perspectives. *Harvard Educational Review, 66,* 496–524.

U.S. Congress, Senate Committee on Labor and Public Welfare, Special Subcommittee on Indian Education. (1969). *The study of the education of Indian children, Part 3.* Washington, DC: U.S. Government Printing Office.

U.S. Department of Education (1991). *Indian Nations at risk: An educational strategy for action. Final report of the Indian Nations at Risk Task Force.* Washington, DC: U.S. Department of Education.

Valdés, G. (1996). *Con respeto—Bridging the distances between culturally diverse families and schools, an ethnographic portrait.* New York: Teachers College Press.

Valdés, G., & Figueroa, R. (1994). *Bilingualism and testing: A special case of bias.* Norwood, NJ: Ablex Publishing Corp.

Van Maanen, J. (1995). An end to innocence: The ethnography of ethnography. In J. Van Maanen (Ed.), *Representation in ethnography* (pp. 1–35). Thousand Oaks & London: Sage Publications.

Varenne, H., & McDermott, R. (Eds.), with Goldman, S., Naddeo, M., & Rizzo-Tolk, R. (1999). *Successful failure: The school America builds.* Boulder, CO: Westview Press.

Vogt, L. A., & Au, K. H. P. (1995). The role of teachers' guided reflection in effecting positive program change. *The Bilingual Research Journal, 19,* 101–120.

Vogt, L. A., Jordan, C., & Tharp, R. G. (1993). Explaining school failure, producing school success: Two cases. In E. Jacob & C. Jordan (Eds.), *Minority education: Anthropological perspectives* (pp. 53–65). Norwood, NJ: Ablex Publishing Corp.

Warner, S. L. N. (1999). *Kuleana:* The right, responsibility, and authority of indigenous peoples to speak and make decisions for themselves in language and culture revitalization. *Anthropology & Education Quarterly, 30,* 68–93.

Watahomigie, L. (1998). The language is a gift—A Hualapai language autobiography. *International Journal of the Sociology of Language, 132,* 5–7.

Wax, M. L. (1970). Gophers or gadflies: Indian school boards. *School Review, 79,* 62–71.

Wax, M., Diamond, S., & Gearing, F. O. (Eds.). (1971). *Anthropological perspectives on education.* New York: Basic Books.

Wax, M. L., Wax, R. H., & Dumont, R. V. (1964/1989). *Formal education in an American Indian community: Peer society and the failure of minority education.* Prospect Heights, IL: Waveland Press.

Weis, L. (1996). Foreword. In. B. A. Levinson et al. (Eds.), *The cultural production of the educated person* (pp. ix–xiv). Albany: State University of New York Press.

White House Conference on Indian Education (1992). *The final report of the White House Conference on Indian Education, Vols. 1 & 2.* Washington, DC: White House Conference on Indian Education.

Williams, A. W., Jr. (1970). *Navajo political process.* Washington, DC: Smithsonian Institution Press.

Wilson, R. D. (1969). Bilingual education for Navajo students. *TESOL Quarterly, 3,* 65–69.

Witherspoon, G. (1975). *Navajo kinship and marriage.* Chicago: University of Chicago Press.

Witherspoon, G. (1983). Navajo social organization. In A. Ortiz (Vol. Ed.) & W. C. Sturtevant (Gen. Ed.), *Handbook of North American Indians,* Vol. 10, *Southwest* (pp. 524–535). Washington, DC: Smithsonian Institution.

Wolcott, H. (1967). *A Kwakiutl village and school.* New York: Holt, Rinehart and Winston.

Wolcott, H. (1999). *Ethnography; a way of seeing.* Walnut Creek and London: AltaMira Press.

Woolard, K. A. (1998). Introduction. Language ideology as a field of inquiry. In B. B. Schieffelin, K. A. Woolard, & P. V. Kroskvity, (Eds.), *Language ideologies: Practice and Theory* (pp. 3–47). New York & Oxford: Oxford University Press.

Yazzie, E. (Ed.). (1971). *Navajo history.* Rough Rock, AZ: Navajo Curriculum Center Press.

Young, R. W. (Ed.). (1961). *The Navajo yearbook.* Window Rock, AZ: Navajo Agency.

Young, R. W. (1968). *The role of the Navajo in the Southwestern drama.* Gallup, NM: *The Gallup Independent,* with the Navajo Tribe.

Young, R. W. (1972). *Written Navajo: A brief history. Navajo Reading Study progress report no. 19.* Albuquerque: University of New Mexico.

Young, R. W., & Morgan, W., Sr. (1987). *The Navajo language: A grammar and colloquial dictionary* (rev. ed.). Albuquerque: University of New Mexico Press.

Author Index

215

Subject Index

About the Author

Teresa McCarty is professor and head of the Department of Language, Reading and Culture at the University of Arizona, where she also codirects the American Indian Language Development Institute—an international teacher preparation program for educators of Indigenous youth. From 1980 to 1983, she lived and worked at Rough Rock, Arizona, where she completed her dissertation in social-cultural anthropology and where she continues to conduct collaborative research with bilingual teachers. She has worked as a regional program coordinator for the National Indian Bilingual Center and as a program specialist for the Arizona Department of Education Indian Education Unit. She has been a W. K. Kellogg National Fellow and a Salzburg Seminar Fellow, opportunities that enabled her to study minority language rights in the U.S., Latin America, Canada, and Europe. Her research focuses on Indigenous language loss and reclamation, language planning and policy, linguistic human rights, and ethnographic studies of Indigenous education. Dr. McCarty is active in educational, anthropological, and applied linguistic organizations, and is the current editor of *Anthropology & Education Quarterly.*

About the Photographer

Fred Bia has worked as a freelance artist in oils, pastels, and watercolors. He was raised at Rough Rock, Arizona, and his work depicts the striking landforms, people, and lifestyles of *Diné Bikéyah* (Navajo Country). He attended school at Fort Wingate, New Mexico, and the Institute of American Indian Arts in Santa Fe. Later, he studied with photographers Ansel Adams and Cole Weston. At Rough Rock, he has served as a school board member, illustrator of Navajo children's books, and art teacher. He also is active in the National Indian Rodeo Association. Mr. Bia continues to work for the Rough Rock Community School as an illustrator, photographer, and director of the school's Print Shop.